Billie's Bent Elbow

Billie's Bent Elbow

Exorbitance, Intimacy, and a Nonsensuous Standard

FUMI OKIJI

Stanford University Press
Stanford, California

Stanford University Press
Stanford, California

© 2025 by Fumi Okiji. All rights reserved.

"'All that is Written': Matana Roberts." Black One Shot series, *ASAP/Journal* 15:1 (2020). Published under Creative Commons Attribution License (CC BY 4.0). Parts of this piece were reworked for use in the final chapter.

An early version of a portion of the section "Before love, fascination" appeared in Le Mardi Gras Listening Collective, "Music and Economic Planning," *South Atlantic Quarterly* 119, no. 1 (2020): 133-151. Permission granted by the copyright holder, Duke University Press.

"Aesthetic form in the new thing // aesthetic sociality of musique informelle," in *Black Art and Aesthetics: Relationalities, Interiorities, Reckonings*, edited by Michael Kelly and Monique Roelofs (London: Bloomsbury, 2023). Parts of this piece were reworked for use in the final chapter. Permission granted by the copyright holder, Bloomsbury Press.

"Billie's Bent Elbow," in *Heirloom*, edited by Karsten Lund (Chicago: University of Chicago, 2022). Parts of this essay were reworked for use in the final chapter. Permission granted by The Renaissance Society at the University of Chicago.

"Oriki for Don Cherry; To be Part of a Gathering Work," in *Organic Music Societies*, edited by Lawrence Kumpf (New York: Blank Forms, 2021). Parts of this essay were reworked for use in the final chapter. Permission granted by Blank Forms.

"Thwarted Possibilities and Subjunctive Moods." *Journal for Adorno Studies* 1, 2024. Parts of this piece were reworked for use in the second chapter. Permission granted.

No part of this book may be reproduced or transmitted in any form or by any means, electronic or mechanical, including photocopying and recording, or in any information storage or retrieval system, without the prior written permission of Stanford University Press.

Printed in the United States of America on acid-free, archival-quality paper

Library of Congress Cataloging-in-Publication Data
Names: Okiji, Fumi, 1976- author.
Title: Billie's bent elbow: exorbitance, intimacy, and a nonsensuous standard / Fumi Okiji.
Description: Stanford, California : Stanford University Press, 2025. | Includes bibliographical references and index.
Identifiers: LCCN 2024012252 (print) | LCCN 2024012253 (ebook) | ISBN 9781503640467 (cloth) | ISBN 9781503641235 (paperback) | ISBN 9781503641242 (epub)
Subjects: LCSH: Aesthetics, Black. | Aesthetics, Modern. | Arts, Black—Philosophy. | Arts, Modern—Philosophy.
Classification: LCC BH301.B53 O43 2025 (print) | LCC BH301.B53 (ebook) | DDC 701/.1708996—dc23/eng/20240805
LC record available at https://lccn.loc.gov/2024012252
LC ebook record available at https://lccn.loc.gov/2024012253Cover design: [designer]

Cover design: Michele Wetherbee
Cover art: © Njideka Akunyili Crosby, *Dwellers: Cosmopolitan Ones*, 2022, acrylic, colored pencil, and transfers on paper, 63 x 60 in. Courtesy of the artist, Victoria Miro, and David Zwirner. Photographed by Kerry McFate.

*For Àdùké Catherine Okiji (1948–2005) and
Fọláṣadé Agnes Okiji (1971–2020)*

Contents

	Preamble	1
Introduction	Constant Departure	5
One	Haiti's Infrasonic Boom	19
Two	Unthinkable Nonsense	33
Three	Cecil's Snuggling	47
Four	Billie's Bent Elbow	75
	Acknowledgments	99
	Notes	101
	Bibliography	157
	Discography	173
	Index	175

Billie's Bent Elbow

Preamble

Walter Benjamin said that History
    not a prisoner of it; should not seek there for the meaning of destiny
had hitherto been written from the standpoint of the victor
    all genres of human collapsed into a single homogenized descriptive statement, based on the West's liberal, monohumanist Man
        "more French than . . . the Frenchmen"
    an ideological fiction: force of the whole
and needed to be written from that of the vanquished,
    a counterhumanism made to measure of the
    colonized-nonwhite-black-poor-incarcerated-jobless
        deactualized to the point of starving to death.
We might add that knowledge must indeed present the fatally rectilinear succession of victory and defeat, but should also address itself to those things which were not embraced by this dynamic,
    our alogical logic, our exorbitance, its unruly spread,
    temporal incongruity
    jerk and reject, diasporic collision and caress
    our extraterritoriality, our statelessness
that which fell by the wayside—what might be called the waste products and blind spots that have escaped the dialectic
    our refusal what has been refused us
        radical praxis of refusal to contain blackness in dialectical form
        Frantz Fanon's refusal of dialectics,
        Cedric Robinson's tracing of black radical tradition,

Hortense Spillers's figuring of flesh as zero degree of signification,
Saidiya Hartman's refusal to rehearse racial violence as moment of black subjectification,
Denise Ferreira da Silva's rendering of the negativating task of wounded, captive body in the scene of subjection,
Fred Moten refusing simple reconciliation with categories of modern thought
    Ọlábíyìí Yáì's *oríkì-ìtàn-ọ̀rọ̀* complex
      in appositional collision
        and snuggle
          or scrambled refrain
      in *Verwandtschaft* with our other kin.

What transcends the ruling society is not only the potentiality it develops
    those real possibilities that exist hidden within the actual
but also all that which did not fit properly into the laws of historical movement
    our failure to be sufficiently disturbed by contradiction
    our untimely, unthinkable possibilities
      blackness's submerged span
      and African pan, *ìtàn*.
Theory must needs deal with cross-grained, opaque, unassimilated material
    that surreal presence of material spirit,
      fantastic, unreal possibilities of imagination gone wild
which, as such, admittedly has from the start an anachronistic quality but is not wholly obsolete since it has outwitted the historical dynamic. This can most readily be seen in art
    making something appear that does not exist, in our not fitting into this world, self-consciously posing our unreality
      I want to contribute to the world a text about impossibility, blackness
        as a space of impossibility
          perhaps an artistic
            gbẹ́nagbẹ́nu undertaking

Preamble

    an aesthetic sociality of/toward brilliance.
The very grandeur of logical deductions may inadvertently take on a provincial quality. Benjamin's writings are an attempt in ever new ways to make philosophically fruitful what has not yet been foreclosed by great intentions
    such as broken, coded documents that sanction walking in another world while passing through this one, graphically discording administered scarcity,
        flouting logical frugality.
The task he bequeathed was not to abandon such an attempt to the estranging enigmas
of [European] thought alone, but to bring the intentionless
    nonidentical, unthinkable, collective body-space
within the realm of concepts: the obligation to think at the same time dialectically and un- or paradialectically.[1]

Introduction

Constant Departure

I am compelled (irrationally so, I would say) to set forth a vignette of black noncitizenry, to outline the topography of that liminal living. I often write to humor this itch, with Theodor Adorno providing the conceptual staging and props (a selection dictated by training and habit rather than imperative). These might make it seem as though immanent critique is taking place, and perhaps it is, but the porosity of black conceptual space makes for a leaky, untrue "whole"—one in which neither necessity nor fidelity nor watertight reliability are privileged.[1] The particular play in the realm of impossibility that blackness is breaches the boundaries of an analytic trained on mining Western modernity's contradictions for critical resource even as this remains somewhat of a preoccupation. As someone whose vista of these aforementioned inadequacies of the European world is German critical thought, I often sound as if I am running Adorno (and Walter Benjamin to a lesser extent) through a variably wet multimodal effect pedal. At times, my engagement with that tradition merely fattens (or flattens) its tone, the sheen taken off its insights by an irrepressible blackness even as I write in overwhelming agreement. At others, all that tradition will hear is heavy distortion, its discourse engaged but drowned out by an approach that cannot but exceed its limits of permissibility. Mine is a play of someone passing through the corridors of the Frankfurt School but whose head is above the clouds, breathing in the atmosphere of our "specific inspiration"—to borrow from Cedric J. Robinson—what Adorno would dismiss as an impossible second, secret world.[2] Needless to say, I'm not tied to immanence, to determinacy, to bringing us to bear on this European world. In fact, I'll be self-consciously posing our unreality, leaning into our modal anomaly, attempting to make something appear that does not exist. I want to show that it is not only that the course of this world cannot admit black life or black sociality or genuine black participation but that it is also the case that *no* prudent European world could allow for the spread of possibility that this contradictory being and its social life generates. A blackened world would require more than black actualization (if such were possible for black life in all its ontological exorbitance). It would be the promotion of a full spectrum of possibility from the real possibilities contained in the actual through to the fantastic. Iain Macdonald characterizes Adorno's understanding of philosophy's project as being to "critique and unmask the general and particular structures of the ideological fiction of the 'force of the whole' in such a way as to open up the possibility of determinate alternatives."[3] We might say that black study, while sympathetic to such, is more concerned with finding ways to share, model, and perform the "cross-g[r]ained [*quere*], opaque, unassimilated material" of the indeterminate.[4] Our peculiar modality is also distinct from that which orients Adorno's ethical imperative, the latter being strictly limited to what is understood as unfulfilled *real* possibilities. In a world in which the fantastic is taken seriously, actuality, or real possibility, loosens its force. A blackened world would require more than actualization. It would be the promotion of a full spectrum of possibility. It would require an expansive appreciation of the mere, the abstract, and the fantastic alongside the actual. In this way, black modality—even as it enacts the critique of "the force of the whole" that also orients Adorno—more closely resembles, in form if not intention, the characteristic coincidence of the material/real and form/fantastic we find in artwork.

In his introduction to W. E. B. Du Bois's long-neglected 1905 text "Sociology Hesitant," R. A. Judy tells us that the "celebrated 'doubleness' of the Negro is about being in a situation of ceaseless movement and ruses. Being a problem, being the Negro problem, that is, involves style." He speaks of black being "generating complexities and complications" rather than being motivated by the resolution of any doubleness or contradiction.⁵ Black life will not settle down. This doubleness is not just being black and American or of Africa and Europe but, more pertinently, *"the sense of being* . . . richly and fundamentally double," as Nahum Dimitri Chandler puts it.⁶ Indeed, as Chandler goes to such lengths to impress on us in his essay "Of Exorbitance: The Problem of the Negro as a Problem for Thought," the ontological contradiction at the heart of black life and its accompanying Weltanschauung, the "identity" or "identification" that moves by way of "double consciousness," throws into doubt the grounding certainties of the prespeculative European outlook—namely, the laws of noncontradiction and those of self-same identity necessary for individuation. In the essay, a portrait of the exorbitant, unthinkable figure of the Negro, multifariously and incessantly (placed) outside of human being, its ethical codes, and universal history, gives way to a black identification with (and orientation by) exorbitance. We might say that black being unfolds or, more broadly, moves by way of exorbitance—a most striking manifestation and formulation of such, appearing by way of Du Bois's double gesture, the "agonistic . . . maintenance of ambivalence" fractured across his various methods and formal experimentation. Eschewing the traditional analytics for race that tend to rely on metrics of purity and simplicity, Du Bois uncovers an "original sense of being in the world" defined by its historicity.⁷ Ensuring we do not miss the contradiction at the heart of this formulation, Chandler underscores that for Du Bois,

> having no strictly delimitable scene of origin or presumptively final sense of habitus, the African American subject is quite often "both/and," as well as "neither/nor." . . . A simple yes/no or either/or question will simply not suffice to situate this identity or determine the sense of identification of this being. The undecidable status of such a sense not only contradicts the conservative understanding of the law of identity formulated in the Aristotelian principle of noncontradiction, which is a philosophical statement of the kind of ontological presupposition that remains the deepest ideal, formal, or logical—that is metaphysical—resource of the discourses of the project of purity . . . but accounting for the *alogical logic* that organizes the structure of appearance of such a being, perhaps, displaces the ultimate pertinence of that principle. It marks the scene of a *certain exorbitance*.⁸

Chandler, by way of Du Bois, works out the exorbitance of black life historiologically—both sketching a philosophy of history that cannot proceed by way of the laws of movement that Adorno refers to in the preamble due to its unbounded origin and insufficient telos *and* a sense of being that is historical rather than essential. (A deep appreciation of the doubleness of black being, embodied by the figure of the slave, is facilitated by the pathbreaking work of Saidiya V. Hartman—the slave being a *willful thing*, not human but also just human enough to be subject to legal apparatus. The excavation of this *alogical logic* has been extended and deepened by a generation of black theorists, most recently by Denise Ferreira da Silva's interrogation of the critical resource this figure that "holds the Human and the Thing in extreme tension" offers.)[9] Here, we should understand *exorbitance* as emergent from a world-historical scene—that is, from violent encounter, from within a world history in which (black) human beings emerge from enslavement and colonization.

A specific preoccupation of this book is the exploration of how this exorbitance of black being, thought, and expression is echoed in an African—or more specifically, Yorùbá—epistemic comportment. Even as black and Yorùbá sense of being might hold a resemblance, I am keen not to collapse this black call/response to projects of white purity into a Yorùbá sense of being (although, this latter has been and continues to be, along with black life, unthinkable from the perspective of Western modernity—the Yorùbá are also an exorbitance for European thought). In the paucity of both archive and theoretical resource, I cannot claim that an African "sense of world," or African common sense, orients black doubleness, which, as I've pointed out, needs to be understood as emergent from the arena of the so-called world-historical peoples. The notion of an African propensity orienting the black sense of being Du Bois and Chandler bring into focus cannot be supported. With that caveat in mind now and throughout the book, I want to indulge my fascination with how, in a Yorùbá sense of being, there is what has been described—in language that at times offends my critical sensibility—as a "unity in contradictory situations," a "harmony in contradiction."[10] I want to draw into a collective narration of black statelessness a consideration of a way to world and thought that can, without crisis, find a place for a jealous, possessive god within (and/or beside) its nonexclusive, open-ended pantheon.¹¹ I am wondering if this might shed light on a common capacity for holding contradiction. Alongside a short, cropped-frame clip of Billie Holiday's undulating arm, to which I've devoted a chapter, Èṣù, the òrìshà of liminality, equivocation, and contradiction, has been a talisman for this project. In "Unthinkable Nonsense," I fixate on a verse of their *oríkì* that describes Èṣù in pairs of contradictory statements—contradictions that are held together by seemingly unsuitable conjunctives: "The short and tall one / Whose head is barely visible when [they] walk through a peanut farm / *Thanks to the fact* that [they are] very tall."¹² It is this genre of alogical logic, this ontoepistemic comportment, that is not adequately disturbed by contradiction that I'm to share with you. This being double, seeing double, or in 3D, this constant negotiation, this "blur," "swarm's swoon," as Fred Moten would say, is what Judy terms, in more sober language, the "meditation of boundaries."¹³ Crucially, this meditation is not necessarily mediation. It is, moreover, a spectrum of maneuvers of contiguity and snuggle, crash, clash, and collusion. It is also the maintenance of such liminality—the "undocumenting" that is part and parcel of this mode of doubling (not committed to sublation and/or pushing through to greater determination); it is the maintenance of ditches and craters by way of our incessant talk (that is, our *òrò*) coming around this matter at hand that we call, for convenience's sake, blackness.¹⁴

For Adorno, a radical revisioning of historical movement should not only rescue the particular subsumed moments and people worked into the historical progression against their particularities but also attend to "those things which were not embraced by this dynamic, which fell by the wayside—what might be called the waste products and blind spots that have escaped the dialectic." He goes on, usefully clarifying that it *is* the extra-, un-, or nondialectical that he has in mind. Such theory might uncover not only that which the system overcomes in order to proceed and succeed but also "that which did not fit properly into the laws of historical movement," meaning the illegible, unthinkable, obscure material, that the system must reject due to its fundamental incompatibility.¹⁵ As such, the thoughts unfolded here contribute to what da Silva refers to as a "radical praxis of refusal to contain blackness in the dialectical form."¹⁶ This refusal is not an attempt to escape but rather, to paraphrase Stefano Harney and Fred Moten, is a refusal of what has been refused us.¹⁷ Frantz Fanon articulates it this way: "I am not a prisoner of History [*l'Histoire*]. I should not seek there for the meaning of my destiny."¹⁸ I too read Georg Wilhelm Friedrich Hegel as an irascible African should. The study explores this shared posture and sense. And yet to track the logical exorbitance that the book is claiming characterizes black being and thought, it is a propensity to operate within distinct temporalities concurrently, much more than the presence of an alternate pulse, that the unfolding thoughts are most keen to impress. The historical laws of movement proper to black life and thought do not, in fact, reject the dialectical form. The movement of black life and thought, marked particularly by the doubling discussed above, might well find itself in moments of dialectical unfolding. This is to say that we are already at the business of thinking both dialectically and nondialectically and, relatedly but separately, already at the business of the fantastic and formal, engaged in exploration of life orientated by *could* rather than *must* or even *ought*, with all the lack of insistence, and the *this and that*, cubist-perspectival comportment, that brings. Significantly, these (de)ranged maneuvers of thought (and the incongruity in thought that Adorno calls for at the end of "Bequest"—"to think at the same time dialectically and undialectically"—is an outstanding instance of such) are generative of a logical exorbitance that fails to trigger a crisis, this want of despair, which, from the perspective of modern German thought, is a debilitating inadequacy, seeing the important role it plays as a catalyst for critical intervention.¹⁹ The education of African beings, these potentially (black) human beings, by way of enslavement and colonialism, as proposed by Hegel, can be read as an attempt to effect a break with such epistemic imprudence. Such lawlessness, or, better, legal insouciance, is a falling short of the resolve necessary for the effective development of consciousness and the adjunctive recognitive capacity.²⁰ We are (to be) taught necessity, fidelity, and parsimony in thought.²¹ This is all to say that we are already operating within a logical contradiction that might break with an attachment to stories of victors and that also broadens its vista to think beyond a history of the vanquished.²² In a manner bequeathed by Ọlábíyí B. Yái (for whom *itàn*, often reduced in translation to "history," [un]folds spatially as much as temporally and, in its inextricable poetics, should also be understood as a sort of epistemological comportment) as much as Walter Benjamin, these meditations unfold mimetically and topographically by turns alongside, within, and against the dialectical tide of critical narration and organization.[23] *Billie's Bent Elbow* contributes to existing scholarship in providing groundwork, by demonstration as much as exposition, for exploration of a way to world and thought that could be described, in its confluence of approaches, its overload/overlap of incongruous laws of historical movement, as incoherent and underdetermined—a way to world and thought encouraging of ill-fit, overlapping, at times contradictory, other times overdetermined deposits, one that writes gluttonous histories. Once we understand immanent critique in black thought and being as just one modality of many, when we understand the active reconfiguring of various congregations (a spread and convergence of/in prayer and anamnestic evocation, of trinkets strung out along ever-snarling flow) as a central preoccupation of black thought, the significance of Judy's spotlight of style (or form or poetics, the subjunctive, a "subjunctive poetics," as Laura Harris offers) comes ever more clearly to view.[24]

Opening an *oríkì* masquerading as an academic article devoted to the recently departed Yáì, fellow theorist of the Yorùbá arts Adéléké Adéẹ̀kọ́ recites the following verse: "Gbẹ́nàgbẹ́nà ṣe tirẹ̀ tán; ó ku ti gbẹ́nugbẹ́nu. (The carving artist is done carving; the remaining lot concerns the mouth carver.)"[25] "Here ends the work of the sculptor / Let the critic start his own."[26] The verse concerns *gbẹ́nàgbẹ́nà* translated as "sculptor," the archetypical Yorùbá artist, but referring more broadly to all cultural and artistic expression, and *gbẹ́nugbẹ́nu*, poorly translated as "critic" but which literally means "'one who carves with one's mouth (voice)'—a sculptor of words . . . *gbẹ́nugbẹ́nu* by necessity are artists."[27] The *gbẹ́nugbẹ́nu* is called upon to "carve" words out of the unfolding work to which their commentary becomes a part. We find the critic make themselves at home in it, "continu[ing] the work of the sculptors by other means."[28] The *gbẹ́nàgbẹ́nà*'s provocation in wood or iron (or lyric, rhythm, tone, *àdìrẹ*, etc.) calls on the *gbẹ́nugbẹ́nu* to "incomplete" its "document."[29] In launching his *oríkì*-cum-article this way, Adéẹ̀kọ́ is signaling a doubling, or rather the multiple doublings, that can be read at various registers of Yáì's work. What Adéẹ̀kọ́ dramatizes for us in his citational play is indeterminacy, on the one hand—an entanglement, or confusion, of *gbẹ́nàgbẹ́nà* and *gbẹ́nugbẹ́nu*, embodied by Yáì (but how Yorùbá artistic and cultural production more broadly comes about and is sustained)—and, on the other, a maintenance of a distinction between these two figures—in this case, presented by Yáì and Adéẹ̀kọ́ as the artist whose work is "done" and the "critic" who must "start his own," respectively. Yáì was quite fond of this sort of metacriticism, and so these formal and performative aspects provide additional "lines" to the *oríkì*. I do not think that it is much of a departure from Adéẹ̀kọ́'s own intention for me to suggest that the late scholar's corpus provides a *gbẹ́nàgbẹ́nà*-like provocation for Adéẹ̀kọ́'s *gbẹ́nugbẹ́nu oríkì* posing as an article. Compounding the complexity of these divergent coincidences, we learn that Adéẹ̀kọ́ lifted the line of praise (a common lyric that he would have undoubtably been familiar) from Yáì's 1999 "Tradition and the Yorùbá Artist," maintaining the Yorùbá of Yáì's rendition (although he recuperates accents and other diacritics) but providing an alternate translation. "The carving artist is done carving; the remaining lot concerns the mouth carver," he offers.[30] What Adéẹ̀kọ́'s demonstration makes quite clear is that, as Yáì puts it, the "sculpting words that beautifully invoke the carver, his work, the orisa, the patrons, actual and potential admirers and the *gbẹ́nugbẹ́nu* [him]self" is *both and at the same time* a recursive working over a common ground, a tilling of, or a fixation on, a particular object of concern, a fascination, *and* a departure, a meandering address that leads astray or spreads out or hatches. Yáì's phrase "constant departure" captures this aporetic motion.[31] Throughout Adéẹ̀kọ́'s piece and particularly in a passage toward the end in which he spotlights the more irreverent modes of narrativity (those "metonymic selections," or constellations, acknowledged by Yáì but whose "fecund unruliness" tends to be [curbed] in his account), we hear Adéẹ̀kọ́, the *gbẹ́nugbẹ́nu*, tease out improvisations of (co)habitation and departure as a sort of dancing on the spot, or treading water, *and* egress.[32] Just how one goes about departing and, crucially, how one concurrently departs and remains make up the guiding concern of Yorùbá artistic production, which Yáì's own body of work and Adéẹ̀kọ́'s *oríkì* attest to.

The most striking features of Yorùbá artistic production, as Yáì understands it, might be traced to its predominately metonymic orientation. In his "apical" rendition of the "metonym," an *oríkì* that (appropriately and inevitably) spans several essays, the theorist of Yorùbá arts speaks of a class of practice that is preoccupied with the creation, arrangement, and traversal of discursive space—the production and recognition of modes of collision, contiguity, and tarrying.³³ Metonym as a figure of speech in which a related concept or phenomenon is made to stand in for another is clearly a much narrower sense than Yáì is mobilizing. Rather, as Adéẹ̀kọ́ suggests, Yáì is not really interested in the substitutive capacity of the metonym. Indeed, the conceptual efficiency that a metonym, as conventionally understood, facilitates is positively eschewed. Rather, we find Yáì's "metonym" serves a metonymic role in its naming practices of (de)forming of discursive space by way of processes of fragmentation, correspondence, and assemblage. Adéẹ̀kọ́ writes that for Yáì, "*àṣà* (traditions) are metonymic selections and bits (*ẹ̀ya*) reconstituted from dispersed parts of other aggregations (*ẹ̀ya* and *ẹ̀yà*)." Yáì's *oríkì* for the metonym, which is a wonderful demonstration of its capacity, is for an artistic and discursive orientation that improvises forms in which constituents (fragments, participants) might find ways to and away from each other and might explore the myriad modes of cohabitation.³⁴ The formal experiments of an approach like this seem to be oriented by the conundrum of how one is to stray *and* remain contiguous (entangled, even). Consider the following from Karin Barber on the *oríkì* practices of a community of women in Okuku, Nigeria:

> Almost any verbal formulation in *oríkì* can be broken off, made to stand on its own, and jammed up against other formulations in a manner which positively exaggerates the discontinuity between them. In this sense the style of *oríkì* is essentially disjunctive. But almost any gap, by the same token, can be bridged. The links may be solid planks of structural symmetry, laid out in parallelism and repetition. Or they may be so fragile as to look like sleight of hand on the performer's part: a single stray word, not prominent in one unit, may become the key word of the next, or a chance resemblance in sound may be enough to set her off in a new direction. . . .
> The predominant impression is of utterances that "go together" in one way or another without having been composed exclusively for each other. . . . If her materials are a repertoire of potentially or actually free-standing utter-

ances, not grammatically linked to the utterances that co-exist with them in her repertoire, then her skill is to play with disjunction. The underlying presence of the gap is the grounds and condition of possibility of her art. It is the gap which makes her performance exciting, as she throws out one fragile and temporary bridge after another. There are no rules about how this is to be done.[35]

I have provided this long quotation as it touches upon so much that Yáì's indispensable but dispersed meditation on "metonym," or *ẹya/ẹyà*, offers: the various and improvised modes of transport and correspondence, including those that frustrate analysis in their nonsensuousness, those that crash and snuggle, the infidelity of the bits, their profuse rehearsal coupled with happenstance and sleights of hand, the encouragement of a sort of vandalism. And so Yáì's "metonym," which might be word, verse, sculpture, *oríkì*, person, or collective, is what I understand to be a placeholder, a vexillum, or a name (even when it comes to us visually or embodied) for the assemblage of parts or bits that hold together by way of a spectrum of (sometimes tenuous) correspondence. The production and recognition of correspondences—both those that are readily available to us through our sensory apparatus as well as those that must be felt—constitute a methodological and performative preoccupation of *Billie's Bent Elbow*.[36]

It was about a century ago that Walter Benjamin, in his writing on the second-manifesto surrealists and friends (André Breton, Louis Aragon, Pierre Naville, et al.), struggled to reconcile the revolutionary organization ("the dictatorial side") with the "radical concept of freedom" that was so important to the life practices of those artist-thinkers (a contradiction that harassed them all the way through the postwar years).[37] By the end of his 1929 essay, Benjamin seems to have exhausted available avenues to address the conundrum. He ends with an advocacy of organization but not of or toward a political party. Rather, he calls for an organization of pessimism, meaning "nothing other than to expel moral metaphor from politics and to discover in political action a sphere reserved one hundred per cent for images," this counterrepresentational eruption being akin to the "radical untimeliness" of Frantz Fanon's leap of invention, which, as David Marriott reminds us, "cannot be anticipated, nor can it be prepared for, nor can it be traced back to a prior historical moment to be interrogated as such."[38] In a discussion of the incongruity of political organization and "revolutionary spontaneity," which echoes Benjamin's own, Marriott highlights Fanon's rejection of political expedience and his vision of a politics that is neither means nor ends (or, with Benjamin, a coincidence of means and ends), one that frustrates and "calls into doubt the classical determinations of politics, i.e. reformism, classism, racialism, vitalism, etc." Fanon's advocacy of the violence of spontaneity coupled with his rejection of party politics, of dialectical fatalism masquerading as development, and any sort of "preconstituted identity" resonates so brilliantly with Benjamin's nonrepresentational, revolutionary image space, which emerges from and orients the body space of an ever-renewing collective.[39] For Benjamin—against the aestheticization of politics, from political sloganeering to the brutality of sociopolitical engineering that must be part of any nation's craft—practices of *political art* cannot be instrumentalized.[40] The collective body space, which only emerges as such in its interpenetration with the image space it brings about, calls for a way with time that is patient and unexpectant but poised for those flashes of emergence. Neither this body space nor its orientation and methods of formation represent a political position. Those impossible-to-anticipate moments of embodied insurrection *are* "political action," committed exclusively to bringing itself about. The challenge, and what keeps Benjamin's pessimism renewed, is the precarity of this form of politics. As Sami Khatib reads, "The entrance into the image-space [the form that this political action must take] cannot be intentionally found but only unintentionally opened up by threshold experience, Freudian slips, and other unexpected deviation of collective political action."[41] In the surrealism essay, Benjamin points to opium and hashish as portals through which one might stumble upon profane illumination, only to demote such intoxicating experiences in favor of the fanning thought supplies. And yet, ultimately, it is by way of a heterogeneity of possible sites, phenomena, people, and ideas that an improvised choreography of constellating correspondence might come about. This is a domain, Khatib tells us, within which "things and words, individuality and collectivity, enlightened consciousness and dream-like fantasies coincide, or more precisely, collide."[42] Practices of mimetic correspondence of the nonsensuous—where similar and dissimilar alike might snuggle and crash, through which the miscellaneous might rub each other up the wrong (or the "right") way—constitute the emergence of the collective political body.

How does one cultivate practices for what cannot be anticipated or prepared for? My commitment is to this sphere, to luxuriate in the abundance of possibility (both real and fantastic) that blackness opens to, to practice fascination and correspondence in the "generative indeterminacy" of that surreal.[43] I've already confessed that the statement of noncitizenry is a petty whim that threatens to overshadow all else that the book is. All I really want to do is practice this space of impossibility, this "black methodology," and extend an invitation of sorts—an invitation to an unfurl/enfold practice that you might already be engaged with.[44] This book ends with a standard, a nonsensuous standard, that travels under the name "Billie's Bent Elbow."[45] It is a standard that resounds through *Billie's Bent Elbow* but finds its true voice in the closing chapter. In it, I gather contributions that I've stumbled upon during the writing of the book that joined me with/at Billie's elbow as she downs the pint or casts the spell or tells the unbounded expanse of our play. This image names and provides a placeholder for the experiments in array and placement that take place within each of those assembled sites and/or fragments and across the rendition that the chapter holds. In *Jazz as Critique*, I work with an understanding of the standard as being quite distinct from the Tin Pan Alley composition that provides the vehicle for soloing in jazz performance. Rather, along the lines that Benjamin proposes for the story, the standard becomes a site of gathering significance, an open-ended work of ad hoc contribution. It is temporally (and geographically) dispersed heterophony and paratactical or palimpsestic layered montage, a dance of musical cross dissolves and closed envelope crashes, a site of "massive concentrations of Black experiential energy," a topology of black mass "maintained in folding, bending, crumpling, and tearing, too," ditches and craters, and underdocuments of the doubling, the undocumenting that doubling does, of the glut, the exorbitance that is black life.[46] And so when pianist and poet Cecil Taylor choreographs a gestural Tower of Babel in the liner notes that accompany his 1966 *Unit Structures* ("Billie's right arm bent at breast moving as light touch" nestled within a cluster of wonderfully miscellaneous lyrics—"from anacrusis to plain," "dancing protoplasm," "God's scream," "knighted tongue enshrouding teeth," "vocal cords . . . strummed," "a 'Gilgamesh' to wine lilacs mania," "mother tongue at bridge scattering Black"), or when pianist Pat Thomas joins XT and Will Holder to continue a cross-media conversation begun by the Cecil Taylor Unit some many moons ago on *Akisakila*, or when Matthew Shipp sets Cecil Taylor alongside other fellow "black mystery pianists" in a school of iconoclastic "code" (pianists whose affinity lay under the crust of any sonic or musical resemblance) that "somehow gets passed down," here also we are faced with the standard.[47] The mimetic openness of unstable, uncertain gatherings of the nonidentical, the nonsensuous subterranean affinity (that moves under the cover of resemblance, disparity, and analogue) is *Billie's Bent Elbow*'s fascination. Perhaps one way to understand the meditations brought together in this book is as demonstration and discussion of this black method of "endless inventiveness"—a practice in the spectra of possibility, rehearsals of leaping and falling, sun-kissed by felicitous, often fugacious happenings.[48] It is an incessant organization of pessimism, thrown-together parties that will break up upon impact with any grounding certainty. The organization demanded for political legibility is frustrated by the movement of our inevitable, unreliable revolt, and yet even as this agitation is not necessarily organized opposition, it cannot but send tremors through the order of politicality, troubling Western thought, common sense and speculative, in its play within the volcanic crossings of possibility. This is a practice of revolutionary intoxication, and—to borrow from Jared Sexton—"there has never been anything else worth the trouble."[49]

One

Haiti's Infrasonic Boom

A company of soldiers is gathered on the upper floor of a plantation house set on a promontory of Saint-Domingue's northern coast. These troops are among the remaining seven thousand of the more than sixty-five thousand sent by Napoleon on what was, purportedly, an expedition to "pacify" their troubled colony.[1] *The house was fortified and punctured with loopholes not for the usual combat or defense purposes but rather as part of the strategic directive from the metropole, this directive amounting to little more than "frighten the ... cowardly and disorganized Blacks" into submission. Hundreds of blockhouses had been planned toward this aim, and some several months later, with the descent into total war (this "struggle to the death between Black and White"), the chain of ill-placed holes, too high up the walls to be of use, taunt these fatigued troops.*[2]

In this closing chapter, Vertières has become a site of strategic importance, heavily defended and otherwise hedged in by a barbed blockade of aloe and vines. Ineffectual loopholes notwithstanding, it had been the ideal last holdout, although this turn of season is betraying its fragility. Rain seeps through the roof and through the ceiling onto these malnourished, exhausted soldiers, already damp with humidity, by now acquiescent to the mosquitoes that had arrived with the rain. Among the last orders given by General de Rochambeau before resigning his post in anticipation of this disaster was to plant the fields over the other side of the estuary with peas. But this was too little, too late. Not much had been eaten this past week even as dozens of prisoners in the Cap-Français area, mainly black, were "take[n] . . . board" (a French military euphemism for "execution by drowning") as a way to deal with food shortage.[3] This is the very last gasp of Napoleon's attempt to reestablish, if not slavery, the racial order it was indexed to. And if not that, then to raze the newly formed society, no longer colony but not yet state.[4]

These soldiers—damp from the rain and air, weary from hunger, perhaps a little drunk from the dregs of brandy and rum, which had been prescribed to ease the disquiet of these last days—awaited what was clearly inevitable. It is now daybreak, and two more of them are taken with fever. It is in this most miserable of conditions that the soldiers hear the sound of "awful howling" coming over the lush hills of Charrier and Pierre-Michel.[5] As this confusion of rhythm, of what sounds like (and might well be) a cacophony of drums and conch shells, approaches, it gradually metamorphosizes into song, intricate but bleared counterpoints, cabalistic, crepuscular.[6] Closer still the music comes, and among the indiscernible, the utterly outlandish, one of the soldiers in the holdout swears he hears "La Marseillaise," the anthem of their own revolution.[7] They all strain to listen. And sure enough, fighting against the polyphonic blur, albeit in accents that deform and jog, they make out the words

> Arise, children of the Fatherland,
> The day of glory has arrived!
> Against us, tyranny's
> Bloody standard is raised,
> Do you hear, in the countryside,
> The roar of those ferocious soldiers?
> They're coming right into your arms
> To cut the throats of your sons, your women!

They hear their anthem and wonder who they are fighting against.[8]

1. Consider the following from Slavoj Žižek:

> When black slaves in Haiti recognized themselves as the subjects of human rights declared by the French Revolution, they of course in some sense "missed the point"—the fact that, although universal in their form ("all men"), human rights effectively privileged white men of property; however, this very "misreading" had explosive emancipatory consequences. This is what Hegel's Cunning of Reason is about: human rights were "really meant" to be accepted only by white men of property, but their universal form was their truth. It was thus the first interpellation which was wrong, but the true interpellation could only actualize itself through the false one, as its secondary misreading.⁹

I appreciate that Žižek's rhetorical disposition demands that he wear his politics on his sleeve, allowing us to readily access critical theory as an "anthropological object" (to borrow a formulation from Nadia Yala Kisukidi).¹⁰ Its candor gives away the so-often covert overrepresentation of this genre of critical thought. The universalism it advocates for is proposed in disarming transparency. In this case, we are told outright that the Haitians were mistaken to believe that the 1789 Declaration of the Rights of Man—the French Republic's very first article, on the inalienable right to freedom—was written with them in mind. They "miss the point." They mistake themselves as addressees of the interpellation. Theirs is a response in the absence of an actual invitation. Indeed—to borrow from Saidiya Hartman—as far as the Western world was concerned, the Haitians' response—as of "beings who [were] sentient but socially dead ... occur[ing] in the default of the political, in the absence of the rights of man or the assurances of the self-possessed individual, and perhaps even without a 'person,' in the usual meaning of the term"—registered as noise, as nonsense.¹¹ What is exciting for Žižek is how this "mistake" gets to the truth of the declaration. It repairs it, reinstating the universality that its French permutation had attenuated. Reason, or the "truth" of the ideal, escapes its containment by the successful racial education of the declaration's authors and propagators. The more serious error of the absent interpellation is corrected by a response into a void. With their mistake, Haitians write themselves into universal history, renovating the modern European ideal and contributing in an unprecedented way to the unfurling of Spirit.

2. There is something quite satisfying about this scene in which the dialectical rover roamed across to the Antilles, staying just long enough to kiss the first black nation-state to life, about how these voices from the margins and below answer an invitation not meant for them and, in so doing, perfect the First Republic's freedom song. And yet there is another way to read the scene. We might consider inspirations of another world orienting the conjuring that we call the Haitian Revolution even as this patently unfolds within the "social cauldron" that is Western modernity.[12] Perhaps the Haitians were not mistaken; perhaps they had not misread. Perhaps they only acted as though they believed the declaration was meant for them. In fact, at the risk of stating the obvious, in light of the catalog of technologies of dehumanization working at the interface of the black African slave and white French landowner (the maintenance of such being essential to the wealth and security of colony and empire), the ignorance assumed in Žižek's account should not be accepted without question. Perhaps they only *acted* as if they believed that liberty, equality, and fraternity were extended to them. After all, these were a people that incubated not only the "organisation and discipline of a trained army" but also "all the tricks and dodges of guerrillas."[13] C. L. R. James recounts one such instance:

> A black appeared among [Jean] Boudet's soldiers, claiming to be a deserter. As Boudet in the midst of his guard questioned him, he seemed overwhelmed with fear. But he was a scout, and having learned all he wanted to know he made a dash for safety. Boudet, who saw his movement first, tried to stop him. But the black nearly bit off his thumb. Then, dashing beneath the legs of a horse, he overthrew the soldiers who tried to stop him, plunged into the river, and escaped amid a shower of bullets. He was struck, for on the opposite bank he collapsed, but a party of his own people carried him off.[14]

Histories of the Haitian Revolution are replete with such tales of confidence trickery, misdirection, and mimicry performed by the rebellion army and their equally astute maroon counterparts. Perhaps the cunning was not *all* reason's.[15] With this in mind, perhaps the Haitians' "La Marseillaise" was not fortuitous ignorance but rather a guileful mobilization of the critical potential encoded in the "richly and fundamentally double . . . *sense of being* of the Negro"—to borrow Nahum Dimitri Chandler's gloss of W. E. B. Du Bois's essential formulation.[16] As an aside but one that aids an appreciation of the contemporary stakes of this insight and to take another pass at the matter with Žižek—although, this time, not with the Haitians but with the contemporary black scholar—we might say it looks like we've "missed the point" of the university's solicitation "Knowledge for all." One might see us with our monographs, seminars, and professorships and assume that we have misconstrued the call. The secularization of the *studia humanitatis*, its democratization, did not extend to us barbarians at the gate. We are responding into a void. But this mistake of ours is beautifully revelatory of the "true interpellation" to which we are party, Žižek would argue. Our genuine misreading of the false interpellation ("we say that this is open to anyone but of course we did not mean the African") would correct it, make it live up to the truth of its words that is obscured by its intention. The cunning of reason finds a way even when faced with such limitations and ignorance on either side. And yet rather than misreading the *studia*'s call, on closer or more patient reflection, you will find that so many of us have a duplicitous relationship to the university. We haven't missed the point in seeming to pledge ourselves to academe. We are shady; we do so under false pretenses. Our acting as though we inhabit the space is how we (can) "inhabit" the space. We act as if we believe that the world can hear us, but we're well aware that our abrasive contribution, when tuned to, might register as nonsense (wanting in precision, determination, parsimony, discipline). We realize that the disorganized complexity of our ineluctable embodied critique might only gain legibility when reduced to shades of Karl Marx or Hegel or Michel Foucault or Adorno. It looks as though we are correcting the false interpellation by way of our ignorance, but we proceed in the understanding that our wonky formulations, our irregular equations, tend to register as a sort of conceptual vandalism (in fact, our bad form is only partly a response, only partly explained as an "acting out," helping to relieve the nausea critical immanence can induce—such demonic agitation is also revelry in an endless improvisation of homegrown methods, which are utterly fit for purpose but tend not to travel well). Our deceit is that we act as though the world can hear us, as if we understand the world to hear us, that we believe the university might (want to) know our blackness—those ways to world and thought that, it seems, must remain opaque or inscrutable in order that the health and coherence of the European world be maintained. We do not embrace the "universal form" authentically.

3. It is their singing "La Marseillaise" that is most readily taken up—this apocryphal image of self-liberated slaves adopting the anthem of the French Revolution, that emblem of the modern ideal of liberty, equality, and fraternity, this emancipatory ideal "imitated" and "perfected" by African captives (their education by way of colonial conquest and enslavement, as prescribed by Hegel in his lectures on the philosophy of history, exceeding all expectations). Their refusal to revert to the legal status of enslavement, enshrined in an astounding performance of their oppressor's freedom song—that song being a testament and aspiration they adopt as their own. For Žižek, Haitians singing the anthem represents a case not of propagation by force, an imposition, or what Denise Ferreira da Silva would understand to be a technology of "engulfment."[17] This is an instance of the spread of ideals that became a commons of an international project of liberty, a "humanist ode to the brotherhood of all people," preceding Ludwig van Beethoven's Ninth Symphony by some twenty years, that demonstrates how—borrowing from Susan Buck-Morss—"common humanity exists in spite of culture and its differences."[18] And incidentally, Žižek tells us, it only gets us into the right ball park to interpret "the message of the Haitian soldiers' *Marseillaise* [as] ... 'even we, the primitive blacks, are able to assimilate ourselves to your high culture and politics, to imitate it as a model!'" More exactly, their rendition tells Žižek that "we [the Haitians] are more French than . . . the Frenchmen," an improved version of the European ideal.[19] The ventriloquism is a mind-bending confusion of originals and impersonations—Žižek speaking the project of European modernity through the Haitians, attributing to them sentiments more closely matched, I would imagine, to those of the auditors in the blockhouse. We are removed from the scene of those black voices raised in song and placed within a mood of appropriate universalism. The universal is French and dialectical even as it comes of age at the margins of the empire, at the edge of the world. The war to prevent the reinstatement of the Code Noir (if not the chattel slavery that it helped secure) and the declaration of a black "universal" (contained in Jean-Jacques Dessalines's article 14), which marked the end of the conflict, were not considered consistent

with an unfolding of world consciousness. The engine of world history hastily vacated the island in the wake of Toussaint L'Ouverture's capture and exile, moving onto the next site of eruption or, from the looks of things, into remission, awaiting further improvement on the brilliance of the governor-general's Saint-Domingue.[20]

4. Žižek also moves on too quickly—he from the scene of French soldiers in the blockhouse and the soundtrack of their opponents' voices raised in song. There is a sonic confusion to be addressed. For some time before recognizing the anthem, the French company heard "tribal war chants" and "awful howling."[21] Are we to put this down to the metonymic chain we heard Žižek stumble upon a moment ago that links black skin to the primitive? Perhaps due to such conditioning, the soldiers only imagined they heard howling. Moreover, might we reconstruct a listening experience in which such imaginaries comingle with the hearing of the unfamiliar prosody of these recently shipped Africans? To borrow a historical note from Jean-Pierre Le Glaunec, "In the confusion of that November day, some Creole and French words could be heard along with African [ones]."[22] Žižek does not register this polyglot chorus, the acknowledgment of which would have allowed for a less vaudevillian sketch. He does not appreciate that the African and Creole accents' disfigurement of the French language provides a metaphor for the dialectical movement of the unfolding of freedom in this age of revolution. The manner in which these dialects break and reset the language speaks to how the Haitian revolutionary forces offer a reconstituted understanding of liberty to the world. Europe's anthem is disarticulated by Africa's sound, practically unrecognizable. French freedom is transfigured by *literal* enslavement and race, by a place at the margins, by illegitimate participants (from the perspective of Europe, thoroughly ill prepared for the occasion). In this way, the Haitians contribute to the standard that is revolution—a standard that exists only insofar as it can be found in these various articulations, a standard that has no original blueprint but instances of which are lit up in France and in Haiti. This is an ever-emergent notion of freedom, a rootless notion, that is broken up upon impact at each particular rendition. It is a creolization whether we are listening to Haiti or to the revolution in the metropole that preceded it.[23] Indeed, this is what Žižek is insisting upon in

his reproach of what is seen as a decolonial knee-jerk rejection of the European universal. This European universal—the unfurling of freedom that is the specific inspiration of that world historical—allows and actually insists on it being reconstituted by the material circumstances it encounters. Žižek writes, "Every dialectical passage is thus a form of dislocation: the previous Substance is dislocated into a new encompassing universality. It is not the same Universality which passes from one to another particular form—in each passage, Universality itself is dislocated, it is reduced to a subordinate moment of a new Universality."[24] Haiti becomes not a subsidiary, a mere dialect of the world historical, but, for a time, the paragon, in relation to which Europe becomes a mere precursory accent.

5. In his essay "Not in Between," Fred Moten writes,

> Toussaint, all hooked up and bound to the French, trapped in the no-man's-land between liberty (abstract-subjective-telic-white) and independence (national-objective-present-black: the position Dessalines seemingly naturally slips into) hips us, by way of James, to the need for something not in between these formulations. For James, the desire is for something not in between darkness and enlightenment, something not in between Dessalines and Toussaint. And we've got to think what it means not just for Dessalines to take the men into his confidence *but to talk to them*. We've got to think the form of that talk as well as its content, in untutored and broken dialect, unretouched, addressed to his followers and not to the French, sounded and not written and rewritten, seemingly unmediated by the graphic, and, finally, concerned not with liberty but with independence. The opposition between Toussaint and Dessalines, between (the desire for what is called) enlightenment and (the adherence to what is called) darkness, between direction to the French and direction to the slaves, is also between speech and writing. Dessalines leaps forward; he jumps into the ditch, sounding, descending. That jumping descent is coded as a jumping forward. Another dialectic. It's what James's phrasing does to the sentence. Oscillation, bridging over to leaping forward, jumping into. This is a question of music.[25]

At first glance, we might understand the image concept that Moten offers of Dessalines jumping into a ditch at the climax of the battle for Crête-à-Pierrot as something of this "dislocating" dialectic.[26] The episode of military cunning that supplies the seed of Moten's thought tells of Dessalines staging a retreat only to lure Jean-François-Joseph Debelle and his troops into an open field ambush. It is the leap rather than the attack on which we should focus, but this "descending" leap into the dugout—Dessalines's shortsighted genius, his taking the *bossales* into his confidence as he brings the notion of a black state into existence—is distinct from the supposedly great leaps of European radicalism and is to be appraised as extrinsic to the rollout of the universal freedom project.[27] Furthermore, Dessalines's leap not only speaks of a reconfiguration of this particular dialectic, culminating in universal emancipation—its apotheosis occurring in the colony, advanced by African slaves. It also provides an image of a discombobulating "dose of dialect" that might transform the dialectical method itself. This phrase "dose of dialect" is a modification that David Scott makes to poet and scholar Edward Kamau Brathwaite's "maroon" imploration for "some dialect to go along with the dialectic" of a Third World Marxism. Brathwaite is writing in reference to Walter Rodney's *How Europe Underdeveloped Africa*, which he considered "truly revolutionary... a verbal bomb and bullet," even as he calls attention to a dampening of the book's radical impulse by its reliance on the "modernist/progressive dialectic" proper to the European world.[28] Kevin Okoth also adopts a version of the phrase in his discussion of the "ontological totality," seemingly reading against Cedric Robinson's grain. The "ontological totality," an indispensable idea, loosely sketched in Robinson's *Black Marxism: The Making of the Black Radical Tradition*, refers to a nonlocal, transgenerational "collective being" oriented by an extraterritorial world of inspiration, set apart from that within which the European freedom project unfolds. (It is inextricable entanglement of a dispersed gathering, or, in long reverberation of Hortense Spillers seminal work, what thinkers in black study have in more recent years explored by way of the notion of "flesh."[29] Robinson speaks of this as the "collective consciousness" of an "outlandish people" whose "epistemology granted supremacy to metaphysics not the material."[30]) It is a "structure of mind... more charismatic than political." Robinson's underdrawing of the notion (which in *Black Marxism* gets jammed on the nature of its violence) is found in snatches, constelled throughout his work, but we might say that the "preser[vation] [of] the ontological totality" is the theorist's foremost motivation.[31] This commitment is demonstrated in his interrogation of the "order of politicality" and his skepticism concerning the pertinence of this sphere of action and thought to an appreciation of black collectivity. We hear it in his insistence on the centrality of a certain complementarity of the contrary, a state of being in which "all are equally incomplete."[32] In distinction, for Okoth, the ontological totality is taken to be "an attempt to inject a dose of dialect into the Marxian dialectic"—this word "injection" suggestive of a therapeutic intervention, a corrective retention of a universalizing orientation that Robinson is keen to devalorize.[33] In Žižek, this "dose of dialect" manifests as a chromosomal alteration, and, importantly, one the dialectic constitutively allows for. As we heard earlier, "in a dialectical process predicate always passes into subject: what was at the beginning a subordinate particular moment of the process asserts itself as its subject and retroactively posits its presuppositions as its own moments ('predicates')." Toussaint's Haiti does not (only) become of the European universal. In fact, the latter "is reduced to a subordinate moment of a new Universality."[34] This constellates with the notion of the "free pulse of a *new* dialect/ic," which Moten hears in both the form and theme of James's *The Black Jacobins: Toussaint L'Ouverture and the San Domingo Revolution*.[35] A demonstration of another mode of "oscillation," a "suspension and propulsion," a dislocation of the synthesizing trajectory of European engulfment (what Žižek might commend as a more faithful rendering of the dialectic than the decolonialist typically allows for). By way of the form of *The Black Jacobins* and the content provided for it by Haiti's emergence, we observe a "lyric disruption of a certain Europeanized notion of public/national history and historical trajectory" taking place. We hear a twang, an interiorized swing that tests the plasticity of the dialectic; a ghosting imposition of Africa that sounds in accents, that can, seemingly, be exorcised through the writing and rewriting of letters; that cannot be contained in the written French. But I think that it is important to underscore that dialect does more than break and reset the dialectic, its infiltrating syncopation rendering the historical engine unrecognizable to previous hosts. Dialects and accents (only recoverable in their sounding) *might* come along with the unfolding of (universal) freedom *and/or* take another mode of transport. The unchartable African accents that are the potholed ground of possibility for the pile up of grammars from which dialect emerges and that form the excess or exhaust that resist letters, written and rewritten for prosperity (forever a ghostly taunt of what that archive can't have), certainly sound for revolutionary and independence movements. Yet this conference and its *òrò*, taking place in the "ditch of *Vodun* ritual," does not (only or always) come along with the irruptive syncopation it supplies.[36]

6. Those thick accents escaped Žižek's attention, and so it is of little surprise that he also fails to hear from those same voices (or from voices in their company) anthems in other languages (Congolese, Yorùbá, or Creole, for instance); he does not hear the polyrhythmic pulsation of a confluence of "independent syntaxes and outer noises"—to borrow from Moten.[37] To acknowledge such, one does not need to deny the rendition of the French standard; we do not need to reject the notion that Haiti serves as a perfection of a European ideal or that it appears to move dialectically (at moments or from a particular perspective). We do not need to deny that it performs universality through sublative reconstitution—the universal that *really* matters to Žižek. I am, however, suggesting that the confusion of sound from which "La Marseillaise" finally emerges is significant. I am suggesting that this fabulous soundscape, palpitating with the spectra of various languages, dialects, accents, chants, and songs, provides an intriguing conceptual accessory through which to consider alternative laws of historical movement. When we broaden our audition out from the Francophile Toussaint (so useful to the European universalist project) to take in the activities of the laboring *bossales* as well as those of the black nationalist, alongside the well-known history of victors and vanquished, we hear those who—to borrow language from Theodor Adorno—"were not embraced by this dynamic," those of the "blind spots that have escaped the dialectic," those of the "cross-grained, opaque, unassimilated material," those who move by way of infrasonic, outer noise.[38] The struggles for continued liberty rub up against those for independence and, crucially, are also contiguous with the socialities from which a nation of community not compatible with the universal freedom project continues to spread and be nurtured. As Jean Casimir is at pains to show in his recent

history, to truly understand Haiti's formation, it is not enough to spotlight the war of independence and the black nationalism that followed. One must appreciate that from the start of the 1790s through the insurrections in the name of liberty from enslavement and those for independence that followed, a "Guinean communal order" (one which frustrated both (anti)colonial bureaucracy and nation building alike) was being disseminated by/about the laboring class. This "social life [that] didn't correspond to Western norms" was, from the perspective of the (anti)colonial administration, a reckless improvidence. These "newly freed," with their "embarrassing atavisms," their African "organization of settlements, language, religion, music and song, and customs," promoted an irresponsible tolerance for "flagrant disobedience . . . laziness and vagabondage."³⁹ Most important here is not so much the unruliness of this liminal sociality but the apposition of the distinct orders—"a muddled mosaic of contrary forces."⁴⁰ The two orders motivated by different laws of historical movement, contrary projects and directions, "exist[ed] alongside each other without creating uncontrollable fires of conflict . . . enabl[ing] the coexistence of secession and revolution."⁴¹ The Haitians dislocative maneuvers as evidenced in Casimir and that Rocío Zambrana is keen to unfurl at a more conceptual register in her essay "Hegelian History Interrupted" are not (only) part of reconfigurations proper to a functioning dialectic.⁴² The Haitians particular mode of disarticulation is indexed to the contiguity of the development of a "nation" of community, on the one hand, and the formation of a state, on the other. What Zambrana and Casimir highlight in their holding apart of state and nation is that the necessary development from nation/people to state is disrupted or inoperable in the Haitian case. Indeed, the persistence of a certain statelessness is a defining characteristic of the emergent nation/state. They are not so much disputing the sublative dislocation of the revolution in Haiti but rather are keen to show that the dialectic (and sublation, as its key mechanics) loses its explanatory sufficiency in the face of the simultaneity of "the people" and state (state-building violence against "the people" notwithstanding). We might say that what Zambrana, through Casimir, is getting at is that the pulse, or the laws of movement (and/or the narration of such) of Haiti's revolution (and that of its war of independence), is not exhausted or adequately/appropriately covered by recourse to sublation. The emergence of Haiti (nation, state, and/or community) needs to be understood as more involved than an injection of dialect into the dialectic or a dislocation of the dialectical process of freedom by that of independence. Limiting the intervention of the African accent to it merely facilitating a perfection of modernity's "sublime communism" turns us away from a distinct mode of narrative transport, the distinct pulsation of Brathwaite's paratactical suggestion. To misuse Moten just a little, Haiti emerges as much by "appositional collision [and snuggle]" as it does sublative confrontation.[43]

7. Dialect and dialectic. Dialect/ic. The marsupial relationship of the lexicon reflects a conceptual correspondence fulsome enough to avail itself both to those who insist that the Hegelian dialectic is an instrument of engulfment and its defenders, who remind us that the dialectic demands the dislocation of any given category, that it is always already dialect, the out inside forcing dialectic's essential and continuous reconstitution, that this dislocation ensures that the dialectic is never the Queen's English but always pidgin, broken (and reset) upon contact with virgin soil or ears. The poetic seduction in pairing the two terms, the way one consumes the other, the way one irrupts from the other, should not blind us to Brathwaite's, Robinson's, and Moten's invocations signposting a distinct tendency. This epistemic orientation is characterized by patulous cadency that cannot be contained within the prevalent movement of critical thought in the Western humanities. The distinction is not of language, cannot be closed by translation or by ears more attuned to the canorous, thick accents of its critique, but is to do with its tolerance for the riot of time signatures encountered when simultaneously traveling by way of multiple sets of laws of historical movement. An ability to play in distinct temporalities concurrently, rather (or much more) than the presence of an alternate pulse, is what identifies this mode of thought and being. As Moten writes of black study, an important site of this competency, "its broken, coded documents sanction *walking in another world while passing through this one*, graphically disordering the administered scarcity," flouting Western administration's logical frugality. It presents as heterogenous, unruly spread (blackness's "submerged span" and/or Afri-

can pan, *ìtàn*), as temporal incompatibility/incongruity, as jerk and reject.[44] The movement of black thought might well find itself in moments of dialectical unfolding. Yet these moments, against the context of the infidelity flaunted by the exuberant traverse of this world and that, lack the thriftiness that dialectical movement demands. The specific genre of contradiction— which might more precisely be understood as a sort of logical gluttony—is one in which Western speculative thought is played through, its "common sense" seemingly adhered to but (perhaps) ultimately in bad faith and with an irreverence that might be mistaken for sophistry or the negative turn of a dialogical round. The West is "pass[ed] through"—through to its bitter conclusions. But at the same time, this other Weltanschauung, one that moves for the sake of and in pursuance of the "surreal presence" of "material spirit," "walk[s] in another world"—a world that calls for (and forth) the ability to move through multiple worlds.[45] This distinctive epistemic orientation is both an alternate pulse and a faculty for the play in multiple temporalities. Does this not unite much of the field of black study? This extraterritorial black thought with its *critical* interest in a world that strains toward ever-greater determination, control, and "inclusivity" performs the impossible (or at least acts as if it does), fulfilling the "obligation to think at the same time dialectically and undialectically."[46]

Two
Unthinkable Nonsense

8. To introduce this contribution by way of a pickup that will set its key and mood, I spin to reverse Claudia Rankine's aphorism indexing the European world's supposedly wild imagination and black death and say that it is because the West is *compelled* to "police its imagination" that "black people are dying."[1] This world, which valorizes the actual, feels crushing despair in the face of our alogical logic. It suffers acute anxiety when met by the walking, talking contradictions that condition its founding.[2] Confrontation with the relative ease and proficiency in resting in/with aporia must be experienced as an affront. The dialectic's cravings for contradiction notwithstanding (and perhaps the very point), the world's impulse is toward urgent resolution. As Kevin Quashie puts it, "the world's lack of imagination for black being" precipitates "brutal enactments against such being."[3] The possibilities we hold must be met with force. We are modally anomalous. We can be without actuality. We will not or cannot regulate our semblance, cannot or will not actualize our fantastic every day or groom our indeterminations, our "this-way-and-that" multiperspective modality, our revelry in could-ness.[4]

This is the mood from which I approach Sylvia Wynter's ceremony finding.[5] And indeed, one way to read her documentation of the pursuit is as remonstrance against the emergence and maintenance of an epistemic locus that cultures a profound want of imagination. Wynter tells us that our current way of "being human" is such that the "ceremonies ... cannot be found" that might "wed the Earth to the Moon, [allow] Othello to remain wedded to Desdemona, for Bon to marry a 'negro.'"[6] That is to say that the hierarchical oppositions and the neurobiological reward system that maintain them, instituted by our current ontoepistemological formation, must not be violated. Crucially, these structural oppositions were/are not put in place by "speaking/behaving subjects" but rather have emerged from the "ratiomorphic apparatus generic to the human"; the defect is inherent in "natural reason."[7] It is a deficiency that afflicts all societies. It is a universal obstinance, a cosmogonically, neurochemically induced compulsion to fortify one's own "genre-specific autopoietic field" and the hierarchical oppositions that constitute it.[8] This poverty of imagination is also, at the same time, a more temporally local consequence of the socialization or engulfment of "all forms of human being into a single homogenized descriptive statement that is based on the figure of the West's liberal monohumanist *Man*."[9] While "all human systems, from that of the royal dynasty of Iron Age East Africa to that of Christian medieval Europe or to that of our own" delay, disrupt, or destroy any prospective ceremony that might disturb or confuse this societal geometry, the modern European is exceptional—sucking much of the globe into its vortex, its human/(b)lack "behavior-orienting opposition" curbing the possibilities that such diversity should bring.[10] Indeed, for Wynter, "we all remain submitted to a memory, that of Western bourgeois *Man*, and to the logic of its stacked deck and dealt cards which dictates that any such concrete realisation on the part of the masses, and thereby, on the part also of the majority of the peoples of Africa, must continue to be thwarted."[11] Black people are dying, and black life is thwarted, due to an inability to consider possibilities beyond those that might be actualized from these conditions.

Prescribed is "a new science of the Word," a curative scripting of a human text that would allow for—to borrow from Adorno—"the thought of the many [to] no longer [be] inimical."[12] This telling of new stories has a neurobiological imperative. The renovation of the second set of instructions, the storytelling, overturning "representations of origin" will inform this evolutionary first. And a rallying of the "damned of the earth" to jointly respond to the open invitation to contribute to this autopoietic unfolding that we call human is crucial to the telling and becoming of a *"counterhumanism—one now ecumenically 'made to the measure of the world.'"*[13] If this *is* a politics of representation, it is one markedly distinct from that which registers its demand in equity, diversity, and inclusion mission statements, commitments to affirmation by engulfment. It is not to do with recognition but rather with actualization. Or to put it a different way, Wynter alerts us to the fact that the problem of African and black actualization is not, at bottom, a problem of recognition—not a deficit to be addressed within the political sphere, not a problem solved by more equitable representation in a court of law or cinematic arena or, if we're feeling optimistic, by way of a war of positions that, at best (for us), ends in impasse, that, if we are fortunate, terminates in a caesura of unproductive contradiction irresolvable under present socioeconomic conditions (irresolvable under the perhaps perennial conditions of this world dependent on African and black liminality).[14] She is alerting us to the fact that modernity—that biocentric cosmogony, genre, or understanding of the human—is just a story. It is just a story and yet a story that *makes* us, "self-inscripting and inscripted flesh."[15] And as we, the historically disenfranchised, are storytellers also, there is cause to be cautiously optimistic. Wynter is pointing out the responsibility that the black thinker, the black artist, the black storyteller are faced with, to set down in ink what we are all about, our *nommo*, our Word becoming flesh—becoming human.[16] She wants to assure us that even in our most focused dismantling and vandalism of Western civilization—something of a compulsion and disproportionate preoccupation for us—we are rewriting *our* mythos.

9. The swash of the overture is thrilling. The universalist program toward the ecumenically human (or toward our becoming ecumenically human), being led by those on the margins (at the vestibule) and from below (perhaps due to our second sight or to it being our round or to our removal from Man's epicenter), is incredibly seductive.[17] How long have we been wondering whether the desire for African (and black) actualization could ever be ful-

filled in the West and whether it would, in fact, make for a blackened world? (I'd say since before Jena Hegel if our Haitian forerunners are anything to go by).[18] We spend an inordinate amount of time ruminating on this question—whether a blackening of the European world, past the superficial incorporation of bodies plucked from their geographical seeding ground and then primed (a crude whitewashing into its common sense), could ever occur. Hegel's infamous prescription for African participation in Spirit, an education of these persons by way of enslavement and colonialism, has not made for a European world inflected with African orientations. For Wynter, this might be explained by the attenuation of the human that secularization exacted, a handy but unnecessary and ultimately unsustainable concentration of representation—emancipation from divine providence coupled with (in fact, indexed to) subjugation of those ill prepared (and unpreparable) for the coming consciousness, to splice with Hegel's philosophy of history. And yet for Wynter, even if this discrepancy in representation were addressable, if African ways to world had not been displaced by those of the white West or if the emancipatory project of the *studia*'s heresy had not been dependent upon African subjugation (perhaps allowing African ways with time and to world to impinge on its script), the need for a new heresy would remain. The adherence of *all* societies, regardless of their metaphysical outlook, to a paradigm that sees their autopoietic imperative motored by the dialectical churning of "significant ill" and "cure," is an inadequacy of our being human, which requires maturation.[19] Necessary is a brand-new Word to become flesh that breaks with the "structural oppositions" our still primitive hybridity relies on.

It is this universalizing move, sweeping the whole world into a European common sense and its particular difficulties with diversity, opposition, and contradiction, that is a sticking point for me.[20] Do *"all* peoples of the world" have these same limitations? Are we compelled to only read them as they appear in the "memory" of "our contemporary Western world system"?[21] Might the supposed ontoepistemological *sufficiency* of the "governing code of symbolic life and death," the code that drives and explains our current way of "being human," not be scrutinized as a technology of engulfment? This is to query the notion that the "transcultural" code by which "positively/negatively marked representations" are developed and maintained, exhaustively accounts for the diversity of symbolic correspondence engaged by "all peoples of the world."[22] It is not to deny the uses to which these other peoples are put in the furnishing of this monocultural memory, just as I would assent to Buck-Morss's assertion of the Haitian Revolution as the perfecting of modern European ideals. It is to register that this surrogacy does not displace commitments more local, where the contradictory nature of life from which these categories of antagonisms emerge might not demand a mechanics for determinate resolution/negation. Indeed, the capacity to satisfy the interests of both worlds—that which Cedric Robinson evocatively terms the "social cauldron" and that of our "specific inspiration"—is a defining distinction.[23] This is the point of divergence that anchors the unfolding thought of this chapter.

10. Contradiction is something like a litmus test here. How a structure of mind, a particular common sense, deals with it is incredibly revelatory. In anticipation of a more sustained discussion of the topic that will take place in the next chapter and to dip into the notion further downstream, I want to share how my understanding of how this capacity to satisfy the interests of both worlds, which I consider of defining significance for black thought, necessarily questions Wynter's inattention to the persistent significance of polytheism. This is to say that the objective of this fragment toggles between saying something about the contradictory nature of this ambidextrous *"walking in another world while passing through this one,"* as Fred Moten puts it, and drawing attention toward persistently polythetic black thought.[24] It would be a mistake to identify Wynter's own universalism with that of Man, a universalism which she traces back to the advent of monotheism, the "high point in the evolution of human cognitive mechanisms" (this progressive inclusivity being the apotheosis of a distinctly human concern whose beginnings were to be found in the "relatively closed aesthetic orders of the particularistic Paleolithic groups").[25] In fact, I might even suggest that Wynter's ecumenically human and the "colonized-nonwhite-black-poor-incarcerated-jobless peoples"—these anticipated heretics, its vanguard—are a manifestation of the polytheism of African thought.[26] My main point here is that an

insistence that the advent of Islam, and later of Christianity, in many parts of the African continent led to a "displace[ment] and reoccupa[tion] [of] the traditional religions of Africa and their . . . local polytheistic and essentially agrarian strategies of identity, self-conception and . . . consciousness" might miss a critical resource that Africa supplies.[27] The arrival of Islam and Christianity was not necessarily a case of supplantation. As Andrew Apter writes, "In the context of Christianity and colonial rule, the totalizing transpositions of òrìṣà worship appropriated church and state, together with more familiar forms of uncultivated chaos, within the metaphysical horizons of the cults"—monotheism found its place within polytheistic ways to world but "certainly did not displace" them.[28] In fact, the polytheistic orientation (and I will join Apter and descend to a more local claim now) of, say, the Yorùbá—with its practices of diasporic collision and caress, in which "to split or break the tradition . . . to depart" from it, is integral to that tradition's modus operandi—is constitutively prepared for breach.[29] Theirs is a way to world that need not capitulate nor resist. For the Yorùbá universe, with its large, hospitable, expansive pantheon, to find a place for another "cult" requires no contortion. Perhaps what is less clear and requires a little more thought is the accommodation of a member that insists on its singularity, that insists on exclusivity. How is monotheism held within a polythetic outlook? What does such lack of insistence do with the autocratic discursive operations of these so-called world religions?[30] How does this orientation accommodate a movement of thought that insists on finding oneself in the other, mutual engulfment when it itself does not demand any such thing, when it is characterized by a lack of insistence?

Here, I take leave of Wynter's project, heartened by her rally of us—those voices below. I bring her cosmological wheelhouse along awhile, as I focus on the second side of this discursive coin—the contradictory nature of a black sense of being. The seeming impossibility of holding both monotheism and polytheism at once has caught my attention. Speaking of his experience of this, Wole Soyinka describes the practice of the *babaláwo* of his childhood in 1950s Yorùbáland as a "rite of continuity between the two 'worlds.'" Christian and Muslim patrons turned to the "roots, barks, jars of concentrates," the palm nuts, cowrie chains, and incantation of Ifá, a supplement that incompletes their monotheistic side—a supplementation that belies a particular way with contradictory commitments, that in fact orients their way to world, that permits this alogical "easy cohabitation, one that contradicted the actual Christian sermonizing—separatist in creed and injunctions."[31] This is an approach to the contradictory nature of existence that does not readily find a place in Western thought. It is a practice with possibilities that are not made to "sink to the ground."[32] Their coexistence exceeds what is taken to be logical for European common sense and speculative thought. This holding of monotheism within a polytheistic outlook does not provoke despair in the African. As will be explored in the next chapter, this want of despair is, from the perspective of modern German thought, a disadvantage, a defect even—despair being a crucial motivational engine for that tradition. From this view, contradiction without the compulsion to determine or improve is inexcusably improvident, rendering the energy source that fuels universal history and thought redundant.[33]

Mati Diop's 2019 film *Atlantics* is a meditation of migration and love in which the spirits of young Senegalese men who had lost their lives in the Mediterranean as they journeyed to find work join the sleeping bodies of the women they left behind. During a postscreening conversation, a question concerning the significance of what was read as an incorporation of the fantasy genre into an African film was posed. Diop replied, with a certain amount of impatience, "You don't make a fantasy film in Africa.... Fantasy is part of reality. Western culture puts a very strong border between visible, invisible, irrational, rational. I try, as a French-African person, not to apprehend Africa from the prism of my Western culture. And so it was interesting as a filmmaker to deconstruct that and to propose a film where fantasy and reality are intertwined."[34] What is this structure of thought that enables or allows for this invasion of the fantastic? Or more precisely, what is this way to thought and world in which fantasy and reality cohabitate with such ease? What way to world is this in which the actual appears demoted and in which the fantastic is of the everyday? This entwinement (sometimes collision, sometimes caress) of fantasy and reality requires some distance from the demands of epistemological realism. This is the very same common sense whose pantheon finds a place for a "jealous god" demanding complete and exclusive fidelity. To invite the "one, true God," the universal self-sufficient, into the four hundred plus one (this number signaling an expectation of, but not insistence on, expansion, deformation, embrace, and release—an openness) requires an ease with contradiction that only one versed or socialized in fantastic possibility is able to stand.

11. The Ibo philosopher Chris O. Ijiomah tells us that the "African worldview . . . accepts the coexistence of seemingly opposing realities which however complement each other. This is what is expressed in the proverb, 'wherever something stands, something also will stand beside it.'"[35] From this point of view, "two contrary realities can unite without producing a contradiction," or, to attune to language more consonant with a European sensibility, we could say that the law of noncontradiction is suspended or not insisted upon; contradictory qualities or positions can hold together without anxiety, without the need to push through to greater determination.[36] Consider this verse of *oríkì* in praise of Èṣù, the Yorùbá *òrìshà* who presides over the principle of contradiction, twoness (what Moten might call the "blur"), and indeterminacy:

> The short and tall one
> Whose head is barely visible when [they] walk through a peanut farm
> Thanks to the fact that [they are] very tall
> But Èṣù must climb the hearthstone in order to put salt in the soup pot.[37]

Èṣù is not merely one *òrìshà* among many—being the messenger and the portal through which one must pass in order that supplication to other *òrìshà* is received. This inordinate footfall across Èṣù's realm allows, according to Soyinka, much opportunity for engagement with the "exploits that surround [their] manifold presences or intrusions."[38] They embody "a cautionary lesson to humankind not to trust too readily to appearances but to learn to negotiate the infinite possibilities, and thus, the pitfalls of seemingly factual evidence or apparent normality," such as that which European ordinary thought most often insists and depends on. Èṣù's exhortation is to, "in short, learn to be constantly on guard for the revelation of reality as only another aspect of liminality."³⁹ The liminal takes priority here. Along with verses and visual media that depict Èṣù being simultaneously buoyant youth and elder, as holding two genders, or as bearing two heads facing in opposite directions, there are various verses highlighting their contradictory height.⁴⁰ This version quoted above is fascinating as it not only itemizes/enumerates the pairs of contradiction (Èṣù being both tall and short) but also uses conjunctives that compound the seeming alogicality of the statement. We are not merely presented with paratactical statements but phrases that want to hold the contradiction together to suggest some sort of appositional complementarity. Their face is barely visible in and among the low shrubbery of a peanut field *because* they are so tall. Furthermore, even as they tower, they are small enough to need to climb as an insect might onto the hearthstone to season the stew. In a discussion of Èṣù's customary black-and-white harlequin, Durotoye Adeleke suggests that there is a decided "unity in contradictory situations within Yoruba Society," that there is—in language that offends our critical sensibility—"harmony in contradiction," and—in a turn of phrase that is almost Hegelian—that for the Yorùbá, "existence or survival has its basis in contradictions."⁴¹

Within this African perspective, as Ada Agada's useful gloss provides, "the law of contradiction loses its strict applicability so that a thing can be what it is and something else even as seemingly opposing propositions can both be true, with contexts taken fully into consideration."⁴² It is this want of crisis that undergirds the contiguity of "Christian sermonizing—separatist in creed and injunctions"—and the *òrìshà* and ancestral worship of the Ifá pantheon.⁴³ To be faced with this and not motivated to move through its contradictions suggests a categorical distinction. Could the European world recognize this Africa without suffering structural collapse? Would its inclusion not be fatal? I am broaching the possibility that the reason this world is incapable of true blackening is not only a consequence of the comprehensive education in racial difference. It is due, moreover, to the modal ambiguity characteristic of African thought. The modes and movements of possibility particular to Africa are incompatible (or make it incompatible) with the European world. Significantly, these (de)ranged maneuvers of African thought are generative of a logical exorbitance that fails to trigger a crisis. This is an orientation anticipatory of breach, which will take in contributions it does not necessarily possess the conditions to support. It is comportment that can welcome what are, for it, fantastic possibilities—possibilities not contained in *its* "actuality," such as the universalizing embrace or grasp of the one true God. This African way to world and thought *might not* refuse what confronts it in intransigence even as the encounter is deeply disturbing for its antipode.

12. The problem of black actualization is often framed as a problem of recognition—a deficit to be addressed within the "order of politicality," a problem solved by better representation in civil society.[44] And yet the world of *real* possibilities (those contained within the actual as potentialities) cannot accommodate African orientation; it is structurally incapable of diversification and transformation by way of vagaries beyond its historical dynamic. It lacks the mechanism for recognizing black life as a real possibility; it does not possess the conditions for black actualization.[45] From the perspective of the white West, black humanity is not a "thwarted" or yet-to-be-fulfilled possibility but rather "fantastic unreal possibilities of our imagination gone wild."[46] In an exploration of Adorno's "modal utopianism," Iain Macdonald rehearses the mechanism for the actualization of possibilities as they appear in Hegel's theory of actuality. Only real possibilities appear or rather are *disappeared* into their actuality. These possibilities *must* (dis)appear. All real possibilities are contained as potentialities within actuality. However, for Marx (and for Adorno), "this totality is shown to be false, to the extent that the historically new possibility of the elimination of socially unnecessary suffering and domination is socially *deactualized* or shunted into mere formal possibility." The obstinance of entrenched forms of social organization impedes the emergence of possibilities threatening its authority; the tyranny of the actual "deactualize[s] moments of possible liberation."[47] The class of possibility that Adorno has in mind is one that lays dormant within a world that has not progressed according

to the promise of its dialectical openness. The reactionary bourgeois intransigence that Adorno identifies as native to such failings is not merely a personal shortcoming of the all-too-human philosopher who could "not resolve the contradiction between his dialectic and his experience."[48] More broadly, it reflects the gerrymandering of a society that in its flinty enlightenment maintains that there is "nothing new under the sun, because all the pieces in the meaningless game have been played out, all the great thoughts have been thought, all possible discoveries can be construed in advance."[49] Hegel, Adorno tells us, "stopped at that boundary [of the actual] because he saw no real historical force on the other side of it." [50] The historical dynamic, with its dialectical impulse, is ridiculed by this constraint on its freedom of movement toward the more radical outcomes contained in the conditions available to it, such as a world in which no one would go hungry or be without health care or somewhere to live. These are real possibilities undone by the "false necessity" of our reality—possibilities denied by a "self-perpetuating actuality that has become an unquestioned and nearly unquestionable second nature."[51]

The ever-repressed potentiality of the colonized African and black slave might feature alongside the worker ("deactualized to the point of starving to death") and could even be said to epitomize it.[52] But as a way to world, a "structure . . . of the mind," established from the contradictory position of *willful thing*, black life is furthermore and more significantly a fantastic possibility.[53] These sentient, incoherent beings feign "ontological resistance."[54] These things act as though they could extend through the world, as though the conditions of their actualization could be marshalled. These willful things are not (primarily) deactualized but rather patently unreal. What sort of possibilities emerge from such a profoundly aporetic state of being? This question goes to a founding predicament of black life and its accompanying Weltanschauung. The "identity" or "identification" that moves by way of "double consciousness" is not simply being a "Negro" and "American" but, as Nahum Chandler puts it, "the *sense of being* of the Negro . . . as richly and fundamentally double," a discombobulating anaglyphic. This doubleness throws into doubt the grounding certainties of the prespeculative European outlook—namely, the law of noncontradiction and its self-same identity necessary for individuation. For Chandler, this figure is marked by an ontological exorbitance that orients its epistemic comportment. It is a figure "quite often 'both/and' as well as 'neither/nor.'"[55] This common "sense of being" is what Frantz Fanon performs in his phenomenology, recognizing himself to be an "object in the midst of other objects" rather than the anticipated meaning maker—this denial ultimately setting him on the path of invention. His narration of this experience of objectification and the associated restrictions on actualization *perform* the alogical logic of black life.[56] Fanon journals his inability to extend through the world as if he were able to extend through the world (this compulsion to "self-consciously pose [one's] unreality" finds a contemporary exemplar in Frank B. Wilderson's autobiographical account of a position of/from noncommunicability). The predicament of the black thinker is a vivid expression of the aporetic constitution being explored in this chapter. This figure registers the constraints—or the impossibilities—that mark its "position of noncommunicability" even as it appears to leap across the abyss.[57] The black scholar writes *as though* they had the capacity for relation; they chart a path of thought *as if* this could be legible to the world and *as though* their formulation might come to hold some authority. The uneasy coincidence of being without standing and authorial voice is a feature of black thought, which, I reckon, closes the gap somewhat and in specific ways between those who urge their coconspirators to not blink in the face of the ongoing violence, to cease thrashing about the hold, and those relentlessly imagining ways out of "no way out."[58] Fantasy in the hold is not only our imaginings of otherwise worlds, not only referring to our dreams of freedom, but more essentially alludes to an inherited structure of thought, our common "sense of being." This subjunctive comportment of the figure, this being without standing that acts as though it had your ear, suggests a mode of possibility distinct from that inherent in Adorno's modal utopianism, although it *does* bear resemblance to what Jay Bernstein has called the "modal anomaly" of the artwork.[59] As with the artwork, the "accent falls on the unreality" of black life. Artworks, Adorno tells us, "have the immanent character of being an act, even if they are carved in stone, and this endows them with the quality of being something momentary and sudden."[60] Or as

Bernstein puts it, artworks "are not 'real' particulars at all; rather they are shot through with 'nonbeing,' with being 'fictions,' 'illusions,' unrealities."[61] In the semblance of their humanlike character, in their making "something appear that does not exist," in their not "fit[ting] into this world" but acting as though they did, black scholars show themselves illegible to the logic of a world of determinate possibilities.[62] We might say, at the risk of the charge of optimism, following Adorno on the artwork, that black life, in positing an unreality, not only contributes a critique of what exists but also, in that break with what exists, embodies a promise of "what could be different."[63]

Three

Cecil's Snuggling

13. Cecil Taylor's is a practice of snuggling the contrariant. It luxuriates in the spillage at the concourse of divergent approaches to the social field we often call *jazz*. His poetics—a synesthetic, anamnestic, polyglottic tongue—demonstrate how we might be together when we are not a given for one another, how we might nurture nonidentity in inseparability.[1] It's not necessary to revisit his 1977 collaboration with Mary Lou Williams to hear this. On home turf, with longtime collaborator Jimmy Lyons, Taylor can be found in various modes of propinquity. Piano and alto convene, often rubbing up against one another, other times entangled in their fascination, and sometimes engaged in more readily accessible antiphonal affiliation. As Mark Bobak observes, "the nature of the ensemble interaction heard in much of Taylor's work" is such that "players in a group may operate quite independently rather than necessarily 'picking up' or collectively developing material played by one group member."[2] Taylor's practice values paratactical communion.[3] It is a play not so much opposed to synthetic unfolding as unreflectively devalorizing of it. Its rehearsal is preoccupied with a way to world in which the thought of the contradictory, of the unruly, of the glut is no longer inimical.[4]

The performance organized by Williams at Carnegie Hall was, by most accounts, disastrous—the length of two grand pianos separating the musicians, a metaphor for the music that was made on that night (this opinion has since been cemented by the near complete separation of the two piano tracks on the recording of the performance, dubiously titled *Embraced*, Williams on the left channel, Taylor on the right).[5] Stylistic incompatibility, generational luxation, and (willful) miscomprehension are the "historiographic" items offered to explain the missed encounter.[6] And while this staging perhaps overstates the autonomy of the players (Benjamin Givan shows that we can find moments where each is somewhat informed by their partner, moments of support, concordance, and correspondence puncturing the plains of disarticulation), such radical estrangement in a music prized for its communitarian impulse cannot but catch one's ear in a sort of morbid fascination.[7] Undercutting the individualist/communitarian thesis somewhat, it is also suggested that a confrontation among understandings of the tradition, idiomatic adherence for Williams, and an (ironically) Ellisonian sociohistorical collectivity in the case of Taylor might help explain the incongruity of the musicians' approaches.[8] That these two philosophies operate on distinct registers, distinct discursive worlds, restricting the dialogue necessary to establish even dispute is notable, but what I'm most interested in highlighting is how it seems to me that Taylor's practice (and, indeed, his appraisal of this particular date lends support) stakes out another distinction, one that groups these two understandings of tradition against what might be understood as a failure to be disturbed by nonrelation—that is, the nurturing of an ease in correspondence not reliant on (not) finding oneself in the other, a comfort with or openness to the exorbitance/underdetermination that the coming together of incompatible approaches / internal laws results in. This, of course, is not an orientation particular to Taylor, and while experimental jazz might hold the most apparent examples (the 1961 double-quartet recording *Free Jazz* through Henry Threadgill's aeriform flute), it is constellated within the practice of apart playing to be found in creative forms across the African world.[9] What we hear is not necessarily an adjournment in musical relation but a practice of sociomusicality that, in its relatively pacific comportment toward the ungiven or contrariant, is devalorizing of a relational ontology monopolized by transformational mutual recognition. More particularly, we might say that the marked stylistic and philosophical divergences between Williams and Taylor provided a forum in which the touching of contraries might be practiced, that the historiographic discrepancies, the missed encounter collisions, give occasion for the cultivation of a mimeticism of nonsensuous correspondence, a coming/being together beyond resemblance (and distinction).[10] While Williams and critics express regret concerning the music's lack of compromise and its want of recognition and dialogic collaboration, Taylor thought the performance—consisting of reams of contiguous, sparingly integrated lines, an abundance of unworked nonrelation—"completely successful."[11]

Want of Despair

14. European thought's fondness for clarity likely explains a tendency to focus on the opposition that the speculative puts up against this common sense at the expense of attention to their continuities.[12] Everyday and formal thinking most often cannot but move to organize contradiction into discrete determinations. "That *is* above, which is *not* below; 'above' is specifically just this, not to be 'below,' and only *is, in so far* as there is a 'below' "—the two diametric, each other's negative, and never to meet.[13] The naïve perspective on the world ensconced in perceptual realism—with its individuating certainties and the lengths that it goes to avoid or to ground contradiction—is met by its seemingly inverted image in Hegel's speculative thought. "All things are in themselves contradictory."[14] Reality is inherently contradictory, "everything stands in opposition," and in reversal of the conventional priority, "if order of precedence were an issue, and the two determinations [identity and contradiction] were to be held separate," then the latter should be understood as the "more profound and the more essential."[15] The law of noncontradiction is seemingly suspended here as well as that of identity, compromised by the self-contradictory. Identity is determinate but of "inert being." Contradiction is the richer source of determination. In fact, it provides the compulsion for movement. It is the "root of all movement and life; it is only in so far as something has a contradiction within it that it moves, is possessed of instinct and activity."[16] And for Hegel, this mode of movement is not an option, a vehicle to be chosen among others. It alone tracks the teleology of the or-

ganic; it alone coincides with how organisms move. The dialectical practice within which contradiction plays such a crucial role is not just one method among many but key to the "organic holism" of Hegel's thought, mirroring and perhaps participating in the workings out of antimonies that configure existence.[17] This is an inverted world from the perspective of the ordinary consciousness that leans so heavily upon grounded certainties.

A patient view on what seems to be a thoroughly antipodal encounter might come to realize how common thinking, in fact, orients the speculative. It may be incompetent, but it provides the orientation for its more considered progeny. Dialectical maneuvers ease open the opaque familiarity of the world as received by ordinary thought. This "presupposed background of philosophical enquiry" is instructed and, in some ways, defended by its "esoteric" tutor, setting the agenda for concerted consideration.[18] For Hegel, Susan Songsuk Hahn tells us, "philosophy must first gain critical distance and independence from common sense . . . and then accept it afterward, but only after certain key philosophical concepts have undergone a transformation."[19] Paul Giladi goes as far as to claim that the central objective of Hegel's philosophy is to vindicate common sense.[20] At the very least, I would say it gives ordinary understanding the determination it so desires and has forgotten (or fails to realize) it doesn't have.[21] The philosophical view is ultimately tasked not (only) with rejecting the ordinary view but seeing it "sublated into philosophy in the *full* sense of the term."[22] In his introductory lectures on the topic, Adorno teases that "there is something of this 'common sense' about the dialectic."[23] What this "something" is shows up for me as a certain attitude or comportment—namely, the anxiety that contradiction generates in ordinary consciousness when faced with the ungiven.

15. Part of the modern subject's praxeological education, we might say its elementary education in this area, is to cultivate an attitude of despair in response to uncertainty. I am thinking, of course, of common sense's abhorrence of contradiction, its need to avoid or ground a volatile immediacy, the anxiety that it recovers from all too quickly to be of productive value, merely a "notion of knowledge," as Hegel puts it.[24] But I am also bringing into view what Robyn Marasco evocatively describes as "dialectical passion"—that is,

the attitude (not the affect) of despair cultivated by the newly speculating consciousness of *The Phenomenology of Spirit*, a transition from commonplace doubt (*Zweifel*) to thoroughgoing despair (*Verweiflung*).[25] This is not a despair that leads to resignation or inertia. On the contrary, it is productive, generating movement of thought and being. It triggers an intensity of intention, of suffering and sacrifice even, according to Marasco. Hegel writes that an awakening skepticism "renders the Spirit for the first time competent to examine what truth is. For it brings about a state of despair about all the so-called natural ideas, thoughts, and opinions, regardless of whether they are one's own or someone else's."[26] The panic assumed when nonrelation is truly engaged, when contradiction is truly triggered, and the radical disintegration that its newly "transcending" state experiences as it starts to reach beyond itself is a catalytic orientation.[27] It inaugurates epistemic "competence." Despair is "the condition for real knowledge and the forms of freedom that come with it."[28] As Marasco reads in her intricate physiognomy, detailing the complexities of natural consciousness on its road of Damascus, "it is undeniable that the entirety of the *Phenomenology* is an exercise in clarifying and completing the view from natural consciousness with a science of Spirit."[29] In keeping with the narrative I am spinning, I do not want to focus on the opposition the "way of despair" puts up against the subjective certainty of common sense. Common sense is not simply opposed but is, in a very emphatic way, renovated by its speculative education. Not being able to abide contradiction, ordinary thinking must endlessly isolate "'above and under,' 'right and left,' 'father and son,' and so on *ad infinitum*."[30] While speculative thinking wants to reveal these sides to be inseparable and dependent on each other for coherence, there is also an acknowledgment of the ordinary's anxiety in the speculative's commitment to administering contradictions that emerge for it. The instabilities of these antimonies might be accepted in absolute knowing but cannot be settled on in these particular moments of thought even as they might be retained in sublated form.[31] There is a restlessness that impels a dialectical working through toward resolution even if a provisional or temporary one and even if this resolution is (merely) a more-determined or better-grounded position. That is to say that brands of anxiety (heightened and "improved" in the case of speculative thought), deportment in the face of the ungiven and contradictory, orient both ordinary consciousness's denial of contradiction and the dialectical mediation that brings consciousness to an acceptance and/or resolution of such.

16. There is a current of evangelical enthusiasm coursing under the ethicophilosophical commitment that despair unleashes in the spiritualizing consciousness—an insistent contradiction-triggered anxiety that presses for resolution, giving over to the "suffering, and sacrifice" that determinate knowledge demands, writhing and wringing of thought and deed toward the eventual peace that is an acceptance of the contradictory state of reality, an absolute susceptibility to change.[32] Marasco speaks of "a restless and energic passion" and "the passions of critique and the energies of everyday life." This is by no means confined to the natural consciousness as we find it at the start of its journey as narrated in *The Phenomenology of Spirit* and could describe an orientation essential to the entire tradition of Hegelian critical thought, albeit that in the latter's case and perhaps increasingly so, the promise of resolution most often assumed as necessary to the system is typically attenuated, at times making contradiction *the* category of reflection at the expense of a more complex picture, which includes moments of resolution. Perhaps this weight toward the negativity of Hegel's philosophy in much recent left-Hegelian scholarship is a symptom of the cresting frustration experienced, particularly in the global North, about the limits on imagining another world, not to mention the cultivation of a necessary coalition toward such. "Critical theory after Hegel constitutes experiments in thinking and doing in despair," Marasco writes, "as things come undone and there is no way out suggested by reason or faith." We might think of these endeavors motivated by the despair that Marasco recognizes as of enduring pertinence to critical theory (even as it no longer "find[s] its answer in philosophy or its refuge in World Spirit"), as placeholding "experiments" in thought as conditions continue to gather for a revolution to come, or as a consolatory focus—the means and perhaps even the end of the contemporary critical project.[33]

This might be one way to understand Slavoj Žižek's commitment to his particular self-proclaiming brand of Eurocentric universality and the aporetic matrix that attends to it.[34] This is a concoction of trumped-up and genuine contradiction emerging from the need to work through conceptual inadequacies and to negotiate the disjuncture between thought and material and historical actuality, as Adam Kotsko tells it.³⁵ This "fascination with contradictions and reversals" is demonstrated in Žižek's remarks on the European "migrant crisis." Disenfranchised citizens of Europe are made culpable victims insofar as they affirm, through electoral participation, democratic systems that continue to fail them. The lion's share of the blame is to be placed on liberal hypocrisy, manifest as "political correctness" and the embrace of multiculturalism (such tolerance is both active cynicism and symptom of repressed racism). Governments are shown to be inhibited by opposed but similar items—on the one hand, ill-placed responsibility for stunted development in Africa and political instability in the Middle East and, on the other, their intractable commitments to neoliberal global capitalism, which create or compound these global structural inequities.³⁶ It is a practice—to borrow from Rei Terada—of being "properly disturbed by non-relation," a generation of antipodal positions, contradictions heightened as they are walked through one another, each worked through (to) its others.³⁷ As Kotsko writes, "These reversals are part of a strategy to keep the thought in motion. Instead of proposing a solution or finding a resting place, Žižek relentlessly seeks out further conflicts and contradictions, carrying out what Marx called 'the ruthless criticism of everything existing.'"³⁸

17. In her essay "Hegel's Racism for Radicals," Terada draws to the surface the most strident strains of radical politics' censure of what is understood to be "racial thinking"—an approach that stands in the way of becoming truly "disturbed by non-relation" or nonidentity or contradiction, a structure of mind that impedes a "tarrying with the negative" so central to recent manifestations of Hegelian left scholarship.³⁹ The idea is that groups that are "stuck in racial thinking" (of which, incidentally, the entire field of black studies might most obviously be accused) are insular and unable to commit to projects of radical openness that speculative thought and its unfolding toward freedom call for.⁴⁰ In a manner that forces the attention away from the enticing, almost-tabloid-like debates around culture clash—the legacy of philosophical shock-jock rhetoric (Hegel through Žižek)—Terada locates the racism of Hegelian radicalism in those features ordinarily lauded as critically generative. Turning to this more obfuscated racism, Terada is alerting us not to the Hegel of (the)

right, the reactionary social theorist, the Hegel of *Philosophy of Right* and *Lectures on the Philosophy of History*, who Adorno writes "resigns himself to reality or appears to vindicate it while sneering at those who would reform the world."[41] Terada's sights are trained on the Hegel of "self-division, aporia, disarticulation . . . negativity" and "radical . . . non-identitarianism," the Hegel of the despairing consciousness of *The Phenomenology of Spirit*, the Hegel of contradiction.[42] I share with Terada a compulsion to read behind the lines, to see what they might inadvertently reveal about circuitously formulated commitments and what a seemingly inexplicable inclusion, a most unreliable rendering of a way to world that Hegel at the outset admits to being incapable of truly appreciating, provides his philosophy of history. I would like to pursue this thought through Hegel on Africa at the gate of universal history, a return I'm yet to convince myself is necessary or wise. The notes from Hegel's lectures read to me like an evangelical pamphlet bringing to life the demand for that particular brand of epistemic virtue detailed in *The Phenomenology of Spirit*—this attitude of despair that drives the emerging consciousness to a point (or multiple points) in which all such nonidentity is engaged and shown to be part and parcel of that consciousness's identity. A most generous retelling of Hegel's reflections on Africa's candidacy for universal history might say that Africa is not in a position (geographically, "topically") to develop the faculty necessary. Africa does, however, provide, in vivid extravagance, a picture of comportmental inadequacy. It is not that the African lacks spiritual potential; it is the case that its inhabitation of an environment that consumes it forecloses a *native* emergence. This "torrid" region is an incompetent incubator for developing consciousness.[43] "We must first take notice of those natural conditions which have to be excluded once and for all from the drama of the World's History. In the Frigid and in the Torrid zone the locality of World-historical peoples cannot be found."[44] These regions are home to populations, organized by kin and tribe, that have yet to cultivate the conditions to move beyond this purportedly homogenous grouping toward a truly unitary will, which dialectical negotiations between individual and the state ignite and sustain. World history pushes off from this statelessness.

18. Hegel plots a desert between the inhospitable geography inhabited by the African consciousness and the ideal "temperate zone" that nurtures the

"ordinary thought" of the European in its emergence. In her essay "On the Limit of Spirit: Hegel's Racism Revisited," Patricia Purtschert suggests that at a glance, there appears to be an intuitive synonymy between the "African consciousness" of the *Philosophy of History* and the "natural consciousness" of *The Phenomenology of Spirit*. Both are on the verge and/or over the edge of the world. Both provide distinct forms of a limit case. The African—within which freedom lays dormant, practically wasted, lacking any potential for realization—is "located at the decisive passage from nature to spirit." It "represents the contradiction of a spirit that is not yet distinguished from nature, even though it is characterized by its potential difference from nature."[45] The natural consciousness is also vestibular, suspended between Spirit and nature, awaiting a catalyst that would propel it into a position from which it would set about "repel[ling] itself from itself, posit[ing] itself as an inner being containing different moments [of consciousness]." The key point of resemblance between the two consciousnesses (although it is also, ultimately, a moment of distinction) for Purtschert's Hegel is a want of progressive movement or reflection. For Purtschert's Hegel, African consciousness and the prespeculative consciousness are without the purposiveness of Spirit that guides thought in its coming to realization of itself through its mediation with the other, its "reflection of otherness within itself."[46] Ultimately, for Purtschert, in what Lucie Mercier might call a *dramaturgy of emergence* (of world history and of spiritualizing consciousness), presented across these two texts, the African and the natural consciousness actually have well-defined, markedly different roles. Africa provides Hegel with an embodiment of "the threshold of World's History" (encapsulated by the following infamous denial: "At this point we leave Africa, not to mention it again. For it is no historical part of the World; it has no movement or development to exhibit"), the exception that proves the rule of Spirit and its dialectical inclusivity.[47] Africa is the perennial nonrelation (thinking with Terada), the forever nonidentical (borrowing language from Adorno) of a system that is absolutely committed to materializing, actualizing, and revealing the identity of identity and nonidentity (or, if preferred, the unity [or approval] of contradiction). Hegel's Africa is a nonrelation, which cannot or will not participate. Or as Terada poses rhetorically, "Do we want to say here that Hegel is insincere, that he doesn't 'really' open up to non-relation, at least as soon as sub-Saharan Africa enters the picture?"[48] Conversely, for its part, natural consciousness is not typecast as the liminal potentiality it finds itself to be at the start of *The Phenomenology of Spirit*. The first act of its arc reaches its apotheosis in dramatic fashion, with the "curtain . . . hanging before the inner world" of a supposedly "undifferentiated selfsame being" drawn to reveal "an inner being containing different moments"—that is, "self-consciousness."[49] The natural consciousness, not "constantly impelled to direct attention [toward] . . . the glowing rays of the sun," is, unlike its African counterpart, not so thoroughly preoccupied with the vagaries of nature.[50] Speaking across texts, the Africa of the lectures on the philosophy of history is a reliable, never-changing reminder of the state of nonreflexivity, of movement that cannot or will not commit to transition, which the developing consciousness of *The Phenomenology of Spirit* has left behind. Africa sets the stage from behind the backdrop to the heroism of the developing consciousness. The African's liminality is not proper to itself, not a kink to be worked through immanently (although impositions of colonialism and enslavement might provide the necessary kickstart). The double billing reveals little about how this African consciousness moves, focusing instead on the function it plays in a story that will never be its own.

19. While I take my lead from Purtschert's reading together the nascent consciousnesses (and the distinct areas of Hegel's work in which we find them), I would suggest—parsing and tuning Terada's commentary of Hegel on Africa to chime with my own—that there are two seemingly contrary but entwined tracks running through Hegel's notes on African consciousness. Alongside that characterization of the African as "man in his immediate existence" in a "completely wild and untamed state," as "animal man in all his savagery and lawlessness"—as a consciousness for which the question of (non)relation and (un)givenness does not arise since it is ensconced in instinctive concerns of the natural world—we *also* find a litany of inhumane *human* offenses that give lie to, or at least question, the totality of African's enmeshment.[51] Terada tells us that for Hegel, if "a people" is not "disturbed by non-relation that alienates the self," it cannot be historical nor political.[52] From Hegel's own notes, we hear of Africans' experience of inter- and intratribal enslavement. We hear that they are susceptible to material loss and that of life and limb

as they and their daughters risk the fate of being sacrificed as part of funeral rituals of their kings. They are also understood to elevate themselves above all other nature and all other beings.[53] And yet the nonrelation that such encounters heighten fails to spark an adequate crisis for the African consciousness. The figure of the African as understood in these lectures (comments concerning its submergence in nature notwithstanding) is not so much lacking the encounters from which transformative potential of contradiction might be practiced. Such encounters, even by Hegel's suspect account, appear to abound. The problem is that it does not develop the appropriate response to such nonrelation. As Terada draws out in her incisive reading, for Hegel, "Africans supposedly do not experience the dismemberment of alienation [negativity], and rather encounter non-relation [negativity] everywhere *but without being disturbed by it*."[54] She cracks open the Polyphemus-like shell of Hegel's African to reveal a consciousness that is bombarded by nonrelation and uncertainty but not properly disturbed by it. And to walk the discussion back to Purtschert's comparative perusal, we might say that the African consciousness does not possess the anxiety that would move it through reflection. It fails to suffer the epistemological despair that the ungiven calls for. It remains jammed midway, surrounded by and experiencing nonrelation but lacking the compulsion to move on through contradiction, lacking the lacerating catalyst that moves the natural consciousness toward self-consciousness, and the associated recognitive relations. The want is not of *opportunity* to develop this capacity for (non)relation. Rather, the problem is that the Africans lack the *comportment* that would compel them to act on the contradictory situations in which they might find themselves. They lack the despair that should, European thought asserts, drive them to resolve the disarticulation (or to come to a more determined acceptance of the contradictory state). Required is not (only) (an awareness of) the presence of nonrelation but to (also) be thoroughly disturbed by it.

20. Consider the following:

> The peculiarly African character is difficult to comprehend, for the very reason that in reference to it, we must quite give up the principle which naturally accompanies all *our* ideas—the category of Universality. In Negro life the characteristic point is the fact that consciousness has not yet attained to the realization

> of any substantial objective existence—as for example, God, or Law—in which the interest of man's volition is involved and in which he realizes his own being. This distinction between himself as an individual and the universality of his essential being, the African in the uniform, undeveloped oneness of his existence has not yet attained; so that the Knowledge of an absolute Being, an Other and a Higher than his individual self, is entirely wanting. The Negro, as already observed, exhibits the natural man in his completely wild and untamed state. We must lay aside all thought of reverence and morality—all that we call feeling—if we would rightly comprehend him; there is nothing harmonious with humanity to be found in this type of character.[55]

Or as H. B. Nisbet's version/translation has it,

> This character is difficult to comprehend, because it is so totally different from our own culture, and so remote and alien in relation to our own mode of consciousness. We must forget all the categories which are fundamental to our own spiritual life, i.e. the forms under which we normally subsume the data which confront us; the difficulty here is that our customary preconceptions will still inevitably intrude in all our deliberations. It must be said in general that, in the interior of Africa, the consciousness of the inhabitants has not yet reached an awareness of any substantial and objective existence. Under the heading of substantial objectivity, we must include God, the eternal, justice, nature, and all natural things. *When the spirit enters into relations with substantial things such as these, it knows that it is dependent upon them; but it realizes at the same time that it is a value in itself in so far as it is capable of such relationships.* But Africans have not yet attained this recognition of the universal; their nature is as yet compressed within itself: what we call religion, the state, that which exists in and for itself and possesses absolute validity—all this is not yet present to them.[56]

Between these two versions, the examples of substantial objective things that the African has not entered into relationship with include God, the law, "an absolute Being, an Other and a Higher than his individual self," "nature, and all natural things," and "the universality of his essential being." I am not interested in adjudicating the charge, amply dealt with in existing scholarship.[57] This enumeration is evidence of the comprehensive incapacity that affects every corner of objective Spirit.[58] My attention is drawn to how the alternative translation/version allows us to calibrate the discussion as a consideration of how universality is indexed to a competence for a certain mode of relation—a "general self-consciousness," an ability to know oneself in the other, or, to adjoin to the language I've been employing, an "awareness of any substantial or objective existence," which depends on a despair-triggered transition, something the African is not compelled by.[59] To not move through contradiction inhibits an experience of universality. "Universal self-consciousness," Hegel tells us, "is the affirmative awareness of self in another self . . . each has 'real' universality in the shape of reciprocity, so far as each knows itself recognised in the other."[60] And in case we get lulled into a false sense that such encounter is all ease and concordance, let us be reminded that, for Hegel, to know oneself is to be profoundly riven by nonrelational encounter or, as Terada puts it, is "to be torn within by non-relation, foundational of relational capacity." It is not enough for a consciousness to have had experience or to be aware of the Other. It must be moved to move through the nonrelation; it must be struck by an urgency to labor upon a common ungivenness. Indeed, for Hegel, as Terada writes, "Non-relation that is not received as laceration of self isn't really received at all. The non-given mustn't be missed, it can't not be concerning, it can't be understood (which must be understood), and it can't be left entirely alone."[61] It should impel some sort of transition and/or determination even if that is (to) another set of contradictory positions.[62] Having this facility or being oriented in this way is what is of absolute necessity for participation in universal history. We might say that the passage on universality intimates a matrix of missing objective spiritual "goods"—God, law, state—but perhaps what is most unfortunate for the African, or principally so, is that the capability for formative relations—which is wrenched from the spiritualizing consciousness so early on its voyage and which these other permutations are cause for refinement and exercise—has not been attained.

21. To shift perspective slightly and to settle more squarely on how the development of consciousness (rather than these sites of objective Spirit) might be read from this threshold, I'd like to trace a line of thought unfolding in Terada's "Impasse as a Figure of Political Space."[63] Terada provides a radical reading of Hegel's bondsman and lord in which the movement is driven "not

[by] the bondsman's choice of life when confronted with the trial by death" but by "the bondsman's *demeanor* toward the object." The focus is shifted from an interaction based on the bondsman being granted recognition in death or, alternately, whether he lives on in radical ignominy (oriented by the possibility of righting this dishonor, while his antagonist struggles to maintain authority) toward the scene of the bondsman dealing with the "ordinary objects and independent beings" that occupy him in labor.[64] Our attention is shifted toward these ordinary objects / independent beings, which bear more than a passing resemblance to the African incapable of relationship. Additionally, and importantly, this shifted focus is also dilated in order that we might imagine the range of ways ordinary objects and bondsman cohabit. Terada helps us appreciate the possibilities that are necessarily rejected by Hegel's relational ontology. She allows us to imagine that the bondsman and independent being have a range of possible comportments that they might cultivate and dedicate themselves to. I will not dwell on the lord. I will only point out that the thought of independent being (nature, thinghood) terrifies him, throws him into a panic, whereas the bondsman who has been relieved of his volition (and considered not quite human) is better placed for an intimacy that the lord must avoid at all costs. What Terada offers tentatively as an "origin myth for labor" is what I would like to claim emphatically as an opening toward undialectical ways to world and to each other. What if rather than heroics on the battlefield, the story being told was that "some are in bondage because before their encounter with the lord, they had not completely destroyed 'being that is independent' around them *out of too much respect for what exists*."[65] Or to put it another way, borrowing from Adorno, a terrifyingly ungiven nature should compel one to mastery; "not-I, *l'autrui*, and finally all that reminds us of nature [must be encountered as] inferior" in order that "self-preserving thought [and deed] may devour it without misgivings."[66] But what if the terrifying disarticulation and our self-preservatory instincts left us with not only "too much respect for what exists" but also our tolerance for a heterogeny of sociality intact. The "implication is that the bondsman 'deal[t] with' independent being only not to the point of annihilation" (and to be clear, having "too much respect for what exists" to participate in lordship is a low bar to clear).[67] All it takes is for one to not aspire to absolute mastery, for one to not cultivate such intractable de-

spair that annihilation of "being that is independent" must follow. Perhaps all it takes is for one not to insist.

Relatedly, our attention is most often drawn to the heroic transformation that comes about through the "habit of laboring." We are distracted by the story of a figure who forms itself out of the earth's resources (which is to say, out of these ordinary things) and who uses "these entities' independence in order to learn pure-being-for-itself" and rid itself of "attachment to natural existence in every single detail."[68] And yet the bondsman, or the not-quite-human being, is /can be other than a sovereign-in-waiting. In fact, if we read not by way of the panic and desires of the lord (most pointedly to become absolute master, "in every single detail," of a terrifying nature) but by way of Terada's alternate narration in which the bondsman might be seen to hold *"esteem for ordinary objects and independent being,"* other correspondences open up to us.[69] When we shift attention from the dramatics of the lord (and bracket the bondsman's narrative of overcoming, which the theater of dialectic spotlights) and toward the disinterested, "independent object" that the lord cannot face directly, when we devote our attention to the mediating bondsman (for whom there is no need or no point in denying or an inability to deny the lack of recognition it receives from the object), other forms of correspondence are permitted to come to light. We can read beyond Hegel and consider that these objects might not be (only) independent but might improvise an array of correspondences, including those that entangle, those that concatenate, those that rest in mimetic but disinterested propinquity, and those earthly, fleshly sites of complete communion that perhaps exceed what can be described as correspondence, even within this broad construal. To not (only) care for your recognition does not mean that I (an ordinary thing) desire to be or am separate from you. It simply intimates that I will not or cannot (only) give nor receive the recognition (or have access to the promise of such) that the master/subject lives for; I need not or cannot (only) see myself in you.[70]

22. A naked, one-eyed, humanlike figure takes center stage of Sebastian Munster's 1554 map of the African continent. He sits on the coastal area that abuts the Gulf of Guinea, the border between what is now Nigeria and Cameroon. In case we happen to miss the allusion, Munster provides a label: *Monoculi*.

We might also call him Polyphemus.[71] It is perhaps beyond superfluous to provide explanation for the Cyclops, son of Poseidon, being chosen from the extensive cast of Greek mythology to represent Africa—a creature ensconced in orality, "abounding in songs and legends," resembling the human but savage, cannibalistic even. A creature incapable of collectivity beyond the family—this protosociety grouping, "self enclos[ed] and kinship-centered."[72] That the association haunts the patchwork of notes, student transcriptions, and editorials that go under the name of Hegel's *Lectures on the Philosophy of History*, compiled a century and a half later, should not surprise us. The European on Africa *still* proceeds from a willed ignorance long solidified into collective consciousness.[73] This is, of course, merely evidence of an inculcation in racial difference, an education so pervasive and accessible that it calls for little more than a surrender of one's curiosity. From the position of the European thinker, the impossibility of African humanity—that is, its coming into consciousness of its inherent freedom (save the reconstitutive educational efforts of colonialism and enslavement)—forces fanciful speculation. To narrate and utilize a black beyond, truly inventive epistemological tools are required. Africanness, rendered as laying outside the realm of world possibility from the start, comes to life in modern German thought as the whimsical and grotesque, as contravention of logical coherence. The African may contain Spirit's freedom (dormant and awaiting the catalyst of Western intervention), but the world was forced to leave the modally anomalous Africa at the vestibule of its history.

23. What of this traipse I'm making through Hegel's counterfactual, his African phantasmagoria? Am I wanting to say that in this rendering of the African as Polyphemus (this contravention of his usual parsimony in thought allowing him to spin tales straining or breaching the bounds of reason, tripping over into mythology, a white mythology that black people are made to bear), Hegel *inadvertently* glimpses a realm of possibility at the limits of world history that exceeds the actual?[74] That for Hegel, the African's antedialectical maneuvers are suggestive of "what could be different"? Perhaps there is some of that. But I do wonder about this reading against the grain I am (I think) too often induced to perform. I hear and struggle against the charge of irreconcilability (although not the contradiction itself). The interrogation of the efficacy of my explicating the inadvertent insights

of a thinker (one already incredibly overrepresented), whose brand of universalism calls into being an antiblackness and/or anti-Africanness, bears on me. I'm not wholly comfortable with engaging Hegel. Terada's own reading against the grain of Hegel's African fantasia, with its immanent critique pulling to the surface of his universalism (or his antiracism, as she has it) an inextricable antiblackness, has a profound politico-theoretical utility. In her formulating the "metaracial" register at work in Hegelian radical politics, she explains the purpose and mechanics of the counterfactual. I, on the other hand, in full awareness of this complex of denial, read *blackness* from the conclusions (although, of course, not the items of adjudication) of Hegel's narration toward a "refusal of what has been refused" us.[75] On my more juvenile days (that killer alchemy of obstinance and insecurity), I tell that inner voice that is critical of an engagement that cannot but help consolidate the narrative I seek to undercut that I am *induced* to set forth a statement of our noncitizenry and that perhaps by way of experience or instinct, I believe that for it to be heard it needs to be delivered in the only language the European critical tradition understands. I'm not buying it today though! To say that—however much I rub him up the wrong way—there is nothing Hegel can tell us about the distinctive African (or, if this generality offends, Yorùbá) ways to world and thought that *oríkì* performers Omoyeni Ashabi or Mayowa Adeyemo cannot is, of course, a gross understatement.[76] It is perverse to allow the exegetically expedient conclusions of his crooked account to chime alongside Cecil Taylor's paratactical commitments. That Hegel's African—with the failure to be adequately disturbed by nonrelation, that tells of a figure whose motion is not bound to transition, whose disjunction is not necessarily harnessed toward a working through or toward greater determination, and that does not "feel the friction" of contradiction that might facilitate "educat[ion] toward the Absolute"—resembles Taylor's improvisation of paratactic form should not suggest affinity between the two.[77] The staging *is* perverse. And yet in those moments of disillusion, sick to the stomach by the pursuit, not entirely sure of its point, I return to Saidiya Hartman, Fred Moten, and Denise Ferreira da Silva. I revisit Robert Bernasconi, James Snead, and Frantz Fanon and their own close-quarter encounters with Hegel's Africa.[78] I am reminded of two things. First, any engagement with the European and Euro-American tradition, critical or not, will face an image of blackness or Africa (even when that image is of a lack, absence, or negativity) that belongs to a white mythology and so is distorted beyond recognition. The negotiation of such is part of the doubling vandalism such thought is called on to perform. More importantly, I am reminded that this compulsion to write against the grain of Hegel's African fantasy has much less to do with the shortcomings of European critical thought than with the cultivation of a practice inspired by a *communitas* out in the nonway—that site of improvised correspondence which I attempt to fall into in "Billie's Bent Elbow," the final chapter of this book.[79]

I leave Hegel on the African, wondering what might have come if he, dissatisfied with the quite preposterous portrayal in Archibald Dalzel's *History of Dahomy* (1793), had traveled to the torrid zone to see for himself.[80] I imagine him out in Òṣun Òṣogbo Grove shrine or at the Oja Èjìgbòmẹkùn in Ilé-Ifẹ̀ watching and listening to the glitching embodied *oríkì* of the earthly and otherworldly correspondences these sites provide a forum for.[81] He might have heard a "history" that moves by way of stuttered flow, a traversal between and within subject positions, a dispersal of elements crossing boundaries in Brownian motion, at times "juxtaposed without one being subordinated to another," sometimes in "ambiguous conjunction." He would have heard "constant departures" of flights, leaps across gaps, ditches, and craters into the open air of invention and the improvisation of transport suited to such shapeshifting law of thought and deed.[82] He might have heard something that sounds like a true contradiction, counterparts absolutely trained on each other, but in and among the improvised modes of correspondences, the exorbitance that compromises any particular law of movement, it would have been impossible to be certain that it was.[83]

Adorno's Snuggling

24. Alongside the "spiritual 'principle of community'" (in the Hegelian sense), of finding one's people (friend and foe) "through a conscious or unconscious act of reflexive identification," there are encounters of contiguity, "being with" that is a "being alongside," a "tarrying" that "linger[s] with

... singularities ... idiomaticities and differences."[84] Adhering to neither a "principle of purity or homogeneity" nor a "mixing" or synthesis, and found apart from a dialectically emergent notion of sociality, we might find a mode of "getting together" that does not insist on or labor on behalf of the identity of identity and nonidentity—a way to world that tends to "not fit properly into [European thought's] laws of historical movement," a sharing that does not insist on our synthesized reconciliation, the parsimony of one in the other, nor a working on/through toward a more determined or complete state of being.[85] There appears, prima facie, to be some distance to cover between failing to be disturbed by the ungiven, contradiction, and nonidentity and a mode of correspondence where we might "snuggle up." Yet it is from this latter, an Adornian rendering of mimesis, that I would like to set out to scout this field of correspondence in which we might "leave each other free" but not alone.[86]

The understanding of mimesis as *anschmiegen*—nestling against, snuggling up, or molding to, a wanting to get with, to draw or bring close to (however far or oppositional, nonidentical, or sensuously, materially dissimilar)—draws attention away from the conventional conception (that is, second-order copies of reality) and inquiry around representation and truth, which this inevitably invites. This latter, a common understanding of mimesis as received from Plato in his denouncement in the *Republic* of the imitative practices of the arts as detrimental to the smooth functioning of a rational society, cannot prepare us for Adorno's formulation.[87] It is entirely appropriate that mimesis be addressed by Adorno in snatches, that those fragments be discontinuous and often contradictory. Andreas Huyssen provides us with five distinct versions of mimesis in Adorno's work: (1) mimesis in relation to "the critique of the commodity form and its powers of reification and deception"; (2) an anthropological account showing mimesis as to do with intimation, an indispensable faculty of human nature; (3) a "biological somatic" permutation "geared toward survival as Adorno had encountered it in Roger Caillois's work"; (4) the "Freudian sense of identification and projection"; and (5) mimesis in an "aesthetic sense that resonates strongly with Benjamin's language theory."[88] Owen Hulatt, who offers a complex rendering of mimesis as part of his project on aesthetic and philosophical truth in Adorno, insists that there are more.[89] This conceptual abundance is an opportunity for creative reconstruction, even as the threat of interpretative proliferation encouraged by such heterogeneity intensifies its blur.

25. Following the lead of Michael Cahn, I approach mimesis in its contiguous guise, drawing attention to Adorno's contravention of the "dubious demand of language that mimesis be always mimesis *of*," restricting its reference to items of mimicry. For Adorno, Cahn writes, "mimesis always goes with 'onto' (*an*, as in *an*schmiegen, *an*bilden)," and while we might want to reserve a little more room than Cahn does for imitative versions of mimesis in Adorno, in light of his commitment to the primacy of the object, the notion of "a flexible and pliant subject [that] entertains an adaptive and correlating behavior" should take precedence in any appreciation of the heterogeneity of the concept.[90] Speaking of the intimacy demanded of critical thinking, Adorno urges, "There is hardly a stronger argument for the fragile primacy of the object and for its being conceivable only in the reciprocal mediation of subject and object than that thinking must snuggle up to an object, even when it does not yet have such an object, even intends to produce it."[91] It is this comportment, facilitating Adorno's nuzzling the object, that might also be said to orient Taylor's approach to the Williams collaboration—a yielding to the unfolding piece, the caustic bill and coo and "caressive crash" of the two demanding the capacity to sit as well with discordance as with attunement, to sit as well with discordance/attunement as with autarky and complete communion.[92] This active acquiescence to what goes on in the music (this relationship, or nonsensuous standard), to a commons into which they might fall (this commons generated by way of disparate material, method, and approach), their want of decorum, a nonperformance of the proper form (that we, within our musicological convention, struggle to rationalize as anything other than misfire), is what I am keen to explicate here.[93] How might we come to a clearer appreciation of these gestures "of touching, nestling, soothing, coaxing" the nonidentical that tell of a way to be that "leaves each other free"?[94]

My own version of Adornian mimesis—trained as it is on this idiosyncratic feature of "snuggling up"—is most resistant to what I understand to be the dialecticization of mimesis, which sees the mimetic impulse transformed into a tool of (proto)rationality in the service of a self-preservatory impulse, a transformation quite pointedly opposed to its rawer incarnation as a drive toward inanimate commonality. We might understand snuggling up as the progeny of an alternate occurrence to the genealogy that passes through sympathetic magic on its way to instrumental reason. Rather than this service to mastery, we find snuggling up is of the "tabooed mimetic traits . . . isolated, shameful residues" in the context of self-preservatory commitments.[95] In his discussion of Franz Kafka's incessantly harassed protagonists yearning to collapse into deep sleep, Matt F. Connell writes that "this sleep, a symbol of infancy, usually comes at the cost of missing something important—perhaps betokening the civilized need to limit the baby-like regression to blissful rest in order to 'get on.' Rest has passed under an obscure taboo. People are often strangely averse to photographs taken while they are asleep, embarrassed at the loss of control, the tender surrender to nature which waking life eschews. In sleep the body adapts itself to nature, snuggling . . . with it like a child in its mother's arms."[96] This surrender, the unguarded susceptibility to nature, is markedly distinct from the calculation that mimetic comportment drawn into rationalistic employment is asked to perform. One observation that this comparison allows is the difference in temporal character of these two tendencies. In fact, it might suggest that left to its own devices, mimesis lacks motivation; it finds its motion and transformative potential only in its adoption by reason. Drawing from Roger Caillois's influential study of anthropological mimesis detailed in a series of articles written in the mid-1930s, Hulatt writes up this missing developmental catalyst as "an impulse toward inactivity and assimilation . . . [a] 'sinking into' nature, an imitative lack of differentiation." He points out that "this base-level form of mimesis . . . is devoid of intrinsic structure, and indeed of an internal motor that could be solely responsible for the developmental narrative of increasing abstraction (the generation of magic and then reason) into which Adorno slots mimesis in his work."[97]

26. In his essay "Mimicry and Legendary Psychasthenia," Caillois writes "that alongside the instinct of self-preservation that somehow attracts beings towards life, there proves to be a very widespread *instinct d'abandon* attracting them toward a kind of diminished existence."[98] Undermining the idea

that imitative practices of animals (taking on the look of other species or the inanimate organic material of their environment) can be exhaustively explained as defense against predators, Caillois tells how "some inedible species (which therefore have nothing to fear) are mimetic," concluding with Lucien Cuénot "that this is an 'epiphenomenon,' whose 'usefulness as a form of defense appears to be nil.'"[99] In these cases, mimesis is not a life-preserving necessity but what Caillois describes as a luxury—"a dangerous luxury" at that or a "beautiful [self-]elimination"—to borrow from Stephen Best and his own engagement with Adorno's snuggle.[100] Mimesis is not an act of cunning in response to the threat posed by fearsome nature but indeed an extravagant impediment to self-defense. As Hulatt points out, this prerational, or arational, mimesis not oriented by survival, progress, or improvement is, for Adorno and Max Horkheimer, "basic open comportment to the world."[101] It is a primary impulse "deeply inherent in living things, the overcoming of which is the mark of all development," the "tendency to lose oneself in one's surroundings instead of actively engaging with them, the inclination to let oneself go, to lapse back into nature," the authors of *Dialectic of Enlightenment* write.[102] This is Caillois's "*le mimétisme*" and what Sigmund Freud terms the "death instinct."[103] Nonrelation, or ungivenness, does not motivate mimesis in the same manner it does self-preservation and rationality. The giddiness, the proprioceptive vertigo brought on by, say, that magnetic vortex of majestic nature, does not trigger a crisis. It does not call for the program of mastery we find reason-infused mimetic tools are put to use toward.

Mimesis does not possess a developmental, or ascendency, telos associated with the dialectical movement of reason. However, snuggling is not "raw" mimesis. A focus on this elemental state is useful in that it averts our attention from the rationalistic uses to which mimesis is put toward self-preservation, but mimesis as *snuggling up* is not a fall into primordial density. We might say that *anschmiegen*, although oriented toward that repose, involves some sort of reason, albeit a mode not in the service of self-preservation. Snuggling (in and among that ensemble of gestures that Adorno and Horkheimer blur it—namely, touching, nestling, soothing, and coaxing, gestures that "mold onto"), particularly when thought through the lens of Yorùbá aesthetics for whom the sculptor is the archetypical artist, might be understood as a practice or as play. Appropriately, these few lines of description have sent me on a momentary multiscene reverie—a cross-fade from spooning my honey to wet clay to the choreography that one performs when petting a cat. This range of creative activity is not without reason, even when its internal laws of operation change from moment to moment (first, I wait for the cat to move in a manner that allows his tail to trail any part of my body that lays in his path; then, I cup the crown of his head as long as it is comfortable), but these constraints (and please note that these are thoroughly mimetic) are not trained toward instrumentality; they are games toward "open comportment." At the risk of getting ahead of myself, it seems an opportune moment to point out that artwork holds a prize of place in Adorno's critical theory due to it providing refuge for a mimeticism free from the imperious drive for self-preservation. As Hulatt affirms, "Art is not a refuge for mimesis simply because it does not contain reason, as often suggested. (Indeed . . . art is . . . reason-laden through and through.)"[104] Rather, artwork constitutes an area of life in which reason—so often the autocrat of the faculties—adapts to art's mimetic commitments. While Adorno and Horkheimer provide a vivid, if somewhat disparate, narrative of mimesis's journey from its raw state through to its service to instrumental reason, no comparable account of reason's adjutancy in the mimetic realm is provided in their work together.[105]

27. I turn to *Death and Mastery: Psychoanalytic Drive Theory and the Subject of Late Capitalism*, in which Benjamin Y. Fong performs a brilliant reconstruction of the rudimentary psychoanalytic foundations provided in *Dialectic of Enlightenment* of the "new anthropological type" emergent with late capitalism. My own interest lies in the drive theory developed in support of this and particularly Fong's reading of Han Loewald's developmental ontogeny, which Fong tells us is better understood as an iteration of Freud's post-1920 metapsychology than a distinct school. Fong writes up Loewald's contribution as a "faithful" translation of the phylogenic psychic development elaborated in *Beyond the Pleasure Principle* into a corresponding ontogeny. Crucially, Loewald is seen to maintain the key elements of Freud's narration of the death drive while insisting that for the infant, reality is not "fundamentally threatening."[106] This key point of distinction (in which Loewald presents the child's inaugural reality as "not primarily outside and

hostile . . . but intimately connected with and originally not even distinguished from it"—a somewhat fantastic reality of complete union) allows the so-called death drive to be appreciated as other than or not merely an annihilation of being.[107] Reading the phenomenon by way of Loewald, one is struck by the inadequacy of the term "death drive." Indeed, the term *primordial density* is preferred.[108] And yet his shift of emphasis toward a compulsion of the child to "be rid of the burden of separateness and to 'return to an enclosure that effectively forecloses the possibility of the hostile external world'"—that is, toward a state in which one is everything/nothing again—coincides perfectly with the inaugural phase of the developing death drive as presented in Freud's "biologistic" narration.[109] The coincidence of the two perspectives (the not-yet-emerged ego and a pre- or neonatal state, whose first reality is of the union of primordial density) is maintained as Freud and Loewald both chart paths from "an endeavor to cancel out what the organism/infant sees as a tension that disturbs an inanimate repose," what Fong usefully terms the "tension-within position," through to the individuating moves that the (mysteriously spontaneous) protective shield of the protoego (Freud) and separation strategies of the infant (Loewald) enact—the "tension-between position."[110] And while the developmental aspect of the relationship should not be dispensed with, it is the simultaneity, or "confusion," of these two positions that I would like to focus on as I continue my portrayal of mimesis as snuggling up.[111]

For Loewald, the "primordial density" that an infant emerges from through birth *and* the gradual separation from its primary caregiver—represented most eloquently by mounting unreliability of the mother's breast—"originates . . . a libidinal flow between infant and mother . . . in an urge toward reestablishing the original unity."[112] In order to satisfy this desire, the child can fantasize that they are also the caregiver, bring the seemingly distant or absent close to themselves, creating something of a superimposition of subject and object (Loewald uses the term *confusion*). The infant might even fashion an imitative body part to assist in the fantasy. Here, mimesis is not primarily a way to deal with a hostile, terrifying world but a practice of drawing close (to) the diverging—the developing a facility for contiguity in response to an impossible-to-satisfy desire for "original unity" (a union as terrifying as it is utterly desirable).[113] The compulsion to be (with) everything/nothing again (the desire to merge with the earth, return to the inorganic) motivates what can be understood as a secondary impulse—a desire for intimacy with a receding coemergent world (the infant's caregiving companion being a prominent gateway). The assimilative activity addressing, most directly, the latter, substitutive impulse is also a response to the loss of "primordial density" expressed in the former. This superimposition, or confusion, of a desire for complete communion and a yearning for proximity (or warmth) helps us appreciate the eccentricity of Adorno's mimesis as *anschmiegen*.

28. In the provinces of life in which mimetic orientation plays a prominent part, such as art, we find that rationalistic aspects at a disadvantage and radically modified by mimesis in a comparable way to how, in the historical movement toward instrumental reason, we see mimesis yield to the preoccupations of rationality and related self-preservatory-oriented activity. Aesthetic form is the mimesis-drenched coming together of a work as an unfolding of truth. It emerges by way of "the nonviolent synthesis of the diffuse," Adorno writes; this orientation "preserves [a work] as what it is in its divergences and contradictions." Aporia in the artwork and those generative tensions between contradictory or divergent particulars at the various registers guiding it to actualization are not repressed or brought to (lasting) resolution. One of the clearest statements on the matter can be found in *Aesthetic Theory* when Adorno writes, "Mimesis in art is the prespiritual; it is contrary to spirit [reason] and yet also that on which spirit ignites. In artworks, spirit has become their principle of construction, although it fulfills its telos only when it emerges *from what is to be constructed, from the mimetic impulses*, by shaping itself to them rather than allowing itself to be imposed on them by sovereign rule. Form objectivates the particular impulses *only when it follows them where they want to go of their own accord*. This alone is the methexis of artworks in reconciliation."[114] In Greek theatrical performance, *methexis* refers to the improvisation of players and audience participants in the assembling of ritual. While the Platonic sense of *methexis* is the correspondence of a particular and its form, I believe Adorno, particularly in relation to artwork, has in mind its more literal rendering: "group sharing."[115] In art, we

find that rationality, ordinarily unrelenting calculation toward ever-greater control (of nature, of material), is oriented by a molding onto or snuggling up of/to the particular, the nonidentical, the contrary, rather than an orchestration of their subsumption or acquisition. Under mimesis's auspices, rationality takes on an unfamiliar lack of insistence; it is oriented by what will not synthesize, what will not cohere. In jazz, with its weak *work* concept, its construction sponsored by a principal of incompletion, its open-ended, never-to-be-complete constitutive code, rationality might be compromised further still. Here, reason experiences even greater mimetic magnetism as the need to actualize the work, to make it cohere, is curtailed. In jazz, the "work" is often quite happy to leave exposed the details of the play or idiosyncratic *methexis* of its particulars. Andrew Kania tells us that the music is "all play and no work."[116] Jazz "work" comes together by way of an explosion, to speak with Vijay Iyer—we experience an abundance of takes, multiseries of alternate decisions, oversubscribed (and so underdetermined) sites of mass concentrations of energy.[117] And in this gathered dispersal of *òrò* (borrowing now from Terada's incisive reading of Hegel's denigration of Africa), "meaningfulness"—an oversubscription of site, as well as logic— "proliferates instead of value."[118] This is to say that jazz "work" is the hoarder's heaven—it retaining in itself, and for us to hear, even that which by its own aesthetic standards falls short. So while "form inevitably limits what has been formed," this "confirmed by the artistic labor of forming, which is always a process of selecting, trimming, renouncing," jazz is not bound to the same extent by the "guilty domination in artworks," which strive for completion.[119] Form is kept open, facilitated by a capacity to tolerate the diffuse, divergent, and contrary. In fact, mimesis is not motivated by formative relations; form, while often delightful and by no means rejected, might be considered somewhat incidental. In jazz (and artwork, for Adorno), we see musicians or material particulars snuggle up to one another and/as the unfolding, unstable "form" that their *methexis* is bringing about.

29. Cecil Taylor might have referred to this as a "black methodology."[120] He demonstrates for us at various focuses: in his individual practice, in his work within bands and in workshops, and also by his participation in temporally

dispersed collaborations of black poetics. In Christopher Felver's film *Cecil Taylor: All the Notes*, the 2004 documentary on Taylor, poet and critic Nathaniel Mackey points to the pianist's insatiable "appetite for intellectual, emotional, aesthetic stimulation and information that cuts across artistic genres." Mackey speaks of the breadth of interests and how they become manifest in the music as "asymmetric equations."[121] Taylor's is a tinker-shop mind. His found material is not only of well-loved/worn motifs and phrases, voicings, and percussive figures but also the racehorse Sea Biscuit, cantilever bridges, dancer Carmen Amaya, and Billie Holiday's bent elbow.[122] Tony Harrington, remaining in strictly musicological terrain, writes that Taylor's "improvisations drew from a vast library of fragments—favorite phrases, motifs, licks and riffs; intervals, inversions and voicings—which he summoned forth into the here and now each time he soloed, reconfiguring and recombining them, impacting them into one another at great speed and with immense force."[123] The fragments that Taylor gathers, in which he becomes absorbed—these sonic textures, angled extremities, structures that take us somewhere, looks and tastes of words—are items that are drawn from an idiosyncratic alphabet, a multimedial language that he welcomes us to as he goes in search of aesthetic form. His arrangement of these fragments in space and time showcases a capacity for recognizing and producing a range of similarities, both those easily perceptible and others that swirl around the immaterial.[124] Other times, Taylor appears to be more ascetic and (as far as we can tell, less apparent correspondences notwithstanding) utilizes single, recurring musical figures. For instance, on "Second Pleasures," from the live album *Always a Pleasure*, a single fragment—a most discrete unit of music—is worked over the entire course of the piece.[125] Or perhaps it would be more accurate to say the fragment unworks the piece as an agent of the mimetic drive that wants to keep it open, the gravitation that pulls these iterations together/apart into constellation toward a point of correspondence that exceeds their undeniable material similarities. Or, to borrow language from Adorno, Taylor's experimentation "is the nonviolent synthesis of the diffuse that nevertheless preserves it as what it is in its divergences and contradictions."[126] It constantly suspends its potential unity. Perhaps my favorite instance of this mimetic comportment, this "black methodology," appears, most unceremoniously, in the first quarter of Felver's film when we find Taylor seated at his grand piano working a motif through a proliferation of microfeels, or microfields, marveling, "Anyone can play looking at that tree move out there. . . . It's wonderful."[127] He adjusts his play somewhat, perhaps toward whatever it is that the branches are gesturing toward, whatever it is that their expression is attempting to get with. While we might choose to understand this as an attempt to represent in sound the branch's movement, as synesthetic imitation, I more readily hear that motivic shift as joining the tree's undulation in constellatory reverie. Taylor's form (fingers, torso, eyes, motif) joins the dancing branches, snuggling toward a nonsensuous standard.[128]

Four

Billie's Bent Elbow

(for Le Mardi Gras Listening Collective)

Nonsensuous Standard

We meet at Billie's Bent Elbow. Billie's bar. Protruding top petal. Vexillum waving us down, interrupting our banter. An undulating, many pointed, anfractuous vexillum. A brushed thing, barely touched, pointed thing. The point. The matter at hand, which is us together, just so, for a while.[1]

In among the compendium of images that populate Cecil Taylor's 1966 poem-essay "Sound Structure of Subculture Becoming Major Breath / Naked Fire Gesture"—those bits of lyric material and tools, a program toward a portrait of relationship, toward practices of relationship, a honing of the mimetic impulse—we find this line: "Billie's right arm bent at breast moving as light touch."[2] The "slipped quadrant," the cauldron of imagistic bits that the notes consist of, supplies the language with which to script a listening of intoxicated gathering. Through and alongside and arrayed with Cecil, I contribute a part. Billie gives a diasporic wave, I say, with a cupped, wine-stained palm. Making a conspiratorial swoosh and Borromean sweeps, an "economy of known material / songs of the mother hand," indicating the expanse of our field.[3] She stirs and casts the spell while nursing the pint, hazy, ungloved, and sends fascinations, corresponding our feelings on the way to *feeling*, on the way to *relationship*. We convene around shared preoccupations—how to make the changes, how to interpret the lyrics, how to get together, how to stay alive—but moreover, we want to "make music," which is to say that we want *Verwandtschaft*: relationship, affinity. Our coming around some matter, composition, lyric, or idea is a vehicle for such. We want to make music, and we know we've made it, only by way of a feeling. I want to write from these inexplicable moments. I want to write from moments of relationship, from the supersensuous, suprahistorical connection I cannot write about—relationship that I can't tell you about but that I will attempt to show how I might have gotten there, knowing even this can only be approached circuitously, improvising parts, and arraying fragments in order that you too might fall into that feeling.

Free Canon

Listen to Matana Roberts's "All Is Written," opening the third installment of the yet-to-be-complete Coin Coin series, the 2015 album *River Run Thee*. At the start, we hear broken chords.[4] Bell peals at a distance that lead to a thrum in voice and alto around staggered G major and minor triads. These two textural centers, bells and expiratory tones, comingle and advance an auditory illusion in which each is transposed into the warp and weft of the other. The mainly sustained chordal hum takes on a tocsin clarity, and dramatic contralto softens the tolls. This binate drone snakes the length of the piece, as much alarm as dirge. (We are both warned and mourned.) It is a galactically metamorphosizing drone, onto which is hooked folk song, memoir, sonic clippings, figures, and phrases. By such lament, the piece is carried along.[5] We are met by a cacophony that frustrates analytic access. Ostensibly, this is a solo recording. It involves layer upon layer of live overdubs, a stacking of sound drawn from an assortment of sources: recitations and samples of the musician's grandfather, abolitionist G. L. Sullivan, Malcolm X, and James Weldon Johnson; snippets and snakes of alto; original lyrics; analog synth; and field recordings. Matana is a collector of secondhand dreams, memories, and happenings. *River Run Thee* is her trove, a bevy of sounds, many of which have been passed around a bit and for a while—spirit companions of analectic counterdialectics, of echoic sediment and decay. Some old, some borrowed, some black blue. It is this ensemblic address, rather than the sea-shanty blues, that gives the piece its folk credentials.[6] An intriguer par excellence, Matana provides the body space for a surfeit of voices, and when in her own, she employs crosstalk, indecipherable mutterings, song, and vocal gesture, adding section after section to the polyphony that swarms the album. This folkic comportment offends the frugality of individuation, upsets the desire for exclusivity, which "originality" supposedly supplies. It breaches the borders of the immortal, sacrificial hero (composer or work) and so could never be tragic. Lament is its stirring, and its moments of fulfilment are not eschatological but—thinking with Walter Benjamin—*musical*. There is no final word to wait for, no rebirth to anticipate.[7] Any fulfilment is inextricable from the ọ̀rọ̀ of the legion she puts forth. Through this speaking together, the diverse and disparate might, over the course of things, happen upon moments of this Benjaminian musicality, although there is no assurance of such.

Nina's Lament

> OK, as a robot gets herself together, and we do it, and we get to the middle, where we have forgotten our feelings of love, you will help me, huh? . . . Come on, let's hit the climax. . . . Feelings! . . . You know this song, come on. . . . Oh-oh-oh-oh-oh, feelings![8]
> —NINA SIMONE

At the close of her set at the 1976 Montreux Jazz Festival, Nina Simone gives a crash course (inaugurates our apprenticeship, really) on *relationship*. It occurs during a medley of Janis Ian's "Stars" and "Feelings" by Morris Albert. The emotional life cycle that takes us from pure sound to language to feeling (lament) in Benjamin's rendering of German *Trauerspiel*—which in (the) mourning play(s), marks three distinct stages—is collapsed into this moment.[9] Toward the end of the piece, Nina sings a strained, ready-to-snap iteration of the chorus, accompanied by the softest, most synthesized chords imaginable. This is not banter, not the ribbing of the audience, this self-proclaimed "looser" Nina took a perverse pleasure in throughout the concert, but a rare moment of shared *relationship*, a rare moment of nonsensuous correspondence between sound, musician, audience, and word—what William Parker calls "the center of the sound" and Don Cherry, "brilliance."[10] In other moments of the seventy-minute set, Nina is exemplary of the choreographing intriguer of the *Trauerspiel* (this widely dismissed tradition of baroque drama but a curiosity for Benjamin, which serves as a vehicle for his meditations on the dereliction of our expressive capacities). Her play of characters includes a Liberian postman, Langston Hughes among the "Black, Yellow, Beige, and Brown" of Harlem, an array of stars (young and amethyst), and a bohemian king visiting a poor girl counting fingers, toes, and raindrops.[11] Èṣù-like in its exorbitance of connotation, the cast is the means by which signification is broken, split, and departed from and from which a plethora of intention is called forth. Danielle C. Heard also hears this: "The laying bare of her 'soul' for the audience to see throughout this concert provides less an entertaining spectacle than an example of the diversity of human personality." Nina does indeed make "it impossible for others to reduce her to an archetype."[12] More pertinently, in her hosting this kaleidoscopic congregation, she frustrates the individuation often imposed on her (both commendations of genius and, I would say, those diagnoses of pathology too).[13] This is not, borrowing from Eli Friedlander on tragedy, the "absorptive individuation of the tragic hero who has made fate his 'inner, self-discovered possession.'"[14] The polyvocality that Nina the intriguer has her hand in performing, along with the diversity of meaning and emotions that arise from her black mass, is that through which an "inner relationship between things that are diverse and disparate" is found. In this flooding of the scene with *òrò*, there is a devaluation of the single voiced hero, a rejection of the "extreme precision . . . that obtains in tragedy" and that allows for incontestable judgements to be made, for resolution to be reached.[15] Nina is not tragic. And in that utterly captivating moment, toward the end of the medley, she opens a punctum of connection. We are touched by the relationship between chord progression and sustained note, alongside/encompassing/orienting our own kinship with/in the musical moment. This is a genre of fulfillment unrecognized within the "individual time" of tragedy.[16] Immediately following this caesura, this exhalation of a phrase that is a pause, that inhales, Nina tells us, "I don't want to leave you so soon and embarrassingly soft," and she invites us to once again accompany her on the chorus.[17]

While "there is no *Trauerspiel* pure and simple, since the diverse feelings of the comic, the terrible, the horrifying, and the many others each take their turn on the floor," the lament from which the form draws its name is singular in its reference to the feeling provoked by the dispersal that language is. What is more, "ultimately everything depends on the ear for lament, for only the most profoundly *heard* lament can become music."[18] It is not the voice but the ear that is profound. This coming together of the dispersed is "a matter for the ear rather than for the voice. Such a dispersion *cannot* be sung. . . . It is a matter of sensing the attunement between different voices, rather than the peaks of passion in the voice of the individual," Friedlander tells us. Relationship, pure feeling, and what Benjamin describes as a sort of musicality occur when the listener (so often also a musician) recognizes "the unity of echoes . . . all those elements [that] belong together despite their utter separation."[19] There is much (often generative) "discontinuity and antagonism" (and, I might add, continuity and synthesis) in our talk (which is also to say our listening), in our òrò, our handling of material, our dealing with matters at hand, in the spectralism of our hearing the disparate together, in our ear's improvised assembly of innumerable overtones (native and completely unanticipated). And yet as Benjamin discovered through his work on the mourning play and we rediscover in Nina's sonographic blackness, in this coming together (and unfolding), "the redemptive mystery is music"—this musicality, feeling, relationship being the "rebirth of the feelings in a supra-sensuous nature."[20]

To Hold One Another / As Other Kin

Julie Mehretu says that her paintings hold one another not as siblings but as other kin—an intimacy that we, from the outside, cannot quite comprehend.[21] Schemata, marks, layers, cauldrons of affinity; make-up and mounds; today's disco eyeshadow; staves hidden beneath expression and phrase, the salty shade. Paintings in search of something together. There's no mistaking that the artist is an intriguer, but she must have approached those paintings with such assiduous care—approached the matter of their possible kinship only obliquely, setting up games and obstacles for them to get lost in one another. Their dragging, scribble, and trawl, hewed and chipped items, guided line and curves, arrayed in order that they might fall into one another, fall upon that feeling. That we fascinated audience participants of these epic plains of standard might fall too. As if monument could be folkic—monumental orality, monumental small talk.

There is a fragment written in 1919 called "Analogy and Relationship" whose job is to disabuse us of the tendency to conflate analogy, similarity, and relationship (affinity, kinship). This short text anticipates Benjamin's discussion in "Doctrine of the Similar" and "On the Mimetic Faculty" of the ontogenetic and phylogenetic development of mimeticism, this most important of capabilities.[22] In these latter works, we hear of a gradual attenuation of the mimetic faculty from the talent enjoyed in childhood (of the individual and of "humankind"), with its easy access to a broad hypersynesthetic palette, to a situation in which language becomes the most reliable medium. The perception and production of "magical correspondences," or what Benjamin also terms "nonsensuous similarity," indexed—as I have shown in the chapter "Cecil's Snuggling"—to what Adorno and Horkheimer write up as mimetic susceptibility, constitute a way to world that frustrates the instrumentalizing tendencies of enlightenment thinking.[23] "Analogy and Relationship" complicates the offerings of these later, better-known essays. For a start, this earlier fragment seems to not have much to say concerning similarity, devoting its attention to analogy and, moreover, that which is the central concern of the text: relationship. Its preliminary remarks apportion some of the confusion that the reader will encounter to the fact that care had not been taken to distinguish *analogy* and *similarity*—the former suggestive of metaphor, and the latter speaking to a more substantial correspondence that terminates in identity. In fact, the role of analogy (and similarity, for that matter) is clearly to provide contrast, however low, for the spotlight on relationship. Compounding this confusion, the "similarity" that we read in the later pieces and particularly its nonsensuous mode might be better understood as what in "Analogy and Relationship" Benjamin assigns *relationship*.²⁴ We are presented with the example of a child and a parent and told that this pair *might* resemble one another but also that they may well not. Their kinship, this relationship, is not determined by a "shared" nose or by the child being the causal result of that parent's intercourse with another. In fact, it might be that adoption or fostering provides its best examples. Here, we avoid the slide into similarity; here, there is no need to set aside genetic identity or disposition. Kinship or relationship does not lend itself to identity thinking; it is difficult to determine or provide evidence for. The relationship is primarily *felt*, Benjamin says.²⁵

Alongside the aforementioned collapse of the distinction between *analogy* and *similarity*, there is a tendency, Benjamin tells us, to confuse *relationship* with *sensuous resemblance*. Similarity, which terminates in identity, "may proclaim relationship," but "analogy can never do this."²⁶ To think of the words *African* and *black* together requires no mediating term. Colony and slave estate are not analogous, although we *might* translate (pre)colonial Africa as slave market and *might* understand slavery's afterlife as a form of colonization.²⁷ Similarly, the diasporic spectrality of *ìtàn* and black life's "imminent departure" / "post-expectan[cy]" is much more a corporeal resemblance than a metaphoric relation.²⁸ And in case it is not clear, this faculty that allows us to recognize continuity also allows us to narrate breach and/or metamorphosis. It is what facilitates the assertion that "Africa and the diaspora are older than blackness. Blackness does not come from Africa."²⁹ It allows us to tell of the violent "liquefaction" of flesh made congruent with racial capital.³⁰ Such narration relies on distinctions between *black* and *African* (or *Bambara, Wolof, Hausa, Ga, Yorùbá, Ibo, Ewe*, etc.). Beside such activity, in which our diasporic disposition is often hastily bifurcated, into "descendants of the Middle Passage" (for whom it is received as violent imposition), and those "left behind" (whose history has always been of dispersal), we find what Benjamin calls "relationship."³¹ We can tell of the many ways that black ontology and Yorùbá episteme resemble one another and how they hold an undeniable similarity, but their kinship needs to be *felt*. Aside from analyses that allow the African to be recognized as the recipient of dishonor and gratuitous violence, as a derivative of the slave, and those that track (or prohibit the pursuit of) African "retentions" in black cultural forms, we might explore an affinity of African thought and black being—that is, *relationship*, which cannot be readily traced or rationalized or accounted for but that flashes up as fleeting feeling *by way of* a sonic, spectral specificity or in a certain tilt of word or gait. Kinship is principally felt. We might say that black nonbeing and African incapacity hold undeniable sensuous similarities *and* that their kinship can only be felt. And we might say that our black jam—that "collective of kinks," that Brownian cavalcade of dread—maintained in our "wandering wonder," or laborious fascination, cannot be grasped.[32] It's all about feel; about musical feel, musicality or soul, or what Moten, following the Queen of Soul, calls "feeling depth."[33]

Òrò òrò òrò

Òrò, the cause of great concern for the wise and experienced elders.
It sounds kù *(making the heart miss a beat)*
Kè *(as a ponderous object hitting the ground)*
Gì *(making the last sound before silence).*
The òrò *that drops from the elderly*
Is stupendous.
It was divined for Òrò-òrò-òrò
Who did not have anyone to communicate with.
And started groaning.

—Recited by D. Adeniji[34]

As the story goes, Ọlọrun, the supreme being, after several thousand years of enduring the "incessant humming" of its loquacious companions, sends Ogbón, Ìmó, and Òye, transported by the transmogrification of their buzz into the sound "*hòò*," to the tangible realm. As might be expected, such cosmic alchemy was commemorated by the heavens with rhapsodic tattoo and pyrotechnics. The universe turned to luscious emulsion; "solid matter . . . became jelly-like." In fact, for some time, these heavenly personalities—now thoroughly enmeshed and going under the name of their sonic transport, Họ̀ọ̀-rọ̀, or, hypocoristically, Ọ̀rọ̀—could be found "suspended in mid-air like an egg." Eventually, Ọ̀rọ̀ fell to the earthly realm and "split (*là*)" in this successive altered state, taking the form of the *òrìshà* Èlà. Rowland

Abiodun tells us that Èlà travels through the world by way of òwe, which translates most literally as "proverb" but needs to be understood as taking in the broadest range of expressive and discursive capacities to include the arts of "sculpture, àrókò [often translated as 'gift,' but I'd like to mobilize it here as the talent for producing and recognizing 'magical correspondences'], dance, drama, song, chant, poetry, incantations."[35] This declension, this sequence of gathered-dispersed descent, from vibration to open vowel through brilliance to its syncopated kù kè gì là, split and spilt into our various expressive forms, is ọ̀rọ̀.

Ọ̀rọ̀ is often translated as "word," but it also means a "matter at hand," a situation that deserves communal consideration, and a dealing of this case in counsel, banter, or gossip—an occasion for sustained reflection, a spot for temporally and geographically dispersed open-housed contemplation. Ọ̀rọ̀ is gathering contribution.[36] Contributors will spin language in congress, grappling with this matter at hand. The inextricable entanglement of thing and practice that is involved in ọ̀rọ̀ (translated, but not exhaustively, as "word," "communication," "orality") compounds the difficulty in rendering its intention in English even though that particular constellation (of *word*, *communication*, and *orality*) is perfectly legitimate, metonymically, in the target language.[37] The business of defining ọ̀rọ̀ is, of course, ọ̀rọ̀ and helps demonstrate the intertwined nature of the substantive and processual in the Yorùbá understanding of the phenomenon. Ọ̀rọ̀ is the thing, the point. Ọ̀rọ̀ is also our talk of it. Ọ̀rọ̀ is that toward which our ọ̀rọ̀ is directed.[38]

The òrìshà Ọ̀rọ̀, Ifá verse tells us, "moves around naked and it is forbidden to see it in that state," and so it dwells within the spots at which our expressive and discursive work congregates, those sites of "massive concentrations of Black experiential energy"—to borrow from literary scholar Stephen Henderson—those mascons providing the cover of darkness under which Hòọ̀-rọ̀ moves.[39] Spend some time with Chris Ofili's àdìrẹ posing as painting if you can. If you wait patiently, settling into his copse, dark in the thick bush of an incessant hum, you might feel it in the noisy silence.[40] Benjamin, in his notes detailing the experiments in intoxication he and his friends conducted in the late 1920s, uses the term "*überspülen*," which means "to spill or wash over" (incidentally, "the opposite of *aufheben*").[41] At that ink spot, roaming freely in the dark intoxication of the thicket, Ọ̀rọ̀/ọ̀rọ̀ washes over me.

Aesthetic Form in the New Thing

i seek another dimension in music.
—WADADA LEO SMITH[42]

The new thing of black music, the midcentury experimentalism of the tradition we often call *jazz*, is an intensified, intentional turn toward what Adorno understands to be *aesthetic form*. Aesthetic form needs to be understood as distinct from, and perhaps even defined in distinction to, *musical* form— *musical* form being that on which most musicological accounts of the emergence of free jazz tend to focus.[43] Musical, or constructionist, form—the working together of sonic stuff—is certainly that by which aesthetic form comes about and becomes sensuously available, albeit obliquely. However, aesthetic form holds a categorical difference in its "transformation of what is given into something *other*, that is, something unreal, nonidentical, outside the grasp of concepts, categories, or distinctions, not to mention purposes, functions, or positions in any standing order of things"—to borrow Gerald L. Brun's useful gloss.[44] Aesthetic form is pursued through the handling, composition, and playing of musical material, through the manipulation of material toward (the) work, which is forever unstable. In phrasing that turns Adorno squarely to jazz, aesthetic form is ultimately processual even when it is encountered in the objectified work thing. It is oriented by a "mimetic impulse," a mode of correspondence that for Adorno, as I have shown, has little to do with imitation but rather might be thought as extrarational constellatory affinity. When Adorno speaks of free and spontaneous *happenings* emerging through and within the unfolding work, he is referring to the formation of material aspects toward momentary communion of/with the work. The music we call *jazz*, despite the undeniable heteronomy of even its more experimental manifestations, is dedicated to this orientation. This is to say that the music—Bessie Smith through to Cecil and beyond—as it works toward its material consummation, or perhaps more appropriately to black poetics, as it carries out its sensuous experiments, is simultaneously engaged in a search for moments when those material/sensuous particulars align in such a way as to happen upon a point of nonsensuous correspondence (we might also call this *relationship* or *feeling*). A work is kept open even as the piece reaches its musicological destination or when the musician has said what they must. Indeed, there can be no assurance these moments of relationship will be found. In fact, the only promise is of caprice and, in the event of success, evanescence. The compulsion toward nonsensuous affinity is antigravitational dark energy—to borrow some terminology from astrophysics—that pulls the piece apart and keeps its experiments in play. The coming together in musical banter and gossip, the charting of polyphonic maps toward brilliance, is *a social toward another order of sociality*. In fact, I would say that aesthetic form is as much the means toward our congregating in performance or rehearsal, practice, or listening as our (co)habitation of musical space is the means to aesthetic form.

Oríkì for Don Cherry

Don Cherry, sitting with *donso n'goni* between his legs, is explaining the spatiotemporal confluence his body space affords.[45] It's a provisional perspective, an image space subject to change, a now-then, here-there, thinking-with, playing-with Don Cherry—a node of our quantum intimacy, sketched out by Cherry playing the blues on the West African harp. Cherry strums a chugging minor seventh ostinato, which he'd adopted from a fellow harpist, and marvels at how familiar the riff, when first heard, had seemed to him, how it had sent him (as he now sends us) to other times, places, and bodies—a scat of calabash blues. Travels facilitated by both modern imposition *and* anamnestic dream and vision—a condition of having to be on both sides of the Atlantic *and* epistemic dwelling (that is, the comportmental coincidence of tarrying and wandering that I speak about in the opening chapter). Cherry tells us, "When he played this rhythm, it was so familiar to me because I could relate it to all the blues players that I heard, like T-Bone Walker, B. B. King, John Lee Hooker. It's like the sound of the railroad train. *Nwaa waa! Oh, the railroad train / Goin a clicky-clacky, clicky-clacky, down the line.*"⁴⁶ In this way, the boundaries between his corporeal body and the collective that his blues-infused, *n'goni*-supplemented body space calls forth are dissolved. The music, or, if I may, the nonsensuous standard(s) it works through, might be understood as a technology in which a sociality is organized. And we might say that Cherry—playing the shunting, two-note figure on the sub-Saharan harp of hunters and storytellers while evoking the spirit of the blues—tests principles of nonlocality for the "aesthetic sociality of blackness."⁴⁷

To speak of this music is to speak for it, and that really means to speak as part of it, not to identify with it necessarily but to join its ensemble. Perhaps the only preparation required is to reach beyond the unease of presuming oneself part of its "anagrammatic" experiments.⁴⁸ Peter Szendy helps us partway when he speaks of the voyeuristic pleasure he takes in listening to musical arrangements from the Romantic era, particularly those of Robert Schumann and Franz Liszt. He "love[s] them more than all the others," he confesses—these musicians who retell a work, who rearrange, who put the work another way, in order that it becomes accessible to an outsider instrument or an anachronistic audience. These "arrangers are signing . . . above all [to] a listening. Their hearing of a work. They . . . write down their listenings, rather than describe them (as critics do)." While I don't subscribe to this bifurcation of interpretation, setting arrangers apart from critics and other listeners, I am intrigued by the arranger's audacious signing of the reworked composition, their name hyphened to that of its composer, their overcoming of any embarrassment, nominating themselves to the joint enterprise, which, in a way, their arrangement inaugurates. This is the idiosyncrasy of the arranger. Their cosigning is the difference. I take the recording of a listening (that which Szendy believes to be the arranger's distinction) to be a pervasive, perhaps even universal, phenomenon of music reception. The layering that our listening performs is the work rewriting itself, comparable to Schumann's and Liszt's "traverse . . . between original and its deformation in the mirror of the orchestra."⁴⁹

To speak as part of the work is not only to place myself in an ensemble but also to cultivate the manners of address appropriate to that site of expressive happening. The event wants my body—resonating chambers, ear drums, kinesics, proprioception. But it *requires* a body space, a node, a point of contact for the transitory assembly/dispersal. To speak as part of the work is not only to provide a listening but to become a host, not for any original work thing but for the sociality constituted by constellations of response to a call I hear after the fact, if at all. Don Cherry says that "it's, actually, not [his] music because it's a combination of different experiences, different cultures, and different composers that involves the music that we play together, or that [he's] playing when [he's] playing alone"—playing together or alone; playing alone together.[50] Urban Lasson's 1978 documentary *It Is Not My Music* begins with Cherry crouched in the Swedish countryside cupping a whistle to his mouth, his ears pricked and tuning, so that he might get with whatever it is the birds' descant gestures toward. This improvised ensemble, the first of many shared in the film, helps to establish the notion as capacious enough to take in a spectrum of animate (and inanimate) contribution. And relatedly, this lays clear the precarity of the congregation: how it is at times barely there, faintly discernible, how it might fly away at any moment, how its refusal or inability to install preeminence compounds this fragility.

Cherry out with the song thrush, Eric Dolphy out with spotted towhees. Cherry and Eric Dolphy out singing with birds sends me back to Cecil Taylor's unfurl/enfold practice and in particular to his piano play with a branch outside his apartment window.[51] It would be a mistake to describe this as mimicry. The encounter might more interestingly and more essentially be understood as evidence of a talent for sounding out quantum propinquity—correspondence with bird and branch toward "complete communion."[52] Of course, their practice *might* be explained as a training of tone and phrase, but it is also a listening to whatever it is bird or branch is straining toward—a listening to their listening. Just as, in free improvisation, we often play with an ear beyond what is sonically available, away from or through dialogue and conversation, through the melding and welding of tone, toward the vestibule just beyond or in the eye of the storm of this sensuousness, Cherry's wanting to get with the birds—his making himself of that scene, providing the body space for a happening to which we too are called—is also a wanting to get with whatever it is the *vox mundi*, the choir of questionable tuning, is looking to lose itself in.

Cherry is ambassador of a way with time and earth, committed to equivocality and oriented by an inability or refusal to make an absolute exception of oneself in relation to the earth and all that is in it. Our way with time that cultivates a stammer to preserve hesitance—it is an inability or refusal to accept that self-preservation subdues our longing for love feasting. Cherry, the wanderer (black and African), for whom—to borrow a fitting sentiment from John Coltrane—"the whole face of the globe is community," travels light.[53] He tells us, "It's actually not my music," and he demonstrates through his practice that, as Fred Moten puts it, "all that we have (and are) is what we hold in our outstretched hands."[54] It is our diasporic disposition that we have to offer, our dispersed assembly, what we are, and all that we have. We arrive empty-handed with nothing to bequeath—no returns, no gifts to present. We arrive in counter-Odyssean empty-handedness, calling for and offering no sacrifice.

Thirteen minutes into Lasson's documentary, we accompany Cherry as he walks through a busy New York City playing his *n'goni*. We see how he provides the body space for a happening that draws passersby in cars and on foot into its orbit. The driver of a brown station wagon—sitting in or holding up traffic with children hanging out of the back-seat window—intermittently doubles up Cherry's vocals. For how long? Ten seconds? Half a minute? I am struck by how quick they are to intimacy, the acute nature of the vicinity hit upon by the passing section. Their deep dive into the portal opens an anamnestic communion, like an involuntary memory of the feel and taste of pressing lips, which could not have possibly met theirs. These participants move out of view, but their song plays on. And the brief encounter, its impossible kiss, no doubt plays on in their imaginations, and it repeats on us too.

This diffused congregation is not confined to the live fragment captured by video; I would say that the thoughts being shared here with you have become part of the lingering happening Cherry's *n'goni*-extended body space instituted. I would like to think he would insist upon my participation, my doubling, my *gbẹ́nugbẹ́nu* spread of our *oríkì*, and so I try to not resist the song that breaks out here and there.⁵⁵ His practice pulls mine into orbit, and I prepare to catch whatever is being spread. The happening makes *us* temporarily (again), but it is not a locus of agreement. Cherry's mood doesn't fuse. The attitude of spread and reach cannot anticipate agreement or identity. We might embrace each other now, but there are no holding patterns. Our "collective body-space" and the communal series it inspires must be incomplete by uncertainty.⁵⁶ It must bank on the unreliability of our brilliance.⁵⁷ Ours is a thrown-together, ill-thought-out reply to an awaited call, the "rub and cyclone . . . eye" of a sound that we could not have possibly heard in advance.⁵⁸ It is a practice of anticipatory delay effect (echo, chorus, reverb, tremolo, flange, feedback, chop, and screw) that scatters and scrambles us until we find our tuning, until we fall momentarily and unfathomably into that portal through which we might become everything/nothing again—a momentary but complete communion that (often) retrospectively orients our material and bodily speaking with one another. A retroactive convocation that exceeds and questions societal bond is our aesthetic sociality, our (under)common *ọ̀rọ̀*, our always-imperfect coincidence, stuttered folkic comportment. Whether in conference with birds or hosting "different experiences . . . cultures . . . and composers," our tenuous assemblies play the range of possibilities of our shared nonidentity in defiance of the actual and its attenuation of the possible to the real.⁵⁹ We speak (alone) together on all manner of fascinating, irreal, and intoxicating things.

Aesthetic Sociality of *Musique Informelle*

In "Vers une musique informelle," Adorno conjures a future music, which remains emancipated from external forms, from conventions of genre and musical material, while being equipped to find its way out of or to avoid the dead end that integral serial and aleatory compositional techniques have led musicians.⁶⁰ *Musique informelle* "mocks . . . all effort of definition," he tells us. Nonetheless, he does provide a rudimentary sketch. Alongside the ever-useful prototype provided by Arnold Schoenberg circa 1910 (which Adorno cannot quite set aside), *musique informelle* is presented as an expressive music of weak, bottom-up, temporary, and/or unstable autopoietic form. It does without "inflexible... external or abstract" formal imposition. It "constitute[s] itself in an objectively compelling way, in the musical substance itself, and not in terms of external laws." It is "a rejection of the mechanical," a return to or rather a reconstitution of an "organic" approach, "a growing unity of parts and whole and not their subsumption under a supreme abstract concept, together with the juxtaposition of the parts."[61]

To supplement this sketch, it is instructive to take a short detour through the art movement of the 1940s and 1950s that lends this "prismatic concept" its name.[62] Adorno intimates that the eponymous gesture was merely "a small token of gratitude towards the nation for whom the tradition of the avant-garde is synonymous with the courage to produce manifestos."[63] Yet as Max Paddison and Joris de Henau show, Adorno's cursory endorsement of Wols (Alfred Otto Wolfgang Schulze), a central proponent of *art informel*, ultimately suggests an appropriation that exceeds the namesake.[64] Referring to the mention of the artist in a key passage concerned with the emergence of a new "organic" approach and the mode of compositional engagement required, de Henau writes that Adorno "was quick to notice the significance of Wols' artistic practice, and saw that it could open up new creative possibilities for composers."[65] A drawing entitled *Injured Head*—in its play between abstraction and representation, coherence and indeterminacy, actual and fantastic possibility, and in the demonstration of material handling toward moments of aesthetic form—provides a bridge from Adorno's bare sketch of an informal music to a more substantial appreciation of the orientation he has in mind. The ink marks are at once noodles (hand leading eye leading mind leading hand) and "rendered... with meticulous care." We might glimpse in this work an apparently "faithful reproduction ... [of an] interwoven web of tissue... a microcosm marked by the process of decay caused by ageing. Various irregularly closed openings and cracks [of] long-healed injuries to a rubbery clump of tissue" become, in time, "hallucinatory excrescence attributable solely to the artist's imagination." (Interestingly, on the website for Städel Museum's digital collection, the drawing is categorized under both "abstract, non-representational art" and "head [human]").[66] Wols's drawing cannot be considered (merely) representational or adhering to a conventional rendering of the phenomena of its fascination, but it also eschews the allergy to mimesis often associated with postrepresentational art. As de Henau writes, "Wols' style does not impose a pre-arranged form, but allows for associations and amalgamations of disparate elements, though at the same time preserving a certain degree of figurative recognizability, however dream-like or alogical their interrelations may appear."⁶⁷ Analogous to the spontaneous play between idiomaticity and autopoiesis that we encounter in free jazz, in Wols's work, we are confronted with periodic breaches of apparent representation and determinate figuration and/or meandering formal operation, which, like clouds, fall (momentarily, felicitously) upon "figurative recognizability."⁶⁸

Another work made about the same time, the watercolor (at times) portrait *Don Juan*, at first glance a perverted *Angelus Novus*, features a dispersed but ridiculously well-feathered, coiffured moustache, seemingly dissembled whisker by whisker.⁶⁹ Barbules splay about the piece, sprouting from all areas of a head resting on what appears to be, to me at least, a pair of pierced (or piercing) bollocks, right eye looking dubiously at said testicles or something else below (possibly out of shot) and left eye in mid-wink. As with *Injured Head*, the viewer is compelled to recompose or improvise the piece. Delphine Biere writes, while Wols's "watercolours are populated with figures, landscapes and characters," they have "no counterpart in the real world, other than certain recurrent clues."⁷⁰ What is more, lest we rush to interpret the approach as a mere play between these two poles, we might consider such work as oriented less by a migration between form and informality than by an anfractuous unmooring toward aesthetic form. To borrow from bassist William Parker, we might say that Wols is oriented by "flow," which "is the spontaneously created map that leads us to . . . the essential house where all beauty resides."⁷¹ Or, to attune to Adorno (and Benjamin), we might understand the work as hosting a mode of experience in which he (and we) might fall upon or glimpse its truth.⁷² What Adorno finds in the artist's work is not a project of strict informality (although we could say that the pieces carry out a sort of material deformation). He does not find a categorical rejection of the figurative or of traditional form. What is found is corroboration for his own denunciation of compositional inflexibility—whether this rigidity is driven by submission to congealed traditional forms, a practice that rigorously organizes prefabricated material, or veneration of novelty. Being oriented by aesthetic form (that which "relates to everything sensuous through which the content of a work of art . . . is realized"), Adorno finds in Wols's pieces an unadulterated pursuit of the mimetically disposed "spiritual element" within the creative process.[73] He finds material formation providing neural pathways to this elusive brilliance of (the) work.

We should keep in view that Adorno's sketch of a future informal music adheres to an understanding of the historical movement of music as quite strictly shaped by the determinate negation of its material and that this progressive development is irreversible.[74] Once the decadence of the material is revealed, it is impossible to "unsee" it; we cannot feign innocence once lost. The organic approach sought must look forward. However, this historiological item—the reality of degenerate, useless forms and the requisite injunction against their restoration—should not be considered the driving motivation of Adorno's proposal. Rather, his advocacy for an open form is in service to the freedom of subjective composition. This subject, "the only component of art that is non-mechanical, truly alive," is essential to the organically evolving "musical substance," or what might be understood as the aesthetic form of music.[75] In response to approaches in midcentury new music that seek to unseat the authority of the imposing composer by way of chance and/or organization, Adorno recasts the musical subject as resident rather than master of the music. What is key to *musique informelle*'s subject is its sensitivity, or one might say devotion, to the unfolding organism (to be of the work "in ignorance of what" it will become). With this relinquishing of sovereignty emerges the "right of subjectivity to be present in the music itself, as the power of its immediate performance, instead of being excluded from it once it has launched."[76] I edge toward the close of these gathered scattered thoughts with a slight "bluesing" of Adorno's intention when he writes in reference to *musique informelle* that "the subject must become an integral part of the organism, something which the organism itself calls for."[77] With this statement in mind, might we not consider Adorno's *musique informelle* a member of the miscellaneous collective of nonsensuous correspondence that I'm bringing together in this closing chapter? For

Adorno, aesthetic form is a key forum for the sustenance of the autonomy of art, and so the notion of a mode of sociality being found there seems an acute departure from his proposition. After all, as Eva Geulen reminds us in gentle reproach of some recent readings that contravene this important position, Adorno understands aesthetic form as that which "distinguishes and separates the artwork from the social world. The new concept of form ignores this fundamental distinction. Instead, everything now turns out to be form."[78] With this vigilance in mind, I want to claim that Adorno—all the while maintaining the significance of the autonomy of art and music from the totally "administered world"—is providing a formulation for what might be understood as an *aesthetic sociality*.[79] We will not find in Adorno's aesthetic sociality an unmediated communion of individuals (for example, between composer and audience or an aesthetic community based on judicial accord). Rather, we find a coming together of subject and aesthetic form or subject in aesthetic form. *Musique informelle* as imagined by Adorno is a model for future reconciliation. For those of us attuned to a broader spectrum of possibility, the omnium-gatherum that is lit up in the coming together toward/as aesthetic form is already at hand.[80]

Before Love, Fascination

Let's question the conditions that foster the pervasive frigidity of this era of socioecological disaster, as Nina Simone does. "Trying to forget all my feelings of love . . ."—the cruelty of the idea arrests her midverse. She ponders for a second or two and then continues, "God damn. . . . What a shame to have to write a song like that. . . . I do not believe the conditions that produced a situation that demanded a song like that!"[81] I, too, do not accept the conditions that demand a denial of feeling—conditions that must short-circuit our rhapsodic ways to one another, that want to straighten out our intoxicated walk and talk on the spot or meander, the intemperance under the cover of which musicality, feeling, soul might move. We might say that the condition that produces this pandemic of apathy is the attenuation of possibilities to only those considered real. The fantastic must be tempered, made to sober up, in order that it be actualized. Lead insoles are slipped into shoes.

Our knotted, gathered dispersal, that extraterritorial dwelling here and here and there, must be straightened and straitened to the course of that world. I cannot accept the conditions that attenuate the spectrum of possibility to that which must be found in this constricted canal. That tautological restriction is the condition of a state of affairs that makes it easier for us to contemplate the end of the world than to imagine a blackened one.

Could this have been a book about love? Listening to Nina Simone while reading early Walter Benjamin almost led me to believe so. And yet contemplating such from the pessimistic mood shared by much theoretical black studies, I reread Adorno's 1966 radio lecture "Education after Auschwitz." "Society in its present form" is based on a profound coldness, he insists. Indeed, "the pursuit of one's interests against the interests of everyone else . . . has settled into the character of people to their innermost center." And so he cannot "preach love." He tells his audience, "I consider it futile to preach it; no one has the right to preach it since the lack of love, as I have already said, is a lack belonging to *all* people without exception as they exist today. To preach love already presupposes in those to whom one appeals a character structure different from the one that needs to be changed. For the people whom one should love are themselves such that they cannot love, and therefore in turn are not at all that lovable."[82] It's Adorno, and so we might want to make an allowance for his customary hyperbole, but those words concerning our desire but unfitness for communal or societal love cut deep. The character structure of a way to world and to thought brought up by market equivalence—one that cannot be weaned off its steady diet of digestible difference, one primed for whenever the fascistic tendency that it hosts, that sits quiet and keen within, calls upon it to quicken the decimation of those earthlings who cannot or will not abide by its extractive drive—is not an agent to entrust such a project. The thing is Adorno's austerity is compounded by an inability to imagine an aesthetic sociality beyond the form of artwork. Benjamin was also guided by pessimism (actually, as I discuss in the introduction, the task of the idiosyncratic politics he cobbled together in "Surrealism: The Last Snapshot of the European Intelligentsia" was nothing other than to "organize pessimism").[83] And yet Benjamin remains a committed votary of the socioaesthetic *communitas* out in the nonway. Luckily for us, he takes inspiration from *Nadja*, André Breton's "banging door" of a novel, to suggest that this motley crew leave the door ajar in order that others might see what goes on there. In opposition to the upwardly mobile virtue of discretion, he tells us, "To live in a glass house is a revolutionary virtue par excellence. It is also an intoxication, a moral exhibitionism, that we badly need."[84] His own practice included hashish experiments with Ernst Bloch, Jean Selz, and other friends—their shared moments of equanimity, shunting between nirvana's "ambiguous wink" and "nothingness, the base and the commonplace," brought to life through an encyclopedic potpourri of fantastic anamnesis.[85] But it is his unremitting trials in thought (this particular gateway to profane illumination was considered "eminently narcotic"), that he considered most revelatory. His beautiful tapestry of a portal frequented by the second-manifesto surrealists is a wonderful example. He traces their "steps of multitudinous flooding back and forth" through the "threshold between waking and sleeping," and shows how the reader might, too.[86] The essay is a Russian nesting doll of lessons on intoxication—each section containing yet other iterations, frequently (but sometimes secretly) correspondent to others, setting off one another in sensuous and nonsensuous coincidence. What we hear is an arraying, stringing together, chasing, and chorusing of often seemingly disparate parts in (non)sensuous configurations in his body space. He invites us to join him in that intimate interpenetration with those gathered bits. If the surrealism essay fails to fascinate you, if it fails to detain you, if you fail to get caught up in it, have you really read it? Before I talk about love, about the need for scholarly empathy, about care, witnessing, or allyship, before we can claim to be "in this together," before you insist on "seeing" or "hearing" me, before we set off to redeem that love at the end of the revolutionary rainbow, I'm going to try to hone my capacity for intoxication.

I first heard "Love for Sale" on the Cannonball Adderley–led quintet cut *Somethin Else*. It is one of those standards (one of the few Cole Porter tunes, despite its lovely melody) that I do not love to sing. Its opening lyrics are as follows:

Love for sale,
Appetizing young love for sale,
Love that's fresh and still unspoiled,
Love that's only slightly soiled. . . .
Who will buy? . . .
Who would like to sample my supply? . . .
Love for sale.[87]

Some learn the tune before these lyrics. In their case, title notwithstanding, the overblown romance of Hank Jones's piano intro could be read as heralding impossible love (impossible, "you-complete-me" love) rather than the promise of that which can be procured in exchange. Jones plays heartstrings, pulling the listener in close. This is no jingle. And what follows, a chirpy read of the head by Miles Davis, is undoubtedly street, but a stroll, not a curb crawl—a trip, trilby tips to Sunday promenaders. Even now, I (choose to) hear "Love for Sale," the standard—despite Porter's show-tune lyrics, taking us to the figure of the sex worker and to making the ordinary seem magical—as being about the tradition working on / with love. Love is not for sale. The trick occurs in the musicians' play between the banality of a show tune with questionable lyrics and the standard(s) that emerges by way of the double character of their sociality—their (co)habitation of musical space being the means to aesthetic form and aesthetic form (that "something else," that nonsensuous love feasting) being an excuse to gather in sociomusical banter.

Ornette Coleman and Don Cherry sound like they are busking it. We hear this on their 1958 debut *Something Else!!!!*, and it is perhaps even more apparent a year later, on *The Shape of Jazz to Come*.[88] In describing them this way, I do not mean to echo deprecation of certain journalists and musicians at the time of the album releases. (These pioneers of the "new thing" knew how to play changes. Listen to "Eventually," a ridiculously fast bebop original. This is not a deviation but rather a loving protraction of Charlie Parker's preoccupations with the drive and shape of melodic line. Their breakout from tonality simply demonstrates that consonance of melody and chord is not necessary to bebop.) Rather, it is to say that they sound out in the open, like they are out busking (it). We wouldn't know to request what they play. They busk not for anyone in particular and perhaps for no one but themselves, but in the refusal of a certain formal disposition (the finish or the brush of their phrases, more than any harmonic-melodic undergirding) that Miles and Cannonball Adderley serve up so effortlessly, Cherry and Ornette sing their hearts out. To say they sound vulnerable, exposed, doesn't get to it. They sound deimmunized, and one might wonder how they went about preparing to sound unprepared. What did they forget to maintain? Which booster did they neglect to administer? It's like they'd planned (not to be ready) for an outbreak.

Buskers can be incredibly versatile. Out on the street, they transform from woodshedding introvert to jukebox from one tune to the next, if they wish. They most often play not knowing whether they will be tipped. They do not play for pay. A gratuity might be given but without obligation. You can listen. They might woo you; they might drown you in love, but you are not obliged to buy. In fact, they are not selling—dropping coins and bills into a musician's case does not complete a transaction. Coins and bills are tokens, fugacious mementos, of the brief encounter. You are not obliged to stay or to stay to the end or to listen if you stay. But if you do, it is possible you catch something that sounds like love.

Acknowledgments

The staggered coincidence of a pandemic, the untimely death of a beloved sister, and a cancer diagnosis mark the most intense period of writing this book. I don't need to paint a picture of that maelstrom of tragedy. I'm sure you can imagine, and most likely you won't need to considering the ubiquity of some (or all) of it. What I do, however, want to share, acknowledge, and give thanks for is the warmth (and dare I say love?) that surrounded me during those long three years. Right after my sister's death and during those early months of the pandemic, our little unit traveled across the country as I took up a position in the Department of Rhetoric at Berkeley, adding an entire continent to the ocean that separated us from our families and friends in the United Kingdom. It wasn't easy being far from them. And so my heart fills as I write these words, thanking my colleagues, fellow travelers, and friends in the Bay Area for the innumerable acts of kindness that continue to sustain us. We arrived in the United States some eight years ago by way of a postdoctoral fellowship I was lucky enough to be selected for. I started my time at Northwestern University, having just completed my first book and feeling around for a new one; I remember that time as an indulgent one of undisturbed exploration. I thank the Departments of Performance Studies and African American Studies for hosting me. To the Lincoln Elementary community, who took us in, we miss you. And to the Chicago-area friends who have given us a family this side of the Atlantic, we are indebted to you in the best possible ways. I would also like to acknowledge my former colleagues at the Women, Gender, and Sexuality Department at the University of Massachusetts Amherst, where I found a place after my time at Northwestern, for the care they extended throughout my time there.

I have been lucky enough to share many of the ideas developed in this book with an eclectic assortment of intellectual communities. I am always amazed that people want to hear what I have to say, and I am grateful for the many, many conversations I've had over the past several years; they have been so important in steering the project toward this publication.

My friends of the Le Mardi Gras Listening Collective, in case it's not clear, I wrote so much of this book with you in mind. Thanks for being the welcome voices in my head. Some of you were able to come and visit at what was undoubtably the lowest point of my treatment year. I was a wreck that day, but sharing the afternoon with you and other dear friends (camped out in an Oakland diner; I could not eat) was sustaining in all sorts of ways.

The book could not have asked for better readers—reports from the three anonymous reviewers, which were able to draw to the surface the project's most pertinent commitments, have helped make this book both more of what I wanted it to be and more than I could have imagined for it. I appreciate the support and encouragement I've received from the editorial team at Stanford University Press, as I stagger toward the finish line. Thanks for holding me steady during those eleventh-hour wobbles.

It's been hard being so far from my dad and brothers, knowing that they are missing my mum and sister too. I appreciate them encouraging me to follow my nose through life (like a proper *àrè*), even as it has taken me away from them.

I don't think I would want to write without the Davis-Kalonaris-Okiji tendency. Thanks for being here with me. I love you.

Notes

Preamble

1. Anticipating the encounters between black study, European critical theory, and Yorùbá aesthetics that this book will stage, I begin with a disfigured passage from Theodor W. Adorno's *Minima Moralia*. Always on the lookout for those moments that I might hear Adorno jump the Hegelian dialectic (theoretically, a jump to lightspeed, a jump into a black hole), "Bequest"—a tribute to fellow traveler Walter Benjamin—has been an indispensable companion from the project's very start. There is a sense in which *Billie's Bent Elbow*, taken as a whole, *dwells* in/with this passage (by *dwelling*, as I write about in *Jazz as Critique* and reiterate here in the introductory "Constant Departure," I mean a simultaneous tarrying and departing from). See Fumi Okiji, *Jazz as Critique: Adorno and Black Expression Revisited* (Stanford, CA: Stanford University Press, 2018). With that quiet agitation between linger and departure, in concert with an array of thinkers mainly in black thought, Adorno's passage explodes for me, its shards becoming part of the polyphonic chorus that surrounds and inhabits it. What the reader hears in this preamble are direct quotations from the sources listed below alongside a handful of phrases of my own that appear in the main body of this text. Theodor W. Adorno, *Minima Moralia: Reflections from Damaged Life*, trans. E. F. N. Jephcott (London: Verso, 2005), 151; Frantz Fanon, *Black Skin, White Masks* (New York: Grove, 2008), 179; Sylvia Wynter and Katherine McKittrick, "Unparalleled Catastrophe for Our Species? Or, to Give Humanness a Different Future: Conversations," in *Sylvia Wynter: On Being Human as Praxis*, ed. Katherine McKittrick (Durham: Duke University Press, 2015), 23, 7;

Slavoj Žižek, *First as Tragedy, Then as Farce* (London, Verso, 2009), 113; Iain Macdonald, *What Would Be Different: Figures of Possibility in Adorno* (Stanford, CA: Stanford University Press, 2019), 101–2; Karl Marx, *The Economic and Philosophic Manuscripts of 1844*, trans. M. Milligan (New York: International Publishers, 1964), 108; Nahum Dimitri Chandler, "Of Exorbitance: The Problem of the Negro as a Problem for Thought," *Criticism* 50, no. 3 (2008): 368–69; J. Kameron Carter, *The Anarchy of Black Religion: A Mystic Song* (Durham: Duke University Press, 2023), 8; Stefano Harney and Fred Moten, *The Undercommons: Fugitive Planning and Black Study* (London: Minor Compositions, 2013), 96; Denise Ferreira da Silva, "1 (Life) ÷ 0 (Blackness) = ∞-∞ or ∞/∞: On Matter beyond the Equation of Value," *E-flux*, no. 79 (2017), https://www.e-flux.com/journal/79/94686/1-life-o-blackness-or-on-matter-beyond-the-equation-of-value/; Denise Ferreira da Silva, *Unpayable Debt* (London: Sternberg Press, 2022), 36; Adéléké Adéẹ̀kọ́, "Decolonization without a Linguistic Turn Is like Drinking Sugar without Tea: Ọlábíyìí Babalọlá Joseph Yáì," *Journal of the African Literature Association* 15, no. 2 (2021): 312; Fred Moten, *Black and Blur* (Durham: Duke University Press, 2017), 2; Walter Benjamin, *Selected Writings*, ed. Marcus Bullock and Michael W. Jennings, 4 vols. (Cambridge, MA: Belknap, 2004–6), 1:207; Rei Terada, "Hegel's Racism for Radicals," *Radical Philosophy* 2, no. 5 (2019): 16; Ọlabiyi Babalọla Yai, "In Praise of Metonymy: The Concepts of 'Tradition' and 'Creativity' in the Transmission of Yoruba Artistry over Time and Space," *Research in African Literatures* 24, no. 4 (1993): 30; Fred Moten, *Stolen Life* (Durham: Duke University Press, 2018), 244, 155; Jay M. Bernstein, *Adorno: Disenchantment and Ethics* (Cambridge: Cambridge University Press, 2001), 435; Frank B. Wilderson III, "Frank Wilderson, Wallowing in the Contradictions, Part 2," interview by Percy Howard, Necessary Angel, July 14, 2010, https://percy3.wordpress.com/2010/07/14/frank-wilderson-wallowing-in-the-contradictions-part-2/; Olabiyi Babalola Yai, "Tradition and the Yorùbá Artist," *African Arts* 32, no. 1 (1999): 32; Laura Harris, "What Happened to the Motley Crew? C. L. R. James, Hélio Oiticica, and the Aesthetic Sociality of Blackness," *Social Text* 30, no. 3 (2012): 53; Walter Benjamin, "Surrealism: The Last Snapshot of the European Intelligentsia," *New Left Review* 108 (1978): 54.

Introduction: Constant Departure

1. Here, I am riffing on Georg W. F. Hegel's and Adorno's contrapuntal "the True is the whole" and "the whole is the untrue." In the preface of *Phenomenology of Spirit*, Hegel tells us, "The True is the whole. But the whole is nothing other than the essence consummating itself through its development. Of the Absolute it must be said that it is essentially a *result*, that only in the *end* is it what it truly is; and that precisely in this consists its nature, viz. to be actual, subject, the spontaneous be-

coming of itself." Georg W. F. Hegel, *Hegel's "Phenomenology of Spirit,"* trans. A. V. Miller (Oxford: Oxford University Press, 2004), 11. Emphasis original. And Adorno responds,

> "The whole is the untrue," not merely because the thesis of totality is itself untruth, being the principle of domination inflated to the absolute; the idea of a positivity that can master everything that opposes it through the superior power of a comprehending spirit is the mirror image of the experience of the superior coercive force inherent in everything that exists by virtue of its consolidation under domination. This is the truth in Hegel's untruth. The force of the whole, which it mobilizes, is not a mere fantasy on the part of spirit; it is the force of the real web of illusion in which all individual existence remains trapped. By specifying, in opposition to Hegel, the negativity of the whole, philosophy satisfies, for the last time, the postulate of determinate negation, which is a positing. The ray of light that reveals the whole to be untrue in all its moments in none other than utopia, the utopia of the whole truth, which is still to be realized.

Theodor W. Adorno, *Hegel: Three Studies*, trans. Shierry Weber Nicholsen (Cambridge, MA: MIT Press, 1994), 87–88.

2. Cedric J. Robinson, *Black Marxism: The Making of the Black Radical Tradition* (Chapel Hill: University of North Carolina Press, 2020), 73. See also Iain Macdonald, "Adorno's Modal Utopianism: Possibility and Actuality in Adorno and Hegel," *Adorno Studies* 1, no. 1 (2017): 1–12.

3. Macdonald, "Adorno's Modal Utopianism," 2.

4. Adorno, *Minima Moralia*, 151. There appears to be a typo in Jephcott's translation, which reads "cross-gained" rather than "cross-grained."

5. R. A. Judy, "Introduction: On W. E. B. Du Bois and Hyperbolic Thinking," *Boundary 2* 27, no. 3 (Fall 2000): 14, 35. See also Tendayi Sithole, *Refiguring in Black* (Cambridge, MA: Polity, 2023).

6. Chandler, "Of Exorbitance," 367. Emphasis original.

7. Chandler, "Of Exorbitance," 352, 369.

8. Chandler, "Of Exorbitance," 368–69. Emphasis added.

9. Da Silva, *Unpayable Debt*, 55. Or to take Zakiyyah I. Jackson's proximate formulation, "Blackness is produced as sub/super/human at once, a form where form shall not hold: potentially 'everything and nothing' at the register of ontology." Zakiyyah I. Jackson, *Becoming Human: Matter and Meaning in an Antiblack World* (New York: New York University Press, 2020), 3.

10. Durotoye A. Adeleke, "The Yorùbá Fool Insignia: Beyond the Shakespearean Tradition," *Journal of Social Sciences* 21, no. 2 (2009): 111.

11. For more on black statelessness, see Carter, *Anarchy of Black Religion*, 6–9.

12. Babatunde Lawal, "Àwòrán: Representing the Self and its Metaphysical Other in Yoruba Art," *Art Bulletin* 83, no. 3 (2001): 502. Emphasis added. Due to Èṣù's androgyny and/or gender fluidity, I have replaced the pronouns here. For more on Èṣù's gender fluidity, see Oyeronke Oyewumi, "The Translation of Cultures: Engendering Yoruba Language, Orature and World-Sense," in *Women, Gender, Religion: A Reader*, ed. Elizabeth A. Castelli and Rosamond C. Rodman (London: Palgrave Macmillan, 2001), 85–86, 89–90.

13. Moten, *Black and Blur*, 231; Fred Moten, "Blackness and Poetry," *Evening Will Come* 55 (July 2015), https://arcade.stanford.edu/content/blackness-and-poetry-0; Fred Moten, *The Universal Machine* (Durham: Duke University Press, 2018), 8; Judy, "Introduction," 14.

14. On "undocumenting," see Laura Harris, "The Subjunctive Poetics of the Undocument: C. L. R. James's American Civilization," *Criticism* 58, no. 2 (2016): 205–30. Ọ̀rọ̀ translates most simply from Yorùbá as "word," "talk," or "conversation." For more on ọ̀rọ̀, see chap. 4, "Billie's Bent Elbow." See also Adélékè Adéẹ̀kọ́, *Arts of Being Yorùbá: Divination, Allegory, Tragedy, Proverb, Panegyric* (Bloomington: Indiana University Press, 2017), 28–32; Rowland Abiodun, "Verbal and Visual Metaphors: Mythical Allusions in Yorùbá Ritualistic Art of *Orí*," *Word and Image* 3, no. 3 (1987): 252–70.

15. Adorno, *Minima Moralia*, 151.

16. Da Silva, "1 (Life) ÷ 0 (Blackness)."

17. Harney and Moten, *Undercommons*, 96.

18. Fanon, *Black Skin, White Masks*, 179. Translation modified in that I follow David Marriott in translating Fanon's *l'Histoire* as "History" rather than "history," which in light of the Hegelian allusion that Fanon follows up with—"I should constantly remind myself that the real *leap* consists in introducing invention into existence"—is not a trivial detail. Ibid. Emphasis original. See also David Marriott, "No Lords A-leaping: Fanon, C. L. R. James, and the Politics of Invention," *Humanities* 3, no. 4 (2014): 518.

19. Adorno, *Minima Moralia*, 152.

20. I'm thinking with Rei Terada here—an inability or refusal to "completely destroy . . . 'being that is independent' around [us], *out of too much respect for what exists*." Or more modestly, we might think of it as lacking a certain single-mindedness that self-preservation supposedly inspires, we who are "passing through" "'deal with' independent being, only not to the point of [the] annihilation" required for mastery. Rei Terada, "Impasse as a Figure of Political Space," *Comparative Literature* 72, no. 2 (2020): 155.

21. For Hegel's parsimony, see Alison Stone, "Adorno, Hegel, and Dialectic," *British Journal for the History of Philosophy* 22, no. 6 (2014): 1123.

22. Thanks to Alexander G. Weheliye, I also have in mind the zoot-suited young men and Tod Clifton's fall out of history in Ralph Ellison's *Invisible Man*. "Forced to bear witness to his friend's violent erasure from history—any history—the protagonist is swept up in a current of doubt, igniting a different historical motor: 'Why should a man deliberately plunge outside history and peddle in obscenity? Why did he choose to plunge . . . into the void of faceless faces, of soundless voices, lying outside of history?' . . . Clifton's death forces the protagonist to acknowledge that Clifton had no choice in 'falling out of history' since there exists no place for black subjects in The Brotherhood's version of history." Alexander G. Weheliye, "The Grooves of Temporality," *Public Culture* 17, no. 2 (2005): 322.

23. For more on *ìtàn*, see Yái, "In Praise of Metonymy."

24. Judy, "Introduction," 14; Harris, "Subjunctive Poetics," 221–24.

25. Adéèkó, "Decolonization," 308. Although the archetypal *gbẹ́nugbẹ́nu* uses words, their response/contribution can be made by way of other media. If I were to write this book again from scratch, I would put, at its heart, a patient unfolding and engagement of two *gbẹ́nugbẹ́nu* contributions to the music of Cecil Taylor: Cecil Taylor, "Cecil Taylor: African Code, Black Methodology," interview by J. B. Figi, *DownBeat*, April 10, 1975, 14; Pat Thomas and XT, *"Akisakila"/Attitudes of Preparation (Mountains, Oceans, Trees)*, Edition Gamut EG01, 2021, 2 LPs. Although the live performance was given by a trio, I would argue that Will Holder's liner notes for the album transforms the work and expands the band. Considering the many sampled voices, there is also a case to be made for considering *Akisakila* a large ensemble piece.

26. Yai, "Tradition," 32.

27. Yai, "Tradition," 32.

28. Yai, "Tradition," 32.

29. Adéèkó, "Decolonization," 310–11. Yái speaks of the encounter as a monument as well as a document. Yai, "Tradition," 32. Due to the "undocumenting," instability, and transitoriness of these "happenings," as well as their porosity and potential for intimacy, I prefer the image of the shrine. Separately, this formulation, in which we see the codependence of *gbẹ́nàgbẹ́nà* and *gbẹ́nugbẹ́nu*, is echoed in Adorno's thoughts on the codependency of artwork and philosophical interpretation. He writes that art's "object is determined negatively, as indeterminable. It is for this reason that art requires philosophy, which interprets it in order to say what it is unable to say, whereas art is only able to say it by not saying it." Theodor W. Adorno, *Aesthetic Theory*, trans. Robert Hullot-Kentor (London: Continuum, 1997), 72. And separately, again, it is the notion of incompleteness that appears in Adéèkó (and Yái) I'm referring to here; although, of course, I also have Stefano Harney, Fred Moten, and Cedric Robinson in mind.

30. Adéẹ̀kọ́, "Decolonization," 308.

31. Yai, "Tradition," 35; Yai, "In Praise of Metonymy," 34. I'm quite taken with this diversity of motion. I particularly like how Yái gets to "hatching": "*Pa ìtàn* (*pìtàn* in contracted form) is often trivially and somewhat inadequately translated into English as 'to tell a story.' *Pa* is also used for such nouns as *èkùrọ́* (kernel) *obì* (kola nut) = to separate the two lobes of the kola nut; *ẹyin, ọmọ* (egg), to hatch; *òwe* (proverb); *àlọ́* (riddle, parable). *Pìtàn* therefore means to produce such a discourse that could constitute the Ariadne thread of the human historical labyrinth, history being equated with a maze or a riddle." Yai, "In Praise of Metonymy," 31. This is a series: constant departure, constant structure, changing same. See Yai, "Tradition," 35. See also Jennie C. Jones and Fred Moten, *Constant Structure* (Chicago: Arts Club of Chicago, 2020); LeRoi Jones (Amiri Baraka), *Black Music* (Brooklyn: Akashic Books, 2010), 205–41. On "tilling," see Jones and Moten, *Constant Structure*, esp. "The Red Sheaves," 28 (but really the entire publication). I also have these lines in mind: "Come on, now. Who, all alone, all, along, don't want to share the open wound, the nasty, gnostic murmur of this constant surfacing, this tilling and aeration, this abduction?" Fred Moten, "Is Alone Together How It Feels to Be Free? Ummm," *Interim* 37, no. 3–4 (Winter 2021), https://www.interimpoetics.org/373374/fred-moten.

32. Adéẹ̀kọ́, "Decolonization," 311, 314. Elsewhere, I delve into the etymology of *dwelling*, which reveals both a tarrying and wandering at play in the word. See Okiji, *Jazz as Critique*. That this contradictory term has proved such a useful one as I attempt to bring light to Yái's contribution to the thoughts recorded here should not surprise me. The paradigmatic artist, the sculptor (*gbẹ́nàgbẹ́nà*), is understood to be what the Yorùbá call *àrè*, or wanderer. Yái constellates this figure with the notion of "constant departure" and what might be understood as an extraterritoriality that characterizes the concept *ìtàn*, this particular modality of becoming (and its narration)—a propensity "to spread, reach, to open up" temporally and geographically. It's a way with time and the earth, comportment that invariably has something poetic about it. Yai, "In Praise of Metonymy," 34.

33. See, e.g., Olabiyi Yai, "African Ethnonymy and Toponymy: Reflections on Decolonization African Ethnonyms and Toponyms," *General History of Africa: Studies and Documents* 6 (1984): 39–50; Olabiyi Babalola Yai, "The Path Is Open: The Legacy of Melville and Frances Herskovits in African Oral Narrative Analysis," *Research in African Literatures* 30, no. 2 (1999): 1–16; Yai, "Tradition"; Yai, "In Praise of Metonymy." For further references, see Adéẹ̀kọ́, "Decolonization."

34. Adéẹ̀kọ́, "Decolonization," 311.

35. Karin Barber, *I Could Speak until Tomorrow: Oriki, Women and the Past in a Yoruba Town* (Edinburgh: Edinburgh University Press, 2020), 269.

36. *Billie's Bent Elbow*, so enabled by Yáì's work, departs from him here—a departure that marks a tarrying. I would say that mimesis (although, the Benjaminian and Adornian rather than Auerbachian variety) is, in fact, precisely what the *gbẹ̀nàgbẹ́nà* and *gbẹ́nugbẹ́nu* are practicing. In chap. 3, "Cecil's Snuggling," I explore Adorno's rejection (or demotion, at least) of the conventional understanding of mimesis as imitation or representation, that "mimesis be always mimesis *of*." Michael Cahn, "Subversive Mimesis: T. W. Adorno and the Modern Impasse of Critique," in *Mimesis in Contemporary Theory: An Interdisciplinary Approach*, ed. Mihai Spariosu (Philadelphia: John Benjamins, 1984), 63n34. Rather, for Adorno, mimesis is a practice of contiguity. In language consonant with the significance granted the figure of sculptor in Yorùbá artistic production, he speaks of mimesis as a molding onto. See Max Horkheimer and Theodor W. Adorno, *Dialectic of Enlightenment*, trans. Edmund Jephcott (Stanford, CA: Stanford University Press, 2002), 50–51. For more on Benjaminian feeling, see chap. 4, "Billie's Bent Elbow," later in this book. Although approaching the issue from a distinct set of questions and literature, Zakiyyah I. Jackson has made comparable use of the term *correspondence* as a more capacious alternative to terminology laden with Hegelian recognitive baggage. Jackson writes, "I use the term *correspondence*, denoting connection, interplay, and communication, in place of and against the normativity that legislates intersubjectivity in the Hegelian terms of the Self-Other relation." Zakiyyah I. Jackson, "Losing Manhood: Animality and Plasticity in the (Neo)slave Narrative," *Qui Parle: Critical Humanities and Social Sciences* 25, no. 1–2 (2016): 120. My own (Benjaminian) slant opens this spectrum a little wider to include array and placement, interested and disinterested (co)habitation.

37. Benjamin, "Surrealism," 54.

38. Benjamin, "Surrealism," 56; Marriott, "No Lords A-leaping," 518.

39. Marriott, "No Lords A-leaping," 532.

40. At the end of "The Work of Art in the Age of Mechanical Reproduction," Benjamin, against the aestheticization of politics by fascism and liberal democracies alike, proposes a politicization of art: "Communism responds by politicizing art." Walter Benjamin, *Illuminations*, trans. Harry Zohn (New York: Schocken Books, 2007), 242. Adorno, in his infamous chiding of his friend, flattens the possibilities suggested into committed art à la Bertolt Brecht. I am not suggesting that activism is absent from the thoughts that unfold in Benjamin's "Work of Art," but I choose to read them through the lens of the figure of the collective body space he writes about at the end of the essay "Surrealism" and to take this site as a focal point for radical living. See Benjamin, "Surrealism."

41. Sami Khatib, "Fantasy, Phantasmagoria, and Image-Space: Walter Benjamin's Politics of Pure Means," paper presented at Die Politik des Phantasmas,

Hebbel am Ufer Theatre, Berlin, Germany, November 23, 2013, 7, https://www.academia.edu/5257726/Fantasy_Phantasmagoria_and_Image_Space_Walter_Benjamins_Politics_of_Pure_Means.

42. Sami Khatib, "'To Win the Energies of Intoxication for the Revolution': Body Politics, Community, and Profane Illumination," *Anthropology and Materialism: A Journal of Social Research* 2 (2014): 13.

43. Harney and Moten, *Undercommons*, 92.

44. Taylor, "Cecil Taylor," 14. For a different path to/through the notion of black methodology, see Katherine McKittrick, "Dear April: The Aesthetics of Black Miscellanea," *Antipode* 54, no. 1 (2022): 3–18.

45. If we were to fold my understanding of the standard another way, we might end up where Brent Hayes Edwards does in his chapter on Henry Threadgill's micropoetics of titles. He writes, "Rather than a 'key,' then, perhaps these titles at least function as something more like John Ashbery's description of poem titles as providing 'a *very small aperture into a larger area*,' a keyhole perhaps, or some way of getting into the poem." Brent Hayes Edwards, *Epistrophies: Jazz and the Literary Imagination* (Cambridge, MA: Harvard University Press, 2017), 182. Emphasis added. "Billie's Bent Elbow" or *Billie's Bent Elbow* or "Billie's elbow bent at breast," possible "titles" of the standard that runs through this book, are better understood as forums or scenes within which the standard unfolds and, better still, as potential puncta, ports, or opportunities through which the readers might encounter the standard. Also see how Samuel Weber interprets *opportunity*, or *Glegenheit*, in Walter Benjamin. He writes that the "moment of opportunity" is one "not to be 'seized' but rather traversed: it is 'port' or 'portal' (lexical root of op*port*unity), which leads not to an ultimate goal but to a multitude of 'carpets.'" Samuel Weber, *Institution and Interpretation*, expanded ed. (Stanford: Stanford University Press, 2001), 230, 235, quoted in Peter Fenves, *Points of Departure: Samuel Weber between Spectrality and Reading* (Evanston, IL: Northwestern University Press, 2016), 3. As Peter Fenves glosses, "The 'port' in *opportunity* opens up an opportunity to alter the standard concept of opportunity, so that it is no longer understood in terms of starting and ending points but is, instead, saturated by *intermittent points of departure*." Ibid., 3. Former emphasis original; latter emphasis added.

46. Stephen Henderson, *Understanding the New Black Poetry: Black Speech and Black Music as Poetic References* (New York, William Morrow, 1973), 44; Fred Moten, "The Red Sheaves," in *Perennial Fashion, Presence Falling* (Seattle: Wave Books, 2023), 14. Thanks to Nick Byers, Slauson Malone's (a.k.a. Jaspar Marsalis) *A Quiet Farwell* is playing. See Slauson Malone, *A Quiet Farwell, 2016–2018 (Crater Speak) / Vergangenheitsbewältigung (Crater Speak)*, Grand Closing GC001, 2022, Bandcamp. I'm also preempting my thinking with C. L. R. James and Fred Moten in chap. 1,

"Haiti's Infrasonic Boom." For work on decadence, a closely associated notion, see David Marriott, "On Decadence: Bling Bling," *E-flux*, no. 79 (2017), https://www.e-flux.com/journal/79/94430/on-decadence-bling-bling/; R. A. Judy, "On the Question of Nigga Authenticity," *Boundary 2* 21, no. 3 (1994): 211–30.

47. Cecil Taylor, "Sound Structure of Subculture Becoming Major Breath / Naked Fire Gesture," liner notes on Cecil Taylor, *Unit Structures*, Blue Note Records BST 84237, 1966, LP; Thomas and XT, *"Akisakila"*; Matthew Shipp, "Black Mystery School Pianists," New Music USA, December 18, 2020, https://nmbx.newmusicusa.org/black-mystery-school-pianists/.

48. Marriott, "No Lords A-leaping," 541.

49. Jared Sexton, "Affirmation in the Dark," *The Comparatist* 43 (2019): 107. Although this book does not directly engage his work, Robin D. Kelley's narration of black radical thought, poetics and politics, and most particularly his bringing to light the black surreal, in its various guises, provides indispensable historical and political context for the thoughts unfolded here. See Robin D. Kelley, *Freedom Dreams: The Black Radical Imagination* (Boston, MA: Beacon, 2022); Robin D. Kelley, "Beyond the 'Real' World, or Why Black Radicals Need to Wake Up and Start Dreaming," *Souls* 4, no. 2 (2002): 51–64; Franklin Rosemont and Robin D. Kelley, *Black, Brown, and Beige: Surrealist Writings from Africa and the Diaspora* (Austin: University of Texas Press, 2009).

Chapter 1: Haiti's Infrasonic Boom

1. John Robert McNeill, *Mosquito Empires: Ecology and War in the Greater Caribbean, 1620–1914* (Cambridge: Cambridge University Press, 2010), 252; Jean-Pierre Le Glaunec, *The Cry of Vertières: Liberation Memory and the Beginning of Haiti*, trans. Jonathan Kaplansky (Kingston: McGill-Queen's University Press, 2020). The official line was that the objective of the expedition was to *assist* the troubled colony following the unrest and immense economic cost exacted by the various struggles of emancipation. The expectation was, in the event of a failure to reestablish slavery, that the racial codes would be upheld and intensified. As Jean-Pierre Le Glaunec writes,

> The expedition was supposed to make it possible to "pacify" the colony. Pacifying, in military doctrine—today we speak of stabilizing—was actually not much like peacemaking. The war ships leaving the European shores for the North, South, and West of the colony in November and December 1801 were loaded with various pieces of ordnance (cannons, mortar, howitzers), projectiles of all sorts (bombs, shells, grenades), as well as rifles, carbines, sabres, pikes, and spears. Napoleon's secret instructions leave little doubt as to the goal of the maneuver, even if [General] Leclerc [Napoleon's brother-in-law] states, in a proclamation

dated 17 February 1802, that he had come to "bring peace and happiness." Once order was restored, the French generals had instructions to arrest and deport black officers. . . . While not re-establishing slavery—at least not right away—the goal was to re-establish, through violence if necessary, the dogma of "race" that structured power relationships in the Ancien Régime.

Ibid., 28.

2. Le Glaunec, *Cry of Vertières*, 39, 28. "'A war of colour,' French General Kerversau called it on 4 November 1802. 'A struggle to the death between Black and White,' as expressed by Officer Pierre Thouvenot in a letter written 21 March 1803 to the minister of the navy and the colonies." Ibid., 28.

3. Le Glaunec, *Cry of Vertières*, 44. See also ibid., 38.

4. Toussaint Louverture's constitution of 1801, a document prohibiting slavery and other forms of race discrimination, transformed Saint-Domingue into an "entity that was no longer exactly a colony and not yet really a sovereign state." Claude Moïse, *Le projet national de Toussaint Louverture: La Consistution de 1801* (Port-au-Prince: Éditions Mémoire, 2001), 26, quoted in Le Glaunec, *Cry of Vertières*, 27.

5. Jean-Pierre Béchaud, "Voyage en Amérique, de Monsieur J. P. Béchaud présentement major du 66e regiment d'infrie: De ligne," letter, July 28, 1803, s.l, s.n. 1807, 75, www.archive.org/details/voyageenamriquoobech, quoted in Le Glaunec, *Cry of Vertières*, 34.

6. Le Glaunec states, "In the confusion of that November day some Creole and French words could be heard along with African words." Le Glaunec, *Cry of Vertières*, 34. Drawing from John Thornton's *Africa and African in the Making of the Atlantic World, 1400–1800*, Le Glaunec suggests that these words were probably Kikongo as most of the African slaves brought over in 1780s were Congolese. In fact, between 1777 and 1791, the Congolese made up less than half of the enslaved population in the North and about a third of those in the West of the island. There were sizeable percentages of Ewe-Fon and Yorùbá and an array of other tribes forming the majority. See David Geggus, "Slave Society in the Sugar Plantation Zones of Saint Domingue and the Revolution of 1791–93," *Slavery and Abolition* 20, no. 2 (1999): 39.

7. C. L. R. James says, "The dishonest political position of the French Army was now taking its toll. The soldiers still thought of themselves as a revolutionary army. Yet at nights they heard the blacks in the fortress singing the Marseillaise, the *Ça Ira*, and the other revolutionary songs." C. L. R. James, *The Black Jacobins: Toussaint L'Ouverture and the San Domingo Revolution* (New York: Vintage, 1989), 317.

8. "Lacroix records how these misguided wretches as they heard the songs started

and looked at the officers as if to say, 'Have our barbarous enemies justice on their side? Are we no longer the soldiers of Republican France? And have we become the crude instruments of policy?'" James, *Black Jacobins*, 317–18.

9. Slavoj Žižek, *Disparities* (London: Bloomsbury, 2016), 64.

10. I acknowledge Rocío Zambrana's 2021 essay for bringing this formulation from Nadia Yala Kisukidi to my attention. See Rocío Zambrana, "Hegelian History Interrupted," *Crisis and Critique* 8, no. 2 (2021): 410–31. "Décoloniser la philosophie, c'est reconnaître son impossible universalisation. Non pas au sens où la raison serait la chose du monde la moins partagée, mais au sens où la philosophie devrait être tenue pour ce qu'elle est, en dehors de ses terres d'élection—à savoir un objet anthropologique, qui renseigne sur une des modalités, parmi d'autres, de la palabre en Occident." Nadia Yala Kisukidi, "Décoloniser la philosophie: Ou de la philosophie comme objet anthropologique," *Présence Africaine* 2 (2015): 96.

11. Saidiya V. Hartman, *Scenes of Subjection: Terror, Slavery, and Self-Making in Nineteenth-Century America* (Oxford: Oxford University Press, 1997), 65.

12. I have this seminal passage from Cedric J. Robinson's *Black Marxism* ringing in my ear here and always:

> The social cauldron of Black radicalism is Western society. Western society, however, has been its location and its objective condition but not—except in a most perverse fashion—its specific inspiration. Black radicalism is a negation of Western civilization, but not in the direct sense of a simple dialectical negation. It is certain that the evolving tradition of Black radicalism owes its peculiar moment to the historical interdiction of African life by European agents. In this sense, the African experience of the past five centuries is simply one element in the mesh of European history: some of the objective requirements for Europe's industrial development were met by the physical and mental exploitation of Asian, African, and native American peoples. This experience, though, was merely the condition for Black radicalism—its immediate reason for and object of being—but not the foundation for its nature or character. Black radicalism, consequently, cannot be understood within the particular context of its genesis. It is not a variant of Western radicalism whose proponents happen to be Black. Rather, it is a specifically African response to an oppression emergent from the immediate determinants of European development in the modern era and framed by orders of human exploitation woven into the interstices of European social life from the inception of Western civilization.

Robinson, *Black Marxism*, 72–3.

13. James, *Black Jacobins*, 317.

14. James, *Black Jacobins*, 317.

15. Here, I also have in mind Fanon on truth and lies in the anticolonial context: "The question of truth must also be taken into consideration. For the people, only fellow nationals are ever owed the truth. No absolute truth, no discourse on the transparency of the soul can erode this position. In answer to the lie of the colonial situation, the colonized subject responds with a lie." Frantz Fanon, *The Wretched of the Earth*, trans. Richard Philcox (New York: Grove, 2004), 14.

16. Nahum Dimitri Chandler, *X—the Problem of the Negro as a Problem for Thought* (New York: Fordham University Press, 2013), 35. Emphasis original. As I intimate in the introduction to this chapter, the Haitians' "La Marseillaise" is also revelatory of that everyday fantastic of an African sense of being. See the next chapter for an unfolding of this idea. There is much to say about how the anticipation or expectation of black actualization falls short of appreciating what a black world would look like. I claim that it would involve an appreciation of how the fantastic should be placed alongside real possibility as essential to a more faithful picture of our existence.

17. Denise Ferreira da Silva, *Toward a Global Idea of Race* (Minneapolis: University of Minnesota, 2007), 32–33.

18. Slavoj Žižek, "Against the Populist Temptation," *Critical Inquiry* 32, no. 3 (2006): 569; Susan Buck-Morss, *Hegel, Haiti, and Universal History* (Pittsburgh: University of Pittsburgh, 2009), 133. Žižek further comments on the Ninth Symphony as a universal anthem:

> The unofficial anthem of the European Union, heard at numerous political, cultural, and sporting events, is the "Ode to Joy" melody from the last movement of Beethoven's Ninth Symphony, a true empty signifier that can stand for anything. In France, it was elevated by Romain Rolland into a humanist ode to the brotherhood of all people ("the Marseillaise of humanity"); in 1938, it was performed as the highpoint of *Reichsmusiktage* and also for Hitler's birthday; during the Cultural Revolution in China, in the atmosphere of rejecting European classics, it was redeemed as a piece of progressive class struggle; and in today's Japan it has achieved cult status, being woven into the very social fabric with its alleged message of joy through suffering.

Žižek, "Against the Populist Temptation," 569.

19. Žižek, *First as Tragedy*, 113.

20. Dessalines's codification of Haiti's universal blackness in the 1804 Declaration of Independence and the war for independence that helped accomplish it marked an absolute break with the empire. This commitment to maintaining the hard-won liberty at any cost is, at times, written up as a retreat from the universal freedom project. Dessalines's assurance given just a month earlier to absentee

"property-owners of Saint-Domingue, who are wandering in foreign lands" that, "in proclaiming . . . independence," the Armée indigène would not inhibit their return was reversed in the most violent manner. Sabine Manigat, *Éventail d'histoire vivante d'Haïti: Des preludes à la revolution de Saint-Domingue jusqu' à nos jours (1789–1999), une contribution à "la nouvelle histoire"* (Port-au-Prince: Collection du CHUDAC, 2001), 418, quoted in Jean Casimir, *The Haitians: A Decolonial History*, trans. Laurent Dubois (Chapel Hill: University of North Carolina, 2020), 16. The "violent elimination of whites signalled [the Haitians] deliberate retreat from universalist principles," which won them the momentary position at the apex of universal history. Buck-Morss, *Hegel, Haiti*, 39. Dessalines's readiness to resort to massacre in order to stabilize the nascent state and/or to wreak vengeance on the island's white inhabitants takes place, for Buck-Morss and Žižek, beyond the frame of a global struggle for freedom and equality even as the brutality of Dessalines's Haiti consolidates its admission into an "inhumanity in common." Ibid., 138. For more on this "retreat" from universal history, see George Ciccariello-Maher, "'So Much the Worse for the Whites': Dialectics of the Haitian Revolution," *Journal of French and Francophone Philosophy* 22, no. 1 (2014): 19–39.

21. Žižek, *First as Tragedy*, 112; Béchaud, "Voyage en Amérique," quoted in Le Glaunec, *Cry of Vertières*, 34. Béchaud was a battalion commander stationed at Gros-Morne, Incidentally, I'm not the only one intrigued by this polyglottic chorus. Historian Jean-Pierre Le Glaunec, whose book has been an indispensable companion as I've worked on this chapter, asks, "Was this rendering of *La Marseillaise* on the hills of Cap-Français faithful to the original lyrics? Was it sung in Creole or in French? Did all the soldiers sing it or did some prefer to sing traditional African or 'Haitian' songs? Voodoo songs perhaps? Which verses did they sing? Did the French fall silent or did they launch into a song praising Napoleon?" Ibid., 5.

22. Le Glaunec, *Cry of Vertières*, 34.

23. Although it is not crystal clear that this is precisely what Žižek is alluding to in his earlier references to Haiti, this is clearly his intention in the more recent "Sublimation and Dislocation," in which he responds to *The Haitians: A Decolonial History*, the recently published book by Jean Casimir, by way of Rocío Zambrana's reading and discussion of what she understands to be the book's "dislocation" of the European freedom project and of dialectical historical movement. There is a refinement in Žižek's thought between *First as Tragedy, Then as Farce* and the recent "Sublimation and Dislocation." In the latter is a desire to attenuate Haiti's distinction by claiming that each eruption in the unfolding of universal freedom involves a dislocation. Dislocation is not particular to Haiti or to postcolonial spaces; the French/European permutation(s) should also be understood as involving dislocation. In his thinking, this is just what the dialectic does. This reworking is a little at odds with

the understanding of Haiti as an improvement and *consummation* of the French attempt. Slavoj Žižek, "Sublimation and Dislocation: A False Choice," *International Journal of Žižek Studies* 16, no. 1 (2022): 1–5; Casimir, *Haitians*; Zambrana, "Hegelian History Interrupted"; Žižek, *First as Tragedy*.

24. Žižek, "Sublimation and Dislocation," 3–4.

25. Moten, *Black and Blur*, 7. Emphasis original.

26. Although, it's important to keep in mind that Dessalines represents, for Žižek, a retreat from the dialectic of freedom rather than further refinement or development.

27. Moten, *Black and Blur*, 7.

28. David Scott, "On the Very Idea of a Black Radical Tradition," *Small Axe: A Caribbean Journal of Criticism* 17, no. 1 (2013): 5; Edward Kamau Brathwaite, "Dialect and Dialectic," *Bulletin of the African Studies Association of the West Indies*, no. 6 (December 1973): 99, 89, 92. I would like to share just a little more of Brathwaite's gentle criticism of Walter Rodney's *How Europe Underdeveloped Africa* (1972):

> It would be a mistake therefore, to take it that European super structures are an end of the matter, bringing man to his highest level of civilization and consciousness. And certain it is that *How Europe Underdeveloped Africa* was not set out to make this point. Very much the contrary. And yet (tyranny of model) this is just what implicitly happens in/to this book. Over and over we find our brother, trapped within his modernist/progressive dialectic, talking about the escalation of African societies from their primal/primitive structures into something newer, more complex, more "efficient" (i.e. exploitative of resources, less subsistent, less like their original model).

Ibid., 92.

29. Robinson, *Black Marxism*, 171. I have most pointedly in mind Ashon T. Crawley's work and particularly his essay "Stayed | Freedom | Hallelujah," which is a meditation on flesh as the source or site of "*otherwise* genres" of human being, an ontoepistemological site of "otherwise possibilities." Ashon T. Crawley, "Stayed | Freedom | Hallelujah," in *Otherwise Worlds: Against Settler Colonialism and Antiblackness*, ed. Tiffany Lethabo King, Jenell Navarro, and Andrea Smith (Durham: Duke University Press, 2020), 29. Emphasis original. In the essay, he suggests that "what remains to be elaborated in Spillers's conception of flesh is the generalizability of such a claim. Flesh is that which has priority before any theological-philosophical mood or movement befalls it, flesh is before the situation of Christian dogma or what Wynter would describe as the 'coloniality of being.'" See also Stefano Harney and Fred Moten, *All Incomplete* (London: Minor Compositions, 2021), 13–18; Carter, *Anarchy of Black Religion*, 18–19; R. A. Judy, *Sentient Flesh: Thinking in Disorder*,

Poiésis in Black (Durham: Duke University Press, 2020), 4–10; Alexander G. Weheliye, *Habeas Viscus: Racializing Assemblages, Biopolitics, and Black Feminist Theories of the Human* (Durham: Duke University Press, 2014).

30. Robinson, *Black Marxism*, 171, 169; Gerald Mullin, *Flight and Rebellion* (New York: Oxford University Press, 1972), 18, quoted in ibid., 170.

31. Robinson, *Black Marxism*, 169, 171.

32. Cedric J. Robinson, *The Terms of Order: Political Science and the Myth of Leadership* (New York: State University of New York, 2016), 196. See also ibid., 7–38.

33. Kevin Okoth, "Resistance from Elsewhere," *London Review of Books* 44, no. 7 (April 2022), https://www.lrb.co.uk/the-paper/v44/n07/kevin-okoth/resistance-from-elsewhere.

34. Žižek, "Sublimation and Dislocation," 3, 4.

35. Moten, *Black and Blur*, 12. Emphasis added.

36. Moten, *Black and Blur*, 7, 10, 9.

37. Moten, *Black and Blur*, 6.

38. Adorno, *Minima Moralia*, 151. I follow the lead of Haitian historian Jean Casimir, who adopts the formerly derogatory term *bossales* in identification and solidarity with the black laborer. *Bossales* is conventionally used to denote the African-born enslaved, who made up the majority in Saint-Domingue at the time of the revolution.

39. Casimir, *Haitians*, 247.

40. Thomas Madiou, *Histoire d'Haïti*, 8 vols. (Port-au-Prince: Imprimerie de Jh. Courtois, 1847–48), 5:111, quoted in Casimir, *Haitians*, 248.

41. Casimir, *Haitians*, 248.

42. Zambrana, "Hegelian History Interrupted."

43. Moten, *Black and Blur*, 2.

44. Moten, *Stolen Life*, 155, 157. Emphasis added. This is just one moment that I pull to the fore the mimetic snuggle of Yorùbá and blackness I allude to in the introduction. Many others are scattered throughout the book.

45. Moten, *Stolen Life*, 155, ix; Moten, *Black and Blur*, 22.

46. Adorno, *Minima Moralia*, 151.

Chapter 2: Unthinkable Nonsense

1. Claudia Rankine, *Citizen: An American Lyric* (Minneapolis, MN: Graywolf, 2014), 135. Rankine writes, "Because white men can't / police their imagination / black people are dying." Ibid. Concerning the misadventures of late modernity, Herbert Marcuse writes, "The willful play with fantastic possibilities, the ability to act with good conscience, *contra naturam*, to experiment with men and things, to convert illusion into reality and fiction into truth, testify to the extent to which

Imagination has become an instrument of progress." Herbert Marcuse, *One-Dimensional Man: Studies in the Ideology of Advanced Industrial Society* (Milton Park: Routledge, 2013), 252. Even though he would not have had antiblack violence in mind, his indictment of the "obscene" fusion of semblance and reality as an instrument of destructive enlightenment tracks Rankine's own intention. While I am in accord, in this chapter, my aim is to draw attention to the myopia of this brutal imagination of the white West. As such, I echo Kevin Quashie when he writes, "What makes 'imagine a black world' so necessary is the exemption of black humanity from our commonsense understanding.... There is no outright assumption of black humanity in the world (the potency of 'Black Lives Matter' as an emblem confirms this), and indeed black humanity has to be argued over and again." Kevin Quashie, *Black Aliveness, or a Poetics of Being* (Durham: Duke University Press, 2021), 2.

2. As I write these lines, two items come to mind. First, Charles Mingus's allegory "The Clown"—a figure whose complexity is reduced to mere slapstick by the mimetic (in the Benjaminian sense) incapacity of its audience. Charles Mingus, "The Clown," on *The Clown*, Rhino Records 8122796415, 1957, compact disc. I also have in mind the criticisms that Mertilla Jones encountered concerning her reactions to the murder of her seven-year-old granddaughter by a Detroit SWAT team. As Tyrone Palmer tells us, "The range of emotions at work in Jones's testimony—grief, shock, despair, rage, depression, vulnerability, disbelief—*are reduced to a hysterical anger, flattened to 'an outburst.'*" Tyrone S. Palmer, "'What Feels More Than Feeling?' Theorizing the Unthinkability of Black Affect," *Critical Ethnic Studies* 3, no. 2 (2017): 31. Emphasis added.

3. Quashie, *Black Aliveness*, 2.

4. Richard Iton writes that the "black fantastic" is that which "refer[s] to the minor-key sensibilities generated from the experiences of the underground, the vagabond, and those constituencies marked as deviant—notions of being that are inevitably aligned within, in conversation with, against, and articulated beyond the boundaries of the modern.... The *black* in black fantastic, in this context, signifies both a generic category of underdeveloped possibilities and the particular 'always there' interpretations of ... agonistic ... visions and practices generated by subaltern populations." Richard Iton, *In Search of the Black Fantastic: Politics and Popular Culture in the Post-civil Rights Era* (Oxford: Oxford University Press, 2008), 16.

5. Sylvia Wynter, "The Ceremony Must Be Found: After Humanism," *Boundary 2* 12–13, no. 3–1 (1984): 19–70; Sylvia Wynter, "The Ceremony Found: Towards the Autopoetic Turn/Overturn, Its Autonomy of Human Agency and Extraterritoriality of (Self-)Cognition," in *Black Knowledges / Black Struggles: Essays in Critical Epistemology*, ed. Jason R. Ambroise and Sabine Broeck (Liverpool: Liverpool University

Press, 2015), 184–252.

6. Wynter, "Ceremony Must Be Found," 27–28.

7. Wynter, "Ceremony Must Be Found," 37.

8. Sylvia Wynter, "Towards the Sociogenic Principle: Fanon, the Puzzle of Conscious Experience, of 'Identity' and What It's Like to Be 'Black,'" in *National Identity and Socio-political Change: Latin America between Marginalisation and Integration*, ed. Mercedes Duran-Cogan and Antonio Gomez-Moriana (New York: Garland, 2000), 43.

9. Wynter and McKittrick, "Unparalleled Catastrophe," 23. Emphasis original. "Man" in Wynter and in this chapter refers to the "overrepresented" genre of the human—supposedly "generic, ostensibly supracultural"—against whom "subjugated Human Others (i.e., Indians and Negroes)" are cast. Sylvia Wynter, "Unsettling the Coloniality of Being/Power/Truth/Freedom: Towards the Human, after Man, Its Overrepresentation—an Argument," *CR: The New Centennial Review* 3, no. 3 (2003): 288.

10. Wynter, "Ceremony Must Be Found," 27, 28.

11. Sylvia Wynter, "Africa, the West and the Analogy of Culture: The Cinematic Text after Man," *Symbolic Narratives / African Cinema: Audiences, Theory and the Moving Image*, ed. June Givanni (London: British Film Institute, 2001), 31. This essay was first presented as the keynote address at the conference Africa and the History of Cinematic Ideas, held in London in 1995. It gathered filmmakers and scholars from across the African world, including Imruh Bakari, Ousmane Sembène, Manthia Diawara, Claire Andrade-Watkins, and John Akomfrah. As such, the essay (and collection) is fascinating as a historical document, pointing to a broader, somewhat stuttered black/African intramural conversation. If permitted to preempt myself, the collection often reads as a snuggling of the contrariant. See the following chapter, "Cecil's Snuggling."

12. Wynter, "Unsettling the Coloniality," 331; Theodor W. Adorno, *Negative Dialectics*, trans. E. B. Ashton (London: Routledge, 1973), 6. Why a science? Wynter writes, "It is only with science, as Riedl and Kaspar (quoting Roman Sexl) observe, that there is ever any true 'victory over the ratiomorphic apparatus'—such as that of Galileo's and his telescope over the abductive logic of the if/then sequence of inference dictated behind the backs of their consciousness to the Aristotelian doctors of philosophy as the speaking subjects of the Christian-medieval system ensemble." Wynter, "Ceremony Must Be Found," 37. And if the term *science* takes us too readily to Isaac Newton, Charles Darwin, and Albert Einstein, we might follow Walter Mignolo's lead and adopt the Latin term *scientia*. See Walter Mignolo, "Sylvia Wynter: What Does It Mean to Be Human?," in *Sylvia Wynter: On Being Human as Praxis*, ed Katherine McKittrick (Durham: Duke University, 2015), 106–23. Adorno's un-

derstanding of what genuine reconciliation would be is one of the most persistent "bits" that this book works with: "Reconcilement would release the nonidentical, would rid it of coercion, including spiritualized coercion; it would open the road to the multiplicity of different things and strip dialectics of its power over them. Reconcilement would be the thought of the many as no longer inimical, a thought that is anathema to subjective reason." Adorno, *Negative Dialectics*, 6.

13. Wynter and McKittrick, "Unparalleled Catastrophe," 37, 11. Emphasis original.

14. Here, I have most pointedly in mind Terada, "Impasse as a Figure." While chewing on these political impossibilities, Frank Wilderson's "Gramsci's Black Marx" is also often in mind. See Frank B. Wilderson III, "Gramsci's Black Marx: Whither the Slave in Civil Society?," *Social Identities* 9, no. 2 (2003): 225–40.

15. Sylvia Wynter, "The Re-enchantment of Humanism: An Interview with Sylvia Wynter," interview by David Scott, *Small Axe* 8, no. 120 (2000): 206.

16. Brathwaite describes *nommo* as the "spirit, force and memory of the Word." Edward Kamau Brathwaite, "Kumina: The Spirit of African Survival in Jamaica," *Jamaica Journal* 42 (September 1978): 47.

17. Rafael Vizcaíno writes,

> What Wynter demands is a theoretical revolution beyond secular modernity. Man was the heresy that unseated God, but Wynter seeks a new heresy that can now unseat Man. And if Man stood outside of God in the theocratic order, then the new heresy is likely to be found among those that find themselves outside the scope of Man. To get at the "true humanism" that can be made "to the measure of the world," one needs an account from those subjects that have suffered the aporetic colonialist/imperialist tyranny of modernity. This is why Wynter roots her work in the "original Fifties/Sixties intentionality" of Black studies that aimed to unmask the conditions enabling a global racial oppressive order. Black studies has this potential for a revolution in thought with the capacity to rewrite knowledge beyond its modern/colonial secularizing status, beyond the false humanism that implicitly dehumanizes the Black (and the Indigenous) as antithetical to Humanity. The task is to be heretical once again. Not toward God, but toward Man himself.

Rafael Vizcaíno, "Sylvia Wynter's New Science of the Word and the Autopoetics of the Flesh," *Comparative and Continental Philosophy* 14, no. 1 (2022): 75.

18. For more on this, see chap. 1, "Haiti's Infrasonic Boom."

19. Wynter, "Unsettling the Coloniality," 265–69. See also Wynter, "Africa," 53–61.

20. Wynter leans on V. Y. Mudimbe's *Invention of Africa* (1988) here, writing,

> While, if as Mudimbe proposed in *The Invention of Africa*, both the world view of autocentric Africa and that of "African traditional systems of thought" rather

than being known and represented "in the framework of their own rationality," have hitherto been known and represented, by both Western and Western-educated African analysts, "by means of . . . conceptual systems which depend on a Western epistemological locus," it would suggest that not even we ourselves, as African and black diaspora critics and filmmakers can, in the normal course of things, be entirely freed from the functioning of these rules; and therefore, from knowing and representing the "cultural universe of Africa" through the same Western "gallery of mirrors" which deform.

Wynter, "Africa," 44.
21. Wynter, "Africa," 27. C. L. R. James and Aime Césaire, from whose *Notebook of a Return to My Native Land* James draws, seem to think not:

In this poem Césaire makes a place for the spiritual realities of the African way of life in any review and reconstruction of the life of modern man. Césaire's whole emphasis is upon the fact that the African way of life is not an anachronism, a primitive survival of history, even of prehistoric ages, which needs to be nursed by unlimited quantities of aid into the means and ways of the supersonic plane, television, the Beatles and accommodation to the nuclear peril. Césaire means exactly the opposite. It is the way of life which the African has not lost which will restore to a new humanity what has been lost by modern life.

C. L. R. James, *Nkrumah and the Ghana Revolution*, ed. Leslie James (Durham: Duke University Press, 2022), 18.
22. Wynter, "Africa," 53, 55, 57.
23. See chap. 1, "Haiti's Infrasonic Boom."
24. Moten, *Stolen Life*, 155. Emphasis added.
25. Wynter, "Ceremony Must Be Found," 25. Wynter is paraphrasing Hayden White here.
26. Wynter and McKittrick, "Unparalleled Catastrophe," 7.
27. Wynter, "Africa," 40. In "Africa, the West and the Analogy of Culture," alongside the repeated claim concerning the subsumption of traditional polytheistic epistemic outlooks by those of Christianity and Islam, Africa (and "peoples of African descent") is given a pride of place as being the location of one of the three "negatively marked categories," with *woman* being the site of the first two. These categories "are imperative to the process by means of which the governing code of symbolic life, and its verbally inscripted 'directive signs,' can be made to override the directive signs of the biological aspect of human 'forms of life' and modes of being." Ibid., 51. I am suggesting another avenue of African criticality.
28. Andrew Apter, *Black Critics and Kings: The Hermeneutics of Power in Yoruba Society* (Chicago: University of Chicago, 1992), 177.

29. Yai, "Tradition," 34.

30. Ada Agada suggests that "instead of attempting to reconcile the antinomy of God's existence in African philosophy of religion, African philosophers should acknowledge the legitimacy of the two conflicting theses constituting the antinomy." Ada Agada, "Bewaji and Fayemi on God, Omnipotence and Evil," *Filosofia Theoretica: Journal of African Philosophy, Culture and Religions* 11, no. 1 (2022): 42–43. Also relevant is the inapplicability of the Judeo-Christian notion of significant ill and redemption/cure, which Wynter extrapolates out to all societies and structures of thought. See Wynter, "Unsettling the Coloniality," 265–66. An orientation like that of the Yorùbá, which has "no concept of sin" and which struggles to find a place for what is understood as evil within the incoming tradition, scrambles the conditions of Wynter's universalism. H. Ulli Beier, "The Historical and Psychological Significance of Yoruba Myths," *Yoruba Studies Review* 1, no. 2 (2017): 210. What to do with a people for whom the only significant ill is the cordoning off of significant ill? For whom the "problem of evil . . . is alien"? Danoye Oguntola-Laguda, "Esu, the Individual, and the Society" (inaugural lecture, Lagos State University, Lagos, Nigeria, January 31, 2017), https://www.lasu.edu.ng/publications/inaugural_lectures/inaugural_57th_lecture_of_professor_danoye_oguntola_laguda.pdf.

31. Wole Soyinka, *Of Africa* (New Haven: Yale University, 2012), 110, 111, 110. This calls to mind Jean Casimir's discussion of one of the contradictions held within emergent Haiti. He writes, "The management of the patriarchal nuclear family promised by marriage expanded the prestige of the couple and served as a trampoline to their social mobility, especially when the wedding was carried out with great ostentation. But this didn't mean that the same couple didn't also operate within communal collectives defined by other kinds of familial and gender relations." He goes on, "The open combination of Christian and Vodou marriages is simply unthinkable. These institutions consecrate diametrically opposed kinds of family relations. . . . Interpersonal behavior in urban or urbanizing contexts unfolded at the border between the two cultural collectives. This confused many foreign observers, who *were incapable of explaining how those who officiated over and participated in a Vodou ceremony on Saturday night made sure not to miss mass on Sunday morning.*" Casimir, *Haitians*, 258. Emphasis added. Or as Billie Holiday puts it in response to a slightly different set of circumstances, "If I go to church on Sunday / And then cabaret all day Monday / Ain't nobody's business if I do." Billie Holiday, "Tain't Nobody's Bizness, If I Do," on *The Complete Original American Decca Recordings*, MCA Records 80100379, 2005, compact disc.

32. Dialectics makes contradiction more palpable to the ordinary consciousness. Contradictions must undertake a dialectical movement in which they "withdraw,"

or "sink to the ground," preserving that which cannot be actualized while appearing in a form more agreeable to ordinary thinking. Nahum Brown writes,

> Contradictions withdraw into the ground, which stabilize and preserve what is too volatile to appear in its own immediacy.... Hegel therefore gives an indication of why ordinary thinking works so hard to separate the sides of contradiction so that real contradictions do not seem to exist, even to the extent that ordinary thinking replaces the law of contradiction with the law of noncontradiction, and then projects this as equivalent to the law of identity. Hegel goes so far as to claim that ordinary thinking abhors contradiction and that we consistently attempt to forget or degrade contradictions wherever they make their mark.

Nahum Brown, *Hegel on Possibility: Dialectics, Contradiction, and Modality* (London: Bloomsbury, 2020), 89.

33. See the following chapter for a discussion of common sense and speculative approaches to contradiction.

34. Mati Diop, *"Atlantics* Director Q&A," TIFF Originals, September 11, 2019, video, 22:30, https://www.youtube.com/watch?v=Azsq_Ghojis&t=1143s.

35. Chris O. Ijiomah, "Harmonious Monism: A System of a Logic in African Thought," *Logic and African Philosophy: Seminal Essays on African Systems of Thought*, ed. Jonathan O. Chimakonam (Wilmington: Vernon Press, 2020), 269. See also Chris O. Ijiomah, *Harmonious Monism: A Philosophical Logic of Explanation for Ontological Issues in Supernaturalism in African Thought* (Bloomington, IN: Xlibris, 2016).

36. Consider this useful gloss of Ezumezu logic by Ada Agada, seeking to shed light on this cohabitation of "seemingly contradictory results." He writes that "in addition to the truth and falsity values, Ezumezu acknowledges a third complemented value characterized by value glut, where the law of contradiction loses its strict applicability so that a thing can be what it is and something else.... Affirmative and negating propositions are sub-contraries rather than contradictories in the Ezumezu system.... *It prioritizes complementarity at the expense of contradiction without invalidating contradiction.*" Ada Agada, "Complementarism and Consolationism: Mapping Out a 21st-Century African Philosophical Trajectory," *Synthesis Philosophica* 35, no. 1 (2020): 145. Emphasis added. I am less interested in the viability of the logic than in the preoccupation with finding a way to understand this failure to be adequately disturbed by nonrelation demonstrated by this common sense.

37. Lawal, "Àwòrán," 502.

38. Wole Soyinka, "Exile: Thresholds of Loss and Identity," *Caliban* 7, no. 1 (2000): 67. It is appropriate and inevitable that Èṣù provides a bridge from Yorùbá/

African aporetic virtuosity to *"poiēsis in black"* (that confluence of African semiosis and the "liquified" Negro). R. A. Judy writes that "in the blues, taking up this *poiesis* is termed *being at the crossroads*, where the figure varyingly called 'the Devil,' 'the Black Man,' 'Exu,' 'Eshu,' and, more widely, 'Legba' dwells. Legba is 'the Black Man' at the crossroads, and the *poiēsis* there with him was instigated when the noise, Negro, was imposed." R. A. Judy, "The Unfungible Flow of Liquid Blackness," *Liquid Blackness* 5, no. 1 (2021): 35. For a detailed unfolding of the ideas presented as a digest in this essay, see Judy, *Sentient Flesh*.

39. Soyinka, "Exile," 67. Such a reality shows up as fantastic for the European, whereas the Yorùbá has "little or no dividing line between [the] fictional world and his/her world." Ayo Bamgbose writes that

> Yoruba believe in the world of the spirits, witches, magic and communication with the dead. A lot of the weirdness in the novels [of D. O. Fagunwa] is reflection of the world view. Thus characters like àrònì, the one-legged fairy, and egbére, a short creature who always sheds tears, which are found in Ògbójú are not merely fictional characters but spirits believed by the Yoruba to exist in the forest.... For those for whom Fagunwa [the novelist] was writing and who basically share this world view, these aspects of the novels are realistic at the level of the reader's consciousness of his world.

Ayo Bamgbose, *The Novels of D. O. Fagunwa* (Benin City: Ethiopia, 1974), 84–85, quoted in Ayo Adeduntan, *What the Forest Told Me: Yoruba Hunter, Culture and Narrative Performance* (Makhanda: National Inquiry Service Center, 2019), 36. For more on Èṣù, see Ayodele Ogundipe, "Esu Elegbara, the Yoruba God of Chance and Uncertainty: A Study in Yoruba Mythology" (PhD diss., Indiana University, 1978).

40. Lawal, "Àwòrán," 501–3; Babatunde Lawal, "Èjìwàpò: The Dialectics of Twoness in Yoruba Art and Culture," *African Arts* 41, no. 1 (2008): 24.

41. Adeleke, "Yorùbá Fool Insignia," 111.

42. Agada "Complementarism and Consolationism," 145.

43. Soyinka, *On Africa*, 110.

44. Robinson, *Terms of Order*, 7. See also Terada, "Impasse as a Figure"; Wilderson, "Gramsci's Black Marx." Frank Wilderson digests his thoughts on the matter in an interview with the Killer Bs (Jared Ball, Todd Steven Burroughs, and Hate): "We cannot enter into a structure of recognition as a being, an incorporation into a community of beings, *without recognition and incorporation being completely destroyed*. We know that we are the antithesis of recognition and incorporation." Frank B. Wilderson III, "We're Trying to Destroy the World," interview by Jared Ball, Todd Steven Burroughs, and Hate, Black Ink, February 10, 2018, https://black-ink.info/2018/02/10/were-trying-to-destroy-the-world/. Emphasis added.

45. "The existence of conditions is the existence of further possibilities, which lie embedded within what is immediately actual. These possibilities are not projections of other worlds. They are real possibilities that exist hidden within the immediately actual. They are contrary only in the sense that they have not yet and might not ever emerge in actuality. But insofar as what is immediately actual already contains them, they exist as further degrees of possibility within the actuality." Brown, *Hegel on Possibility*, 22.

46. Macdonald, *What Would Be Different*, 101–2. Wynter and McKittrick might understand this notion of closed actuality as synonymous with their "cognitively closed terms." Wynter and McKittrick, "Unparalleled Catastrophe," 20. Separately, while I am remaining within Adorno's (and Macdonald's) understanding of Hegel's modality, which reads with an ear cocked toward the spirit of Hegel's writing—occasionally, at the expense of the letter of the law of the text—it is worth noting that some commentators consider "fantastic" possibilities to be already contained in Hegel's notion of actuality. For instance, Brown tells us that while "strange or fantastic possibilities face greater barriers and require more complex conditions to come about in actuality, to the extent that they might seem to be permanently inaccessible and definitively impossible . . . if Hegel is committed to absolute necessity, which brings along with it infinite sets of infinite series of every possibility whatsoever, then he is also committed to the radical contingency that this actual world can become significantly otherwise." Nahum Brown, "Transcendent and Immanent Conceptions of Perfection in Leibniz and Hegel," in *Transcendence, Immanence, and Intercultural Philosophy*, ed. Nahum Brown and William Franke (Cham: Springer, 2016), 203.

47. Macdonald, *What Would Be Different*, 42, 43. Emphasis original.

48. Adorno, *Hegel*, 80. This is elaborated on: "As though the dialectic had become frightened of itself, in the *Philosophy of Right* Hegel broke off such thoughts by abruptly absolutizing one category—the state. This is due to the fact that while his experience did indeed ascertain the limits of bourgeois society, limits contained in its own tendencies, as a bourgeois idealist he stopped at that boundary because he saw no real historical force on the other side of it. He could not resolve the contradiction between his dialectic and his experience: it was this alone that forced Hegel the critic to maintain the affirmative." Ibid.

49. Horkheimer and Adorno, *Dialectic of Enlightenment*, 8. Here is a more substantial quotation:

> The principle of immanence, the explanation of every event as repetition, which enlightenment upholds against mythical imagination, is that of myth itself. The arid wisdom which acknowledges nothing new under the sun, because all the

pieces in the meaningless game have been played out, all the great thoughts have been thought, all possible discoveries can be construed in advance, and human beings are defined by self-preservation through adaptation—this barren wisdom merely reproduces the fantastic doctrine it rejects: the sanction of fate which, through retribution, incessantly reinstates what always was. Whatever might be different is made the same. That is the verdict which critically sets the boundaries to possible experience.

Ibid.
    50. Adorno, *Hegel*, 80.
    51. Macdonald, *What Would Be Different*, 143, 127.
    52. Marx, *Economic and Philosophic Manuscripts*, 108, quoted in Rocío Zambrana, "Actuality in Hegel and Marx," *Hegel Bulletin* 40, no. 1 (2019): 79.
    53. Robinson, *Black Marxism*, 169. I have previously discussed this, drawing from Chandler's seminal work. See Okiji, *Jazz as Critique*. See also da Silva, *Unpayable Debt*.
    54. Fanon, *Black Skin, White Masks*, 83.
    55. Chandler, "Of Exorbitance," 367, 369. Emphasis original. One way to anchor this doubleness in the actual social history of black life is to understand that the slave subject is unable to reconcile—at once human and inhuman (and also American and African). You will find this contradiction explored in several black theoretical works. See, e.g., Hartman, *Scenes of Subjection*; Chandler, *X*; Fred Moten, *In the Break: The Aesthetics of the Black Radical Tradition* (Minneapolis: University of Minnesota Press, 2003); da Silva, *Unpayable Debt*. Also see "Introduction: Constant Departure" herein.
    56. Fanon, *Black Skin, White Masks*, 82.
    57. Frank B. Wilderson III, *Afropessimism* (New York: Liveright, 2020). The "meaning of Blackness," Wilderson tells us, is "not—in the first instance— . . . a variously and unconsciously interpellated *identity* or as a conscious social actor, but as a structural *position* of non-communicability in the face of all other positions." Frank B. Wilderson III, *Red, White and Black: Cinema and the Structure of U.S. Antagonisms* (Durham: Duke University Press, 2008), 58. And to be clear, here, I am not interested in challenging or mounting a direct theoretical defense of the claim of the radical noncommunicability of black being, which undergirds this thought. I stay in the company of many contemporary black scholars across a spectrum of approaches to a common problem and train my attention on proposing a way to appreciate something of how this being without standing seems to act as though it had your ear. On the impossibility, or impossible/otherwise worlds, from one with commitments squarely in Afropessimist thought, consider this exchange:

FW: What I want to contribute to the world is a text about impossibility, Blackness as a space of impossibility. Now having said that, there are things I do to manage myself, to help me be okay, know what the world is saying or whatever, in a place where everyone sees me as their object, you know. One of the things I said in psychoanalysis and another thing that I do is consult regularly with a teacher, *Babalawo*, who consults ancestors to help me. But I'm, I'm a little cautious and uh, uncomfortable with incorporating that into my political analysis and my political philosophy. One, because I don't write about, I don't write the answer to Lenin's question, what is to be done? I think, *I believe that the liberation of Black people is tantamount to moving into an epistemology that we cannot imagine*. Once Blacks become incorporated and recognized I don't think we have the language or the concepts to think of what that is. It's not like moving from Capitalism to Communism, it's like the end of the world.

PH: It's like moving to Mars.

FW: It's like moving to Mars.

Wilderson, "Frank Wilderson."

58. Tiffany Lethabo King, Jenell Navarro, and Andrea Smith, eds., *Otherwise Worlds: Against Settler Colonialism and Anti-blackness* (Durham: Duke University Press, 2020); Axelle Karera, "Paraontology: Interruption, Inheritance, or a Debt One Often Regrets," *Critical Philosophy of Race* 10, no. 2 (2022): 158–97. Also see Frank B. Wilderson III, Selamawit Terrefe, and Joy James, "An Ontology of Betrayal," Williams College, November 16, 2022, video, 2:03:04, https://www.youtube.com/watch?v=8p3At6glozQ&t=5095s.

59. Bernstein, *Disenchantment*, 437. For a more patient meditation on this nexus of black life, artistic production, and history, see Stephen Best, *None like Us: Blackness, Belonging, Aesthetic Life* (Durham: Duke University Press, 2019). On the subjunctive in black being and expression, see Quashie, *Black Aliveness*, 57–82.

60. Adorno, *Aesthetic Theory*, 79.

61. Jay M. Bernstein, "Why Rescue Semblance? Metaphysical Experience and the Possibility of Ethics," in *The Semblance of Subjectivity: Essays in Adorno's Aesthetic Theory*, ed. Tom Huhn and Lambert Zuidervaart (Cambridge, MA: MIT Press, 1997), 179. Incidentally, it is interesting that Bernstein goes on to query how Adorno's attempt to rescue the particular and the object took the artwork as its figure of interest at the expense of a consideration of "ecological habitats or the poor, women, ethnic minorities," these "fully worldly particulars . . . not adequately recognized as being of substance and worth." Ibid.

62. Adorno, *Aesthetic Theory*, 82, 59. See also Bernstein, "Why Rescue Semblance?"; Michael Kelly, *Iconoclasm in Aesthetics* (Cambridge: Cambridge University Press, 2003).

63. Adorno, *Hegel*, 83.

Chapter 3: Cecil's Snuggling

1. See Denise Ferreira da Silva, "On Difference without Separability," in *Incerteza Viva*, ed. Jochen Volz, Júlia Rebouças, and Isabella Rjeille (São Paulo: Bienal Internacional de São Paulo, 2016), exhibition catalog, 57–65.

2. Mark J. Bobak, "The Music of Cecil Taylor: An Analysis of Selected Piano Solos, 1973–1989" (PhD diss., University of Illinois Urbana–Champaign, 1994), 135. I've taken to hearing Taylor's introduction to the 1960 recording of "Air" as a dry run of the Williams-Taylor date. Following Denis Charles's drumroll, Taylor appears to split into three different pianists, running off a series of licks, one after the other, chasing each other's tails, eluding any "synthesizing principle" (Adorno), a pileup rather than an unfolding of form. Cecil Taylor, "Air," on *The World of Cecil Taylor*, Candid CJS 9006, 1961, LP; Theodor W. Adorno, *Notes to Literature*, trans. Shierry Weber Nicholsen, 2 vols. (New York: Columbia University Press, 1991–92), 2:131.

3. One might understand the encounter between Taylor and Mary Lou Williams as a clinch—their restraining one another. I would concede that in a clinch being not quite what it seems, it does bear some comparison. A clinch looks like a hug, but it's a mechanism of restraint, and Taylor's genre of *snuggle* seems anything but a "molding to" (*anschmiegen*) (see the second part of this long chapter for an unfolding of mimesis as *anschmiegen*). I will be suggesting that Taylor's snuggle be understood as paratactical communion, or what Moten might call "caressive crash." Moten, *Black and Blur*, 231. See also Adorno, *Notes to Literature*, 2:109–49.

4. "Reconcilement would be the thought of the many as no longer inimical, a thought that is anathema to subjective reason." Adorno, *Negative Dialectics*, 6. I have repeated this quotation from Adorno's *Negative Dialectics* in various creatively licensed versions throughout the book.

5. Mary Lou Williams and Cecil Taylor, *Embraced*, Pablo Live 2620 108, 1977, LP.

6. Benjamin Givan, "'The Fools Don't Think I Play Jazz': Cecil Taylor Meets Mary Lou Williams," *Journal of Musicology* 35, no. 3 (2018): 397–430; Tammy L. Kernodle, *Soul on Soul: The Life and Music of Mary Lou Williams* (Champaign: University of Illinois Press, 2020); Andrew W. Bartlett, "Cecil Taylor, Identity Energy, and the Avant-Garde African American Body," *Perspectives of New Music* 33, no. 1–2 (1995): 274–93.

7. Givan, "Fools Don't Think."

8. Givan, "Fools Don't Think," 403–7. Ralph Ellison's coolness toward postswing approaches is well known. Speaking of free jazz in a 1965 broadcast, he offers that the "main musical motive of the experimentalism is to absorb—to Americanize—the most recent developments of European classical music. . . . The music of Cecil Taylor is, I think, a most interesting illustration of that struggle."

Ralph Ellison, "Rare Footage of Charles Mingus for Your Listening Pleasure," Brian Krock, April 22, 2022, video, 29:12, https://www.youtube.com/watch?v=T2KDM6TA6ow, quoted in Ethan Iverson, "All-Star Television: Charles Mingus, Cecil Taylor, Ralph Ellison, Martin Williams," *Journal of Jazz Studies* 13, no. 1 (2022): 49. Several years later, Taylor replies, "You see, what white intellectuals must be confronted with is the black methodology that creates this music. Stravinsky and Bartók made a statement in a certain way, but blacks put it together differently—their way—and Ralph Ellison's notion of the symphonic form as the 'ultimate' is a lie. My purpose . . . is to carry on the tradition of Fletcher Henderson and Duke Ellington and therefore to reaffirm and extend the line of black music that goes back thousands of years." Cecil Taylor, "Cecil Taylor: This Music Is the Face of a Drum," interview by Robert Levin, Robert Levin (website), April 9, 2009, https://robert-levin.com/2009/04/09/cecil-taylor-this-music-is-the-face-of-a-drum/. Also see Ralph Ellison, *Shadow and Act* (New York: Vintage, 2011), esp. 221–32, 247–60.

9. See Robert Farris Thompson, "An Aesthetic of the Cool: West African Dance," *African Forum* 2, no. 2 (1966): 85–122; Benjamin Givan, "Apart Playing: McCoy Tyner and 'Bessie's Blues,'" *Journal of the Society for American Music* 1, no. 2 (2007): 257–80; John M. Chernoff, "The Rhythmic Medium in African Music," *New Literary History* 22, no. 4 (1991): 1093–1102.

10. In "On the Mimetic Faculty," Walter Benjamin speaks of "magical correspondence" and "nonsensuous similarity." It is sensible to steer clear—initially, at least—of the term *similarity*. Within the context of the mimetic faculty, "nonsensuous similarity" tends to refer to that which in other writing he calls "relationship," "affinity," or "kinship." Benjamin, *Selected Writings*, 2:721. See chap. 4, "Billie's Bent Elbow."

11. Cecil Taylor, "Cecil Taylor: Interview," interview by Bob Rusch, *Cadence: The American Review of Jazz and Blues* 4, no. 1 (April 1978): 3, quoted in Bartlett, "Cecil Taylor," 284. "While critic John Litweiler notes the 'demolition of Williams' that Taylor enacted in his 'extremely long, complex lines, turbulent as ever and at his fastest speed' (Litweiler 1984, 217), Taylor regarded the concert as 'completely successful' and thought that the shock Litweiler and other reviewers expressed as a product of their lack of journalistic skills and their faulty 'concepts of music' (Rusch 1978, 3–4)." Ibid. Citations original. The scene calls to mind Thomas Madiou's description of the post-Emancipation coalition of Haitian resistance, made up of neocolonial, anticolonial, and "Guinean" traditions and orientations: "We made up a muddled mosaic of contrary forces." Madiou, *Histoire d'Haïti*, 5:111, quoted in Casimir, *Haitians*, 248. Jean Casimir commentates on this, writing, "The state of 1804 was a tacit agreement that allowed the two poles, with their contradictory directions, to exist alongside each other without creating uncontrollable fires of conflict.

It enabled the coexistence of secession and revolution." Ibid. See also chap. 1, "Haiti's Infrasonic Boom," and chap. 2, "Unthinkable Nonsense."

12. An example is provided when Todd McGowan writes, "Left Hegelianism marks the victory of common sense over philosophy. It seems *self-evident that we strive to overcome contradictions that we confront rather than trying to sustain them*, but philosophy, as Hegel defines it, is the refusal of what presents itself as self-evident. The more self-evident it is, the more it requires thought to unpack." Emphasis added. McGowan also states, "Contradictions seem like problems to overcome, which is why both the traditional interpretation of Hegel's dialectic and Marx's materialist version are so attractive. But Hegel's significance as a thinker derives from his ability to defy common sense, as his claim in the preface to the *Phenomenology of Spirit* that 'what is well known as such, because it is well known, is what is not *cognitively known*' makes clear." Emphasis original. Todd McGowan, *Emancipation after Hegel: Achieving a Contradictory Revolution* (New York: Columbia University Press, 2019), 222n7, 10.

13. Georg W. F. Hegel, *Hegel's "Science of Logic,"* trans. A. V. Miller (New York: Humanities Press, 1976), 441. Emphasis original.

14. Georg W. F. Hegel, *The Science of Logic*, trans. George Di Giovanni (Cambridge: Cambridge University Press, 2010), 381. In case it is not yet clear, I am walking a tightrope in my discussion concerning the centrality of contradiction to Hegel's speculative thought. This acknowledgment of the contradictory nature of existence echoes what I understand to be Yorùbá (if not African) common sense or consciousness. One way to formulate the position as it stands in this point in the proceedings is that Yorùbá common sense bears a close resemblance to this speculative thought. But I want to keep in mind that for Hegel, contradiction is the point of transition—the contrary determinations become contradictory in their being walked through one another. "It [common sense] holds these two determinations over against one another and has in mind *only them*, but not their *transition* [Di Giovanni prefers to translate this as 'determinations of relation'], which is the essential point and which contains the contradiction." Hegel, *Hegel's "Science of Logic,"* 441. Emphasis original. For Giovanni's translation, see Hegel, *Science of Logic*, 383. Contradiction is to be worked through or rather *is* a working through the mutually ungiven. Even as I accept the importance of tarrying with the negative to Hegelian thought, it is hard to ignore the progressive overtones at work here. We might not speak of resolution, but we certainly can speak of greater determination. With this in mind, and to get back to this thin line I am treading, perhaps the key point of distinction is the Yorùbá lack of insistence on this transition. What other modes of movement and shapes emerge when we devalorize this particular response of the encounter of contraries? For two competing interpretations of contradiction in

Hegel, see McGowan, *Emancipation after Hegel*; Susan Songsuk Hahn, *Contradiction in Motion: Hegel's Organic Concept of Life and Value* (Ithaca, NY: Cornell University Press, 2007).

15. Georg W. F. Hegel, *Encyclopedia, Part 1: Hegel's Logic*, trans. T. F. Geraets, W. A. Suchting, and H. S. Harris (Indianapolis: Hackett, 1991), 119, quoted in Hahn, *Contradiction in Motion*, 40; Hegel, *Science of Logic*, 381.

16. Hegel, *Science of Logic*, 382.

17. Hahn, *Contradiction in Motion*, 3.

18. Robert Sinnerbrink, *Understanding Hegelianism* (Milton Park: Routledge, 2014), 17. Also, consider this from Rebecca Comay and Frank Ruda:

> Hegel exhibits a Lutheran commitment to the vernacular.... Philosophy is difficult not because it speaks an esoteric idiom or relies on specialized terminology. It is difficult because it does strange things with the language we take most for granted. Hegel took nothing for granted.... If he can be characterized plausibly as an ordinary language philosopher, this is only because he manages to extract weirdness from the most innocuous particles of everyday speech. Rather than plumbing the depths or revealing the mysteries of being, he brings to light what is already on the surface; he exposes what has become invisible through overexposure.... Hegel invented a "new concept of 'naïveté'" that enabled him not only to revivify the hidden treasures of language—but to unleash the uncanny, undead energy of living speech. This is what it means to write and to read speculatively.

Rebecca Comay and Frank Ruda, *The Dash—the Other Side of Absolute Knowing* (Cambridge, MA: MIT Press, 2018), 6.

19. Hahn, *Contradiction in Motion*, 39n4.

20. Paul Giladi, "Hegel's Philosophy and Common Sense," *European Legacy* 23, no. 3 (2018): 269–85.

21. This is closest in tone to Ralph Palm, who writes, "Speculative thinking is not some mystical mode of thought beyond and irreconcilable with ordinary thinking. Rather, it is a different approach to and focus on the same content. *Speculative thinking simply attempts to prove what ordinary thinking only presupposes.*" Ralph Palm, "Hegel's Contradictions," *Hegel Bulletin* 32, no. 1–2 (2011): 142–43. Emphasis added. And earlier on in the same essay, speaking of the use to which Hegel puts the ordinary and of the technical valences of *aufheben*, Palm states that "one can see how ordinary thinking is not simply external to speculative thinking but is also a part of it. These two ways of thinking are, in effect, opposites, but opposites in the speculative sense; that is, united as much as they are divided." Ibid., 138.

22. Christoph Halbig, "The Philosopher as Polyphemus? Philosophy and

Common Sense in Hegel and Jacobi," *Internationales Jahrbuch des Deutschen Idealismus* 3 (2005): 274. Emphasis original.

23. Theodor W. Adorno, *An Introduction to Dialectics*, trans. Nicholas Walker (Cambridge, MA: Polity, 2017), 33. Later on in the course, Adorno states,

> Of course dialectic does have a good deal to do with sound common sense, and the steps it takes in each individual case are always steps guided by rational reflection. As I have already attempted to show you, it is not as if there were another kind of source of reason, a speculative source, which would itself be separated by a gulf from the merely reflective rationality of the "understanding." But, on the other hand, I emphatically believe that the dialectical mode of thinking is distinguished from the ordinary use of the understanding precisely because it refuses to be satisfied with the givenness we have described, because it properly begins its work exactly there where the given confronts us most inexorably, where dialectical thought attempts to penetrate what is opaque and seemingly impenetrable, and to bring all this into movement.

Ibid., 119.

24. Hegel, *Phenomenology of Spirit*, 49. "Natural consciousness will show itself to be only the Notion of knowledge, or in other words, not to be real knowledge. But since it directly takes itself to be real knowledge, this path has a negative significance for it, and what is in fact the realization of the Notion, counts for it rather as the loss of its own self; for it does lose its truth on this path. The road can therefore be regarded as the pathway of *doubt*, or more precisely as the way of despair." Ibid. Emphasis original.

25. Robyn Marasco, *The Highway of Despair: Critical Theory after Hegel* (New York: Columbia University Press, 2015), 39. As I precede with this slight twist in terminology from ordinary consciousness and common sense to natural consciousness, we might keep in mind a shift of apparent stasis to emergence, a shift from prereflective to a reflective posture. I do believe, however, that the particular point I am making at this juncture, concerning the speculative perspective being motivated by the anxieties of common sense remains intact. Comay and Ruda take doubt and despair to refer to a perspective on reality rather than an attitude or rather that it begins as an attitude and then becomes a perspective. Comay and Ruda, *Dash*, 44–45.

26. Hegel, *Phenomenology of Spirit*, 50. Emphasis added.

27. Marasco, *Highway of Despair*, 41.

28. Marasco, *Highway of Despair*, 39. In this compelling account of the significance of despair to the critical theory tradition, Robyn Marasco makes a clear distinction between natural consciousness and common sense. I accept that the former

is a character not confined to the start of the drama of consciousness's awakening in the way common sense, or ordinary understanding, might be.

29. Marasco, *Highway of Despair*, 28.

30. Hegel, *Science of Logic*, 383.

31. Perhaps I am belaboring this acknowledgment of how compelling (but by no means dominant) contemporary interpretations of dialectical motion privilege its negative moments, but this extended quotation from McGowan is too serviceable not to share. He writes,

> A dialectical advance, as Hegel conceives it, is a step in the direction of absolute contradiction, not a progressive movement toward the elimination of contradiction. The unity that occurs at the end of each dialectical process does not do away with contradiction but enacts a reconciliation with it. Rather than synthesize two opposing positions, what Hegel calls unity involves the recognition that the position is opposed fundamentally to itself, that it involves itself in what it is not. Unity enshrines contradiction as the constitutive form that identity takes. Contradiction both undermines and defines the identity of the subject.
>
> When thought arrives at the absolute and thereby achieves totalization, the status of contradiction undergoes a thoroughgoing transformation. At the point of the absolute, thought can no longer seek the resolution to contradiction through another dialectical movement of thought. At the end of Hegel's philosophy, there is nowhere left to go because Hegel has explored all possible logical resolutions. Though other empirical possibilities surely exist, none promises any novel pathway out of contradiction. The absolute is nothing but the affirmation that contradiction is unsurpassable. At the position of the absolute, we recognize that we cannot ever eliminate contradiction, no matter how long or how hard we strive to do so.

McGowan, *Emancipation after Hegel*, 21.

32. Marasco, *Highway of Despair*, 5. See also McGowan, *Emancipation after Hegel*, 179. For a more conventional reading of the significance of negativity in reflective thought and Hegelian dialectics more particularly, see Palm, "Hegel's Contradictions"; Stone, "Adorno, Hegel, and Dialectic"; James Gordon Finlayson, "Hegel, Adorno and the Origins of Immanent Criticism," *British Journal for the History of Philosophy* 22, no. 6 (2014): 1142–66; Jon Mills, "Psyche as Inner Contradiction," *Continental Thought and Theory* 2, no. 4 (2019): 71–82.

33. Marasco, *Highway of Despair*, 3.

34. This sentence of Etienne Balibar's comes to mind: "The paradox of 'European identity' is that it conceived of itself as the particular site of the invention of the universal and its revelation to the world." Etienne Balibar, "Ideas of Europe: Civili-

zation and Constitution," *Iris: European Journal of Philosophy and Public Debate* 1, no. 1 (2009): 3. See also Slavoj Žižek, "A Leftist Plea for 'Eurocentrism,'" *Critical Inquiry* 24, no. 4 (1998): 988–1009. As I mention in a previous chapter, one of the appeals of Žižek's scholarship from the point of view of the black scholar is it helps facilitate a reading of European thought as an anthropological object. I thank Nadia Yala Kisukidi for this formulation and acknowledge Rocío Zambrana's 2021 essay for bringing it to my attention. See Zambrana, "Hegelian History Interrupted."

35. Adam Kotsko, "How to Read Žižek," *Los Angeles Review of Books*, September 2, 2012, https://lareviewofbooks.org/article/how-to-read-zizek/.

36. Kotsko, "How to Read Žižek"; Žižek, "Leftist Plea."

37. Terada, "Hegel's Racism for Radicals," 16.

38. Kotsko, "How to Read Žižek."

39. Terada, "Hegel's Racism for Radicals," 11, 15; Hegel, *Phenomenology of Spirit*, 19.

40. Terada, "Hegel's Racism for Radicals," 12. Žižek would likely be appreciative of Afropessimism's "courage of hopelessness" (this is the title of his 2017 "chronicles of a year of acting dangerously"). In this book, Žižek states,

> Giorgio Agamben said in an interview that "thought is the courage of hopelessness"—an insight which is especially pertinent for our historical moment, when even the most pessimistic diagnosis as a rule finishes with an uplifting hint at some version of the proverbial light at the end of the tunnel. The true courage is not to imagine an alternative, but to accept the consequences of the fact that there is no clearly discernible alternative: the dream of an alternative is a sign of theoretical cowardice, functioning as a fetish that prevents us from thinking through to the end the deadlock of our predicament.

Slavoj Žižek, *The Courage of Hopelessness: Chronicles of a Year of Acting Dangerously* (London: Penguin, 2017), xi. However, as Zahi Zalloua lays out in his Žižekian appraisal of Afropessimist thought, the latter's "separatist ideology" is likely lamented as a neutralizing of political potential. He writes, "as Žižek points out, 'revolutionary solidarity' happens when 'it is the repressed, the exploited and suffering, the "parts of no-part" of every culture which come together in a shared struggle.' This abundance of '*different proletarian positions*' is and must become the stuff of revolutionary coalitions." Zahi Zalloua, *Žižek on Race: Toward an Anti-racist Future* (London: Bloomsbury, 2020), 143. Emphasis original. See Rei Terada, *Metaracial: Hegel, Antiblackness, and Political Identity* (Chicago: University of Chicago Press, 2023). In it, Terada extends and deepens the ideas sketched in "Hegel's Racism for Radicals" concerning the "antiblack antiracism" of European and Euro-American radical thought. See also Terada, "Hegel's Racism for Radicals."

41. Adorno, *Hegel*, 85. See also ibid., 80.
42. Terada, "Hegel's Racism for Radicals," 12.
43. For a spirited defense of Hegel against accusations of racism, see Sandra Bonetto, "Race and Racism in Hegel—an Analysis," *Minerva: An Internet Journal of Philosophy* 10 (2006): 45–46.
44. Georg W. F. Hegel, *Lectures on the Philosophy of History*, trans. J. Sibree (London: G. Bell and Sons, 1914), 83. For recent black theoretical engagement with the infamous passage, one that works at the intersection of the biopolitical, animal studies, new materialism, and black ontology, see Jackson, *Becoming Human*.
45. Patricia Purtschert, "On the Limit of Spirit: Hegel's Racism Revisited," *Philosophy and Social Criticism* 36, no. 9 (2010): 1041.
46. Hegel, *Phenomenology of Spirit*, 103, 10.
47. Hegel, *Philosophy of History*, 103.
48. Terada, "Hegel's Racism," 16.
49. Hegel, *Phenomenology of Spirit*, 103.
50. Hegel, *Philosophy of History*, 103.
51. Georg W. F. Hegel, *Lectures on the Philosophy of World History*, trans. H. B. Nisbet (Cambridge: Cambridge University Press, 1975), 177; Hegel, *Philosophy of History*, 97.
52. Terada, "Hegel's Racism," 15.
53. Consider this snippet in case you need reminding:

> The undervaluing of humanity among them reaches an incredible degree of intensity. Tyranny is regarded as no wrong, and cannibalism *is* looked upon as quite customary and proper. Among us instinct deters from it, if we can speak of instinct at all as appertaining to man. But with the Negro this is not the case, and the devouring of human flesh is altogether consonant with the general principles of the African race; to the sensual Negro, human flesh is but an object of sense—mere flesh. At the death of a King hundreds are killed and eaten; prisoners are butchered and their flesh sold in the markets; the victor is accustomed to eat the heart of his slain foe. When magical rites are performed, it frequently happens that the sorcerer kills the first that comes in his way and divides his body among the bystanders. Another characteristic fact in reference to the Negroes is Slavery. Negroes are enslaved by Europeans and sold to America. Bad as this may be, their lot in their own land is even worse, since there a slavery quite as absolute exists; for it is the essential principle of slavery, that man has not yet attained a consciousness of his freedom, and consequently sinks down to a mere Thing—an object of no value.

Hegel, *Philosophy of History*, 99–100.

54. Terada, "Hegel's Racism," 15. Emphasis added. For a slightly different version of this quote that prefers the term "negativity," see Terada, *Metaracial*, 30. I have had similar ambivalence in my use of the ensemble of terms that speak of the phenomenon. I've used, or toyed with, *contradiction*, *nonrelation*, *nonidentity*, and *negativity*.

55. Hegel, *Philosophy of History*, 97.

56. Hegel, *Philosophy of World History*, 176–77. Emphasis added.

57. Ronald Kuykendall, "Hegel and Africa: An Evaluation of the Treatment of Africa in the Philosophy of History," *Journal of Black Studies* 23, no. 4 (1993): 571–81; Robert Bernasconi, "With What Must the Philosophy of World History Begin? On the Racial Basis of Hegel's Eurocentrism," *Nineteenth Century Contexts* 22, no. 2 (2000): 171–201; Robert Bernasconi, "Hegel at the Court of the Ashanti," in *Hegel after Derrida*, ed. Stuart Barnett (Milton Park: Routledge, 1998), 41–63.

58. For more on black/Negro/African cognitive incapacity or cognitive spectrality, see R. A. Judy, "Kant and the Negro," *Surfaces* 1, no. 8 (1991): 7–81; da Silva, *Toward a Global Idea*; J. Kameron Carter, *Race: A Theological Account* (New York: Oxford University Press, 2008); Chandler, *X*; Moten, *Stolen Life*, 1–95; Jeffrey Sacks, "Introduction: Nonsense—Critique for the Times," *Critical Times* 6, no. 1 (2023): 1–14.

59. As Heikki Ikäheimo reads it, "'General self-consciousness' as mutual knowing of oneself in a free other is the 'substance' of what makes modes of social life such as 'the family, the fatherland, the state' as well 'virtues, love, friendship, valour, honor, fame' truly 'spiritual.'" Heikki Ikäheimo, "Hegel's Concept of Recognition—What Is It?," in *Recognition—German Idealism as an Ongoing Challenge*, ed. Christian Krijnen (Leiden: Brill, 2014), 24.

60. Georg W. F. Hegel, *Hegel's "Philosophy of Mind*," trans. William Wallace (Oxford: Clarendon Press, 1894), 57.

61. Terada, "Hegel's Racism," 17, 15.

62. I am aware that Hegel's *Science of Logic*, as a view from the standpoint of "God prior to creation," is not concerned with the agreement between individual objects—their qualities or positions—and contradiction, generally referring to a logical breakdown within a category of thought. Even so, the commonsense, or ordinary, understanding—that at a certain (retroactive) register, speculative thought is responding to—does understand contradiction as the sort of nonidentity that I am suggesting here. For more on the view of God precreation, see Comay and Ruda, *Dash*, 42–43.

63. Terada, "Impasse as a Figure."

64. Terada, "Impasse as a Figure," 154, 155. Emphasis added.

65. Terada, "Impasse as a Figure," 155. Emphasis added.

66. Adorno, *Negative Dialectics*, 23.
67. Terada, "Impasse as a Figure," 155.
68. Terada, "Impasse as a Figure," 156; Hegel, *Phenomenology of Spirit*, 117. "Although Hegel projects the bondsman's use of these entities' independence in order to learn pure-being-for-itself and '[rid] himself of his attachment to natural existence in every single detail,' the lord's and the bondsman's past and present indicates quite a different environment populated by various entities and different possibilities than Kojeve's politico-human teleology, rather than having no organization at all." This wonderfully insightful interpretation has great significance. For one, it speaks to the apparent advantage that the bondsman has due to their relation, their learning "being-for-itself" from these objects. It also points to the necessity or insistence that Hegel imputes. The bondsman *must* rid himself of attachment of "every single detail." Additionally, the aloof, disinterested object, set apart from the recognitive drama unfolding in the scene, is shown, nevertheless, to have a distinct bearing on the situation. This move, which brings the object to the center stage of the reading, casts both master and bondsman in a refreshing light. We observe more clearly the master being consumed by anxiety concerning his need for recognition. The bondsman is seen to have access to genres of correspondence with the object that *might* refuse the call to "[rid] himself of his attachment to natural existence in every single detail." Ibid.
69. Terada, "Impasse as a Figure," 155. Emphasis added. The bondsman's relation to the ordinary object is subjugating "only because of the proximate panic of the lord." Ibid., 156.
70. This is also to say that we might correspond in a manner that is not consumed by the discovery of difference and distinction either.
71. The first excursus of *Dialectic of Enlightenment*, "Odysseus or Myth and Enlightenment," has been useful for fleshing out this association. Although it would take me too far out from my concerns in this already long chapter, I am intrigued by Adorno and Horkheimer's sympathetic renovation of Polyphemus. There are gems such as "abundance needs no law, and civilization's accusation of anarchy sounds almost like a denunciation of abundance." Horkheimer and Adorno, *Dialectic of Enlightenment*, 50–51. They suggest that the aspersions cast by Homer are directed not toward patriarchy as such ("each man rules his women and children as he wishes") but toward sociality that is "not yet organized according to the standard of fixed property." Ibid., 51. Compare this to Hegel's complaint in the lectures on philosophy of history that the African "ha[d] no sense of private property, of achieving independence through one's own activity, or of securing one's property through right." Georg Wilhelm Friedrich Hegel, *Die Philosophie der Geschichte: Vorlesungsmitschrift Heimann (Winter 1830/1831)*, ed. Klaus Vieweg (Berlin: Wilhelm Fink,

2005), 61, translated by and quoted in Alison Stone, "Hegel and Colonialism," *Hegel Bulletin* 41, no. 2 (2020): 255. They call attention to the fact that Cyclopes had quite an enviable capacity for sociality, care, and relationship. Not only do Polyphemus's neighbors rally when they hear him cry out (any assistance ultimately thwarted by Odysseus, in his renaming himself Nobody), but also "he puts the young sheep and goats to their mothers' udders, this practical action show[ing] a concern for creaturely life itself, and the famous speech of the blinded Polyphemus in which he calls the leading ram his friend, asking whether it is the last to leave the cave because it is grieving for its master's eye, has a power and poignancy equaled only at the highest point of the Odyssey, when the homecoming Odysseus is recognized by the old dog Argus." Horkheimer and Adorno, *Dialectic of Enlightenment*, 52. Adorno and Horkheimer also draw attention to how the charge of lawlessness, a want of *contract* in the social realm, is echoed in the Cyclops's manner of thought, described as "unsystematic, rhapsodic." Although they do repeat the conventional understanding of Polyphemus as "guileless" and completely wanting of the cunning for which his encounter with Odysseus is known, the care of the portrayal allows for something more than the disposable antagonist Polyphemus is most often cast as. I'm particularly intrigued by this sentence: "Stupidity and lawlessness share a common definition: when Homer calls the Cyclops a 'lawless-minded monster' he does not mean simply that the Cyclops does not respect the laws of morality but that his thinking itself is lawless, unsystematic, rhapsodic." Ibid., 51. I wonder what might emerge from bringing this passage into constellation or dialogue with Moten's indispensable rumination of blackness, imagination, knowledge, and lawlessness in "Knowledge of Freedom" in his *Stolen Life* and R. A. Judy's equally stunning thoughts on the impossibilities of Kant's Negro. See Moten, *Stolen Life*, 1–95; Judy, "Kant and the Negro," 4–70; R. A. Judy, *(Dis)forming the American Canon: African-Arabic Slave Narratives and the Vernacular* (Minneapolis: University of Minnesota Press, 1993).

72. Terada, "Hegel's Racism," 14.

73. Consider Nicolas Sarkozy's 2007(!) remarks during his address at the Cheikh Anta Diop University of Dakar:

> The drama of Africa is that the African man has not entered enough into history. The African peasant, for millennia, lives with the seasons, where the ideal life is to be in harmony with nature, and he knows only the eternal recycling of time marked by the rhythm of repetition without end of the same gestures and the same words. In this imagination, where everything always recycles, there is no place for either human adventure or for the idea of progress.... The challenge for Africa is to enter more into history. It is to draw from within itself the energy, the strength, the desire, the willpower to listen to and to espouse its own history. The problem of Africa is to stop always repeating, to stop always trotting out, to

free itself from, the myth of the eternal return, to understand that the Golden Age, which Africa never stops longing for, will never come back because it never existed.

"US Embassy Cables: Nicolas Sarkozy's Personal Diplomacy in Africa Is Hamfisted," *The Guardian*, August 13, 2008, https://www.theguardian.com/world/us-embassy-cables-documents/165955. Achille Mbembe's response gives some useful context. He writes that "the new French elites do not believe anything different. They share this Hegelian prejudice. Unlike the generation of the 'Papa-Commanders' (de Gaulle, Pompidou, Giscard d'Estaing, Mitterrand, or Chirac), who tacitly espoused the same prejudice whilst avoiding openly offending their interlocutors, France's 'new elites' now consider that one can only address societies so deeply plunged into the night of childhood by speaking unguardedly, with a sort of virgin energy. And that is indeed what they have in mind when they now openly defend the idea of a nation no longer 'hung-up' about its colonial past." Achille Mbembe, "Nicolas Sarkozy's Africa," trans. Melissa Thackway, Africultures, August 7, 2007, https://africultures.com/nicolas-sarkozys-africa-6816/.

74. For Hegel's parsimony, see Stone, "Adorno, Hegel, and Dialectic," 1123.

75. Harney and Moten, *Undercommons*, 96. This formulation has been at the very forefront of my mind at various points in the book, but in the wake of all that Hegel, it seems appropriate to share a little more from that passage. They write, "Can this being together in homelessness, this interplay of the refusal of what has been refused, this undercommon appositionality, be a place from which emerges neither self-consciousness nor knowledge of the other but an improvisation that proceeds from somewhere on the other side of an unasked question?" Ibid.

76. These are two contemporary popular *oríkì* singers. For what remains among the most useful accounts of *oríkì*, see Barber, *I Could Speak*. Adéléke Adéekó's scholarship on the Yorùbá *òrò-oríkì-ìtàn* complex has been an indispensable companion. Adéekó, *Arts of Being Yorùbá*; Adéléke Adéekó, "Oral Poetry and Hegemony: Yorùbá Oríkì," *Dialectical Anthropology* 26 (2001): 181–92.

77. Terada, *Metaracial*, 27. On the important distinction between *resemblance* and *affinity*, see chap. 4, "Billie's Bent Elbow."

78. This practice, something approaching a necessity for black studies, is a response to the awkwardness involved in Europe and Euro-America being the "social cauldron" but not the "inspiration" of black radicalism. Robinson, *Black Marxism*, 72. Or recall Fred Moten writing that black studies is a "walking in another world while passing through this one." Moten, *Stolen Life*, 155. For more on this, see chap. 1, "Haiti's Infrasonic Boom," and chap. 2, "Unthinkable Nonsense." See also Saidiya V. Hartman, "Venus in Two Acts," *Small Axe* 12, no. 2 (2008): 1–14; Moten, *Stolen Life*; da Silva, *Toward a Global Idea*; Bernasconi, "Hegel at the Court"; James A.

Snead, "Repetition as a Figure of Black Culture," in *Black Literature and Literary Theory*, ed. Henry Louis Gates Jr. (Milton Park: Routledge, 2016), 59–80; Fanon, *Black Skin, White Masks*.

79. Nahum Dimitri Chandler, of course, says it better than I ever could: "Such a questioning can unfold only by way of a double gesture: not only must the ground of the dogmatic claim, the assertion of a certain hierarchy (here among certain groups of humans), be brought into question, but the possibility of another kind, or order, of distinction must be posed and the dispersed figurations that become articulable by way of it given their elaboration." Chandler, *X*, 30. The nonway, according to Terada (borrowing from Jacques Derrida), is a huge and "most positive [realm], despite its negative name. It excludes no possibilities except the dividing line of the route. Every other possibility is still there—maybe an infinite number, maybe a condition unassimilable to choice." Terada, "Impasse as a Figure," 146. As the sphere off to the side of political action (whether conservative revolutionary, or of impasse), the nonway might be most readily experienced as an aesthetic sociality. The phrase *Billie's bent elbow* is the shorthand for the particular gathering of thought this book is making an attempt to document.

80. For an appraisal of Hegel's scholarly practice as it pertains to his philosophy of history, see Tom McCaskie, "Exiled from History: Africa in Hegel's Academic Practice," *History in Africa* 46 (2019): 165–94.

81. Ọ̀ṣun Òṣogbo Grove, and the Èjìgbòmẹ̀kùn market in Ilé-Ifẹ̀ are two sites where the interpenetration of the fantastic and actual might be observed. For more on Oja Èjìgbòmẹ̀kùn, see Abiodun Ajayi and Olusegun Rotimi Faturoti, "Èjìgbòmẹ̀kùn Market in Ilé-Ifẹ̀: Investigating the Nexus between the Mythical and Modern Era of the Yorùbá History," *Yoruba Studies Review* 5, no. 1–2 (2020): 1–18. In a chapter entitled "Disjunction and Transition," Karin Barber discusses various approaches to the contiguity (or snuggle) and traversal of *oríkì*. It is important to note that "transition" for Barber is the traversal from one element (phrase, subject position, utterance) to another, at times involving transformation but more often not. It is distinct from the Hegelian understanding of transition that more specifically refers to the walking of contraries into tension through to contradiction and ultimately to reach a more determined state. Barber, *I Could Speak*, 248–91. See also "Introduction: Constant Departure" herein.

82. Barber, *I Could Speak*, 288, 248; Yáì, "In Praise of Metonymy."

83. These few sentences are very much enabled by Barber, Adéẹ̀kọ́, and Yáì. I also have in mind C. L. R. James, Frantz Fanon, David Marriot, and Fred Moten on the significance of the leap within black ways to world and thought. Malone, *Quiet Farewell* is also in mind (thanks to Nick Byers). See C. L. R. James, *Notes on Dialectics: Hegel, Marx, Lenin* (London: Alison and Busby, 1980); Fanon, *Black Skin, White Masks*; Marriott, "No Lords A-leaping"; Moten, *Black and Blur*, 1–27.

84. Balibar, "Ideas of Europe," 5; Gerhard Richter, *Thinking with Adorno: The Uncoercive Gaze* (New York: Fordham University Press, 2019), 38.

85. Balibar, "Ideas of Europe," 5; Adorno, *Minima Moralia*, 151.

86. Hegel, *Phenomenology of Spirit*, 114, quoted in Terada, "Impasse as a Figure," 156. The passage that contains the quote has been influential to my thinking about the extra- and parapolitical stakes of this project. Terada states,

> Hegel writes that if lord and bondsman were to simply perish without having a history to contribute to, as in the catastrophic worst case of *The Communist Manifesto*—and it would be an even worse case, not mentioned there, if the bondsman alone perished—they would "leave each other free only indifferently, like things." Here, Hegel thinks of entities independent of one another as like *dead* ordinary things, dead because not human, *not preserved in history*. Yet, this "leaving each other free" resonates as a possibility that ought to exist—and is being defended against at this textual moment—for people who are not dead.

Ibid. Emphasis original.

87. Martin Jay suggests that this might be a return, somewhat, to "the original Greek use of the term. . . . [T]he expression of an inner state through cultic ritual rather than the reproduction of external reality." Martin Jay, "Mimesis and Mimetology: Adorno and Lacoue-Labarthe," *The Semblance of Subjectivity: Essays in Adorno's Aesthetic Theory*, ed. Tom Huhn and Lambert Zuidervaart (Cambridge, MA: MIT Press, 1997), 32. Interestingly, Catherine Osborne suggests that Plato's criticisms of the arts be read as directed at their apparent reliance on imitation. She writes that "seeking the justification for art, he found that current critical theory had only the notion of imitation to offer"—the implication being that his judgement might have been revisited if new evidence had come to light. Catherine Osborne, "The Repudiation of Representation in Plato's *Republic* and Its Repercussions," *Cambridge Classical Journal* 33 (1987): 56.

88. Andreas Huyssen, "Of Mice and Mimesis: Reading Spiegelman with Adorno," *New German Critique* 81 (2000): 66–67. For another black theoretical engagement with mimesis as snuggling, see Best, *None like Us*, 33–34.

89. Owen Hulatt, "Reason, Mimesis, and Self-Preservation in Adorno," *Journal of the History of Philosophy* 54, no. 1 (2016): 136–37; Owen Hulatt, *Adorno's Theory of Philosophical and Aesthetic Truth* (New York: Columbia University Press, 2016).

90. Cahn, "Subversive Mimesis," 63n34, 63.

91. Theodor W. Adorno, *Critical Models: Interventions and Catchwords*, trans. Henry W. Pickford (New York: Columbia University Press, 2005), 129.

92. "Ofili, Fanon, Ralph Ellison, Louis Armstrong constitute a quartet within a larger plain. Ben Hall sits in, as an arranger [*sic*]. That multistereophonic shmear, its caressive crash, is Hall's *Black and Blur*." Moten, *Black and Blur*, 231. This "ensem-

ble" that Moten pulled together for his 2015 performance lecture at the Museum of Modern Art (which included footage of Armstrong in Ghana in 1956; the soundtrack is etched in my memory) is one of the rickety bridges I've used to get from *Jazz as Critique* to *Billie's Bent Elbow*.

93. For more on nonperformance, see Moten, *Stolen Life*, 241–68.

94. Horkheimer and Adorno, *Dialectic of Enlightenment*, 149; Hegel, *Phenomenology of Spirit*, 114. *Coaxing* is an interesting member of this group. At first, it seems the odd one out. Terms that offer themselves from a short exploration of coaxing and (to a lesser extent) the word used in the original German, *zureden*, include those that are suggestive of either an insincere or a paranormal engagement, such as *cajoled*, *beguiled*, *tempted*, and *fascinated*. And yet the word also took me to the genre of persuasion at work in the lullaby and to Camille Norment's 2016 sound installation *Lull—So Ro*, to the pendulum swing of a cradle, and finally to that percussive pat (bringing to mind rain patter) that cuts the light jog on the spot of a caregiver soothing an infant on his or her chest. Regardless, *coaxing* has the most active connotations and is suggestive of rationalistic employment in the way that *snuggling*, *touching*, and *nestling* do not. "Those blinded by civilization have contact with their own tabooed mimetic traits only through certain gestures and forms of behavior they encounter in others, as isolated, shameful residues in their rationalized environment. What repels them as alien is all too familiar. It lurks in the contagious gestures of an immediacy suppressed by civilization: gestures of touching, nestling, soothing, coaxing." Horkheimer and Adorno, *Dialectic of Enlightenment*, 50–51.

95. Horkheimer and Adorno, *Dialectic of Enlightenment*, 149.

96. Matt F. Connell, "Body, Mimesis and Childhood in Adorno, Kafka and Freud," *Body and Society* 4, no. 4 (1998): 69.

97. Hulatt, "Reason, Mimesis, and Self-Preservation," 138, 138–139.

98. Roger Caillois, "Mimicry and Legendary Psychasthenia," in *The Edge of Surrealism: A Roger Caillois Reader*, ed. Claudine Frank (Durham: Duke University Press, 2003), 102.

99. Caillois, "Mimicry and Legendary Psychasthenia," 97; Lucien Cuénot, *La Genèse des espèces animales* (Paris: Félix Alcan, 1911), 463, quoted in ibid.

100. Caillois, "Mimicry and Legendary Psychasthenia," 97; Best, *None like Us*, 37. Although Stephen Best would likely bristle at the communitarian impulse that courses through *Billie's Bent Elbow*, our projects share an interest in bringing to light comportment and correspondence that go against the general tide of recognitive relations. In fact, in *None like Us*, he calls for a "critical comportment that embraces . . . forms of mimesis," such as Adorno's mimesis as snuggling, toward a "non-sovereign form of critical subjectivity on the idea that art thinks . . . an intellectual or philosophical project" that practices what I would describe as improvised correspondence. Ibid., 33–34.

101. Hulatt, "Reason, Mimesis, and Self-Preservation," 140.
102. Horkheimer and Adorno, *Dialectic of Enlightenment*, 189.
103. Roger Caillois, Le Mythe et l'Homme (Paris: Gallimard, 1938), 125, quoted in Horkheimer and Adorno, *Dialectic of Enlightenment*, 189; Sigmund Freud, Beyond the Pleasure Principle, in The Standard Edition of the Complete Psychological Works of Sigmund Freud, trans. James Strachey, 24 vols. (London: Hogarth Press, 1953–74), 18:44–60.
104. Hulatt, "Reason, Mimesis, and Self-Preservation," 149.
105. For instance, they write, "Civilization replaced the organic adaptation [*Anschmiegung*] to otherness, mimetic behavior proper, firstly, in the magical phase, with the organized manipulation of mimesis, and finally, in the historical phase, with rational praxis, work. Uncontrolled mimesis is proscribed." Horkheimer and Adorno, *Dialectic of Enlightenment*, 148. We do not find much concerning reason's adaption to mimetic comportment in *Dialectic of Enlightenment*. We would need to look to Adorno's unfinished, late work *Aesthetic Theory* for this.
106. Benjamin Y. Fong, *Death and Mastery: Psychoanalytic Drive Theory and the Subject of Late Capitalism* (New York: Columbia University Press, 2016), 19, 43.
107. Hans W. Loewald, *Papers on Psychoanalysis* (New Haven: Yale University Press, 1989), 8. See also Sigmund Freud, *Beyond the Pleasure Principle* (London: Penguin, 2003).
108. Loewald, *Papers on Psychoanalysis*, 203. Fong points out that he is drawing to the surface Loewald's interpretation of those "wild 'biologistic'" passages of *Beyond the Pleasure Principle*, a more explicit interpretation of the death drive. He writes, "Nowhere does Loewald systematically treat the concept of the death drive—a fact that could be related to his aversion to the topics of hatred, aggression, and so forth. He does, however, offer tantalizing hints that he takes Freud's proposal to gesture toward foundational ideas in his own work: For instance, in a short book review, in which he describes the death drive as an 'urge toward the bliss and pain of consuming oneself in the intensity of being lived by the id.'" Benjamin Y. Fong, "Hans Loewald and the Death Drive," *Psychoanalytic Psychology* 31, no. 4 (2014): 525–26.
109. This maturation of the death drive follows the psychic "big bang"—this most original stage, at which the animate quite simply wants to find a way back to the inanimate.
110. Fong, *Death and Mastery*, 30, 33.
111. Here, I am bracketing Freud's and Fong's various solutions to the problem of accounting for what inaugurates the initial motivation away from a comportment that returns the animate to inanimate repose, toward a situation that preserves life. For a detailed discussion of such, see Fong, "Hans Loewald." Loewald's translation of Freud's focus on primordial organism to the figure of the infant avoids the trickier implications of this problem.

112. Loewald, *Papers on Psychoanalysis*, 6.

113. I am departing somewhat from Loewald's language. Loewald understands the mimetic activity of the infant as an identification and an imitating closure of distinction, whereas I am wanting to both lean into the *fantasy* of union and distinguish something that is more like a superimposition of subject and object than an erasure of their difference (Fong's phrase "confusion of subject and object" is one I happily retain). Fong, *Death and Mastery*, 95.

114. Adorno, *Aesthetic Theory*, 143, 118. Emphasis added.

115. For a useful short comment on *methexis*, see José E. Muñoz, "Toward a Methexic Queer Media," *GLQ: A Journal of Lesbian and Gay Studies* 19, no. 4 (2013): 564.

116. Andrew Kania, "All Play and No Work: An Ontology of Jazz," *Journal of Aesthetics and Art Criticism* 69, no. 4 (2011): 391.

117. Vijay Iyer, "Exploding the Narrative in Jazz Improvisation," in *Uptown Conversation: The New Jazz Studies*, ed. Robert O'Meally, Brent Hayes Edwards, and Farah Jasmine Griffin (New York: Columbia University Press, 2004), 393–403.

118. Terada, *Metaracial*, 35. See also chap. 4, "Billie's Bent Elbow."

119. Adorno, *Aesthetic Theory*, 144. This fascination with and commitment to the "blur" of gathered dispersal is captured by Taylor's response to a student who inquired as to where the pulse was in his music: "I asked him how many different rates of breathing there are. I told him that what I'm interested in in my music is the variety of pulses that exist in a given moment." Whitney Balliett, *American Musicians II: Seventy-One Portraits in Jazz* (Jackson: University Press of Mississippi, 2006), 520. Moreover, in case we race to file this under a mere tolerance of diversity, by way of his embrace of the much-maligned four-four (which the new thing is often understood as attempting to extract itself from), Taylor suggests a distended commons hosted by the time signature: "The big chance we had a large part in precipitating was the dispensing of the *overt* manifestation of four. It became a concept that we no longer felt we had the necessity of stating, but understood that we experienced it and that it was, in many ways, the given premise of—or even the motivation of—all that we were going to do." This wide divergence of pulses that feel out (and outside) the four-four together, irreverent pulses that collide and bristle as they collude, is a snuggling up of the contrariant, the play of "bodies of sound" toward a falling into/ with/out of the general four-four. The four-four is the coemergent space of various correspondences. Taylor, "Cecil Taylor," 14. Emphasis added.

120. Taylor, "Cecil Taylor," 14.

121. Christopher Felver, dir., *Cecil Taylor: All the Notes* (Sausalito: Emotion Studios, 2004).

122. Taylor, "Sound Structure"; Cecil Taylor, "Being Matter Ignited: An Inter-

view with Cecil Taylor," interview by Chris Funkhouser, *Hambone* 12 (1995), https://writing.upenn.edu/epc/authors/funkhouser/ceciltaylor.html.

123. Tony Harrington, "Three Seconds in the World of Cecil Taylor," *The Wire*, April 2018, https://www.thewire.co.uk/in-writing/essays/three-seconds-in-the-world-of-cecil-taylor-by-tony-herrington.

124. Here, I stray into Benjaminian terrain, anticipating my discussion of nonsensuous correspondence in chap. 4, "Billie's Bent Elbow."

125. Cecil Taylor, "Second Pleasures," on *Always a Pleasure*, FMP CD69, 1996, compact disc.

126. Adorno, *Aesthetic Theory*, 143.

127. Felver, *Cecil Taylor*.

128. In the context of different configurations of "participants" in his approach to improvisation, Taylor reveals,

> I can have four or five bodies of sound existing in a duality of dimension. In other words, I might decide to have three or four different voices or choirs existing and moving with different weight propelling their ongoing motion.... So that one can have—say that two or three octaves below middle C is the area of the abyss, and the middle range is the surface of the earth, the astral being the upper range—you have three constituted bodies also outlined by a specific range, a specific function of how the innards of these groups relate to themselves and then to each other. You have therefore, what starts out as a linear voice becoming within itself like horizontal because of the plurality of exchange between the voices.

Taylor, "Cecil Taylor," 14, 31.

Chapter 4: Billie's Bent Elbow

1. The constellation of images that, at times, can only be related obliquely (if at all) is some of what I intend by the (nonsensuous) standard (e.g., *vexillum*, which means both the top petal of a papilionaceous flower and a rallying banner, Billie Holiday's undulating elbow, the imaginary pub Billie's Bent Elbow, and the idiom "bend an elbow" are placed alongside imagistic bits that commune in a manner less readily to analysis, such as the correspondence with *Verwandtschaft*—kinship not reliant on resemblance or identity but on a fugacious, adoptive affinity and the communion of participants, contributors, and creative/expressive material toward what has been termed *aesthetic form*, the center of the sound, brilliance, musicality, and feeling). Walter Benjamin gestures toward the very particular temporality involved in the nonsensuous—a sort of patient, unexpectant but attentive poise: "The perception of similarity is in every case bound to a flashing up. It flits past, can possibly

be won again, but cannot really be held fast as can other perceptions. It offers itself to the eye as fleetingly and transitorily as a constellation of stars. The perception of similarities thus seems to be bound to a moment in time. It is like the addition of a third element—the astrologer—to the conjunction of two stars; it must be grasped in an instant. Otherwise the astrologer is cheated of his reward, despite the sharpness of his observational tools." Benjamin, *Selected Writings*, 2:695–96.

In this final chapter, I break with convention (which, incidentally, I follow up until this point) and refer to musicians as they are known colloquially.

2. Taylor, "Sound Structure."

3. Taylor, "Sound Structure."

4. Matana Roberts, "All Is Written," on *River Run Thee*, Coin Coin 3, Constellation Records CST1101, 2015, compact disc.

5. In an earlier permutation of this meditation on "All Is Written," I write about having to resist an urge to interpret the work as the unearthly sound that might have escaped the mouth of the angel of history had the scene of piling catastrophe been unmuted—as a contribution to Walter Benjamin's soulful allegory. I had thought to consider why the angel's sound might be considered black, to *read* the piece in order that some hidden significance might be unlocked. It goes without saying that this approach can be exciting and opens into unexpected avenues for thought, regardless of its veracity. I clearly have not always been able to resist that type of close, or depth, reading. Notwithstanding, my preoccupation in recent work has been with developing an approach to musical works as image space—that is, a node that draws the (often) disparate and (sometimes) contrary into correspondence in order that the arrangement might tell us something—even when seemingly arbitrary and lacking in the determination usually expected of criticism and interpretative approaches, and perhaps that is the point. Relatedly, as a nascent contribution to this still developing approach, in the aforementioned piece on "All Is Written," I made a conscious decision to sit in the piece's opacity/impenetrability. What I do there, and lean into in this present version, is to *retell* the piece as a "bodily collective innervation," rejecting the analyst's search for the "penny slot of meaning" attempting to expel "moral metaphor." For the quotes, see Benjamin, "Surrealism," 47. Part of what that means for me is that the meditation takes itself to be a member of Matana's already-oversubscribed ensemble. Benjamin might understand this anterepresentational eruption, this spontaneous "party," to be a "political" move—as vigilance against political expediency and toward the upkeep of our recalcitrant ensemblic work. Fumi Okiji, "All Is Written," *Black One Shot* 15, no. 1 (2020), https://asapjournal.com/node/15-1-all-is-written-fumi-okiji/.

6. For more on anamnesis as a techne of Africana expressive practices, see Moyo Okediji, *The Shattered Gourd: Yoruba Forms in Twentieth-Century American Art* (Seattle: University of Washington Press, 2003).

7. "The mourning play, on the other hand, is inherently nonunified drama, and the idea of its resolution no longer dwells within the realm of drama itself." Benjamin, *Selected Writings*, 1:57.

8. Nina Simone, Claude Nobs, and Raymond Juassi, *Nina Simone: Live at Montreux 1976*, performed July 3, 1976, DVD, directed by Claude Nobs and Raymond Juassi (London: Eagle Rock Entertainment, 2006).

9. Walter Benjamin, *Origin of the German Trauerspiel* (Cambridge, MA: Harvard University Press, 2019); Benjamin, *Selected Writings*, 1:55–58.

10. William Parker, "William Parker: Everything Is Valid," interview by Eyal Hareuveni, All about Jazz, March 7, 2005, https://www.allaboutjazz.com/william-parker-everything-is-valid-william-parker-by-eyal-hareuveni; Don Cherry, quoted in L. Jones, *Black Music*, 191. In a 2005 interview, Eyal Hareuveni asks William Parker whether he feels "elated every time" he plays. Parker answers,

> That's the fundamental center of the music. Every time that you're playing you are trying to get into the *center of the sound*, bang, right there. That takes a minute, but once you developed that concept, every time you play, it's there. You have to be able to get right in there in an awaked trance state and immediately put yourself into a trance, getting to that area that just opens you up to the other, other worlds. If you don't have that, the music is not going to work, no matter what you are doing. The first time that I had that feeling was with ensemble Muntu at Rashied Ali's place, when one afternoon we played and the bass was lifting me off the ground. And many times we just break through into that area, *the spirit area*, it was a very elated period.

Parker, "William Parker." Emphasis added. Bill Dixon uses an almost identical phrase in discussing his philosophy and free jazz. See Andrew R. Dewar, "Searching for the Center of a Sound: Bill Dixon's Webern, the Unaccompanied Solo, and Compositional Ontology in Post-songform Jazz," *Jazz Perspectives* 4, no. 1 (2010): 59–87. Don Cherry, in conversation with Amiri Baraka, states, "When everybody's got their mind and feelings in tune, it's separate from the presence of the audience. Everybody carries their brightness . . . it makes a sound. Separate yourself, and each time it'll be different. Be at the instance, absolute. The music will have a quality at Its instant absolute. And that will be brilliance." Baraka goes on to explain that "Don uses language the way he plays, with a preciseness based on specific insight. Bright, brightness, brilliant, brilliance, are words he came to again and again hoping that his meaning was clear." L. Jones, *Black Music*, 191.

11. Langston Hughes, *The Panther and the Lash* (Visalia: Vintage, 1992), 9.

12. Danielle C. Heard, "'Don't Let Me Be Misunderstood': Nina Simone's Theater of Invisibility," *Callaloo* 35, no. 4 (2012): 1079, 1075. She goes on, "By playing with the discontinuity between the realm of appearances and reality, Simone makes

it impossible for others to reduce her to an archetype. How can she be 'the angry black woman' when she also sings the vulnerability of a little girl? How can she be the entreating servant when she stands tall as a queen to be revered? How can she be a gun-toting black nationalist when she also preaches love? And is 'Sister Sadie' capable of the deep passion and longing Simone feels for Imojah?" Ibid., 1079.

13. One could make the argument that such porosity of the individual is a pathology, but as will become clear, I am working with a distinct notion of hosting the different and diverse, which draws from Benjaminian ideas around nonsensuous correspondence, mimetic comportment, and the interpenetration of body space and image space.

14. Eli Friedlander, *Walter Benjamin: A Philosophical Portrait* (Cambridge, MA: Harvard University Press, 2012), 119.

15. Eli Friedlander, "On the Musical Gathering of Echoes of the Voice: Walter Benjamin on Opera and the *Trauerspiel*," *Opera Quarterly* 21, no. 4 (2005): 640, 639.

16. Benjamin, *Selected Writings*, 1:56.

17. "Lament . . . is the most undifferentiated impotent expression of language. It contains scarcely more than the sensuous breath." Benjamin, *Selected Writings*, 1:73.

18. Benjamin, *Selected Writings*, 1:61. Emphasis added.

19. Friedlander, "On the Musical Gathering," 641–42. Benjamin writes that "words have a pure emotional life cycle in which they purify themselves by developing from the natural sound to the pure sound of feeling. For such words, language is merely a transitional phase within the entire life cycle, and in them the mourning play finds its voice. It describes the path from natural sound via lament to music." Benjamin, *Selected Writings*, 1:60.

20. Benjamin, *Selected Writings*, 1:61.

21. This fragment is extracted from a piece that I wrote for an event in celebration of Julie Mehretu's midcareer retrospective at the Whitney Museum of American Art in 2021. In preparation, I watched many interviews, one in which she speaks of her paintings as not siblings but other kin. I unfortunately have been unable to find the clip to share with you.

22. Benjamin, *Selected Writings*, 1:207–9, 2:694–98, 2:720–22.

23. Benjamin, *Selected Writings*, 2:721.

24. There is something quite delicious about happening upon a term, complete with conceptual framework, for a phenomenon (or an experience) with which you've been grappling. That sense of satisfaction, of validation even, is very quickly superseded by the dread of the responsibility you experience—obligation not only to the found linguistic and theoretical tools (one inevitably finds have already been at work in the vast network of conscious and not-so-apparent associations, the little world, or the image of the world, that the gift is merely public relations for) but also

to the story of one's own devotion. (How to maintain fidelity to one's intention? Should one be so faithful? Might one not think so monogamously?)

25. "Relationship . . . can be directly perceived only in feeling (neither in intuition, nor in reason)." Although with "rigor" (but only "modestly"), relationship might be "comprehended by reason." Benjamin, *Selected Writings*, 1:208.

26. Benjamin, *Selected Writings*, 1:207.

27. In a 2016 interview as part of an extended response to a question concerning the "field and discipline" of black studies and Afropessimism's place within it, Frank Wilderson says, "Africa is a slave dwelling as well; it's just that it is a slave dwelling at a higher level of abstraction than the cabin. . . . Africa has always been a big slave estate. That has been and still is the global consensus." Frank B. Wilderson III, "'The Inside-Outside of Civil Society': An Interview with Frank B. Wilderson, III," interview by Samira Spatzek and Paula von Gleich, *Black Studies Papers* 2, no. 1 (2016): 8–9.

28. Ọlábíyìí Yáì's exposition of the Yorùbá concept *ìtàn* complicates the conventional understanding of Africa as the discrete, frozen, bounded cradle of humanity and, distinctly, as the inaccessible, impossible origin of the raw material from which the Negro is extracted. The definition of the term is often reduced in translation to "history," robbing *ìtàn* of its spatial register, the expressive tools on which it relies, and its broad application as a sort of epistemological comportment. It is an order of oral or folk practice and also a more fundamental propensity "to spread, reach, to open up" temporally and geographically. Yai, "In Praise of Metonymy," 30. It is a way with time and the earth that invariably has something poetic about it. Yáì understands *ìtàn* as a near synonym to *diaspora*, as both extension *and* coincidence, geographical and temporal shuttles *and* mountings. Also of relevance is that the artist (*gbẹ́nàgbẹ́nà*) in Yorùbá tradition is considered (or is often) *àrè*. "Lagbayi, the paradigmatic Yoruba sculptor, lived as an *àrè*. No etymology of the word has been attempted." But Yáì suggests that *àrè* is likely derive from the verb *re*, which means "to depart." He writes that *"ares* are itinerant individuals, wanderers, permanent strangers precisely because they can be permanent nowhere. *They always seek to depart from current states of affairs.*" Yai, "Tradition," 35. Emphasis added. See also Nathaniel Mackey, *Splay Anthem* (New York: New Directions, 2006), 5; Nathaniel Mackey, *From a Broken Bottle Traces of Perfume Still Emanate* (New York: New Directions, 2010); Okiji, *Jazz as Critique*, 51.

29. Bryan Wagner, *Disturbing the Peace: Black Culture and the Police Power after Slavery* (Cambridge, MA: Harvard University Press, 2009), 1. I would be remiss not to acknowledge Fred Moten's response, which I read as a displacement of the question of temporal priority rather than a reversal of Wagner's dictum. Even as Moten delivers the rebuttal quite plainly—"In contradistinction to Wagner and the wide

acknowledgment he invokes, we might move by way of the assumption that blackness is older than Africa, older than its diaspora, older than racial slavery, older than its beginning, older than its name or its submission to the operation of naming"—I read much of this as maintenance and adornment of Cedric Robinson's utterly indispensable but weatherworn notion of the ontological totality (and the complicated but irrevocable Pan-Africanism this notion speaks on behalf of). Moten, *Stolen Life*, 22. See also Moten, *Black and Blur*; Fred Moten, "Notes on Passage (the New International of Sovereign Feelings)," *Palimpsest: A Journal on Women, Gender, and the Black International* 3, no. 1 (2014): 51–74; Fred Moten, "The Subprime and the Beautiful," *African Identities* 11, no. 2 (2013): 237–45. One of the questions that emerges from such work is how we might think about the terms *African*, *black*, and *diaspora* together without recourse to origin (or telos). The question of temporal priority that Wagner brings to life is perhaps more readily addressed (and addressable) in relation to how the unruliness of blackness calls the West's mechanizations of control and governance into being. As Moten writes, blackness "is the anarchic principle that calls originary nominalization into being and, therefore, into question; it is the subjunctive, substantive, anticipatory accompaniment of every eviscerative indication." Moten, *Stolen Life*, 22.

30. Judy, "Unfungible Flow," 30. R. A. Judy writes that "whatever semiosis the captured souls loaded into the hulls of the slave ship came with—whether Wolof, Bambara, Fulfulde, or Yoruba—were liquefied and remolded into the exchangeable commodity called 'Negro.' The compelling violent force of modernity's liquefaction notwithstanding, elements of those semiosis remained in the stream, as it were. So, with respect to the so-called Negro, we can say there are multiple semiosis in play with inflecting iterations of fluidity, which I call para-semiosis." Ibid.

31. Chad Infante et al., "Other Intimacies: Black Studies Notes on Native/Indigenous Studies," *Postmodern Culture* 31, no. 1 (2020): 6. Ọlábíyìí Yái tells us that "the Yoruba have always conceived of their history as diaspora"; their dispersed-gathering deportment "is neither necessity or lamented accident . . . but the normal order of things historical." Yai, "In Praise of Metonymy," 30. For a study dedicated to the exploration of gathering as a feature of black sociality, see Sarah J. Cervenak, *Black Gathering: Art, Ecology, Ungiven Life* (Durham: Duke University Press, 2021).

32. Harney and Moten, *All Incomplete*, 19; Denise Ferreira da Silva, foreword to *All Incomplete*, by Stefano Harney and Fred Moten (London: Minor Compositions, 2021), 9.

33. Moten, "Red Sheaves," 15. Moten writes,

Feeling-depth is soulful
refusal to separate

practice from what
that was in your hand.
nothing ever comes
of infinite rehearsal.

Ibid.

34. This was recited by D. Adeniji (and translated by Abiodun), who was a research assistant at the Institute of African Studies, University of Ibadan, Ibadan, in March 1976. Abiodun, "Verbal and Visual Metaphors," 253. Please note that the reversal of italicizing convention is reproduced from the source (at this point in Abiodun's text, the first occurrence of the word *òrò* is not given in italics, while the name of the associated *òrìshà*, Òrò, is). Lower diacritics, that I've elected to use throughout the book, are also not used by Abiodun here. Until quite recently, there were several impediments to the use of Yoruba diacritics (particularly lower).

35. Abiodun, "Verbal and Visual Metaphors," 255.

36. Abiodun, "Verbal and Visual Metaphors," 252. Also see Adéẹ̀kọ́, *Arts of Being Yorùbá*, 28–35. For more on the multivalence of *ọ̀rọ̀* and Ọ̀rọ̀, see Oludamini Ogunnaike, *Deep Knowledge: Ways of Knowing in Sufism and Ifa, Two West African Intellectual Traditions* (University Park: Pennsylvania State Press, 2020), 233–39.

37. Adetokunbo F. Borishade, "The Study of African American Sermonics and Protest Rhetoric in Relation to the Yoruba Concepts of Oro (Hoo-ro) and Iwa" (PhD diss., Temple University, 1993); Abiodun, "Verbal and Visual Metaphors," 252–56.

38. Adéẹ̀kọ́, *Arts of Being Yorùbá*, 28–32; Abiodun, "Verbal and Visual Metaphors," 252–70.

39. Henderson, *New Black Poetry*, 44.

40. I've gotten caught up in *Blue Confession (Lady Chancellor)* but any of his indigo paintings will do. In fact, I recently spent time with Ofili's *Seven Deadly Sins* at Victoria Miro in London and was similarly intoxicated. These palimpsestic canvases are delicious pinks (vulva pinks rather than Stuart Semple's Barbie-pink Pinkie), psychedelic purple and turquoise, and browns. Pointillist and broad strokes of color merge (really!), superimpose, and sit beside one another. Once you settle into this cacophony, which is anything but chaotic (more a sort of peaceful euphoria), one glimpses bodies and limbs, otherworldly and earthly, only to lose them almost immediately. In this way, for me, Ofili *dramatizes* Hòọ̀-rò's need for adornment, cover, or opacity. But there were also times in which my attention on all that ornamentation and play between the various layers of ornament and surface allowed me access to "nirvana's . . . ambiguous wink." Walter Benjamin, *On Hashish* (Cambridge, MA: Harvard University Press, 2006), 24. If I am permitted to light up just

one other point of correspondence, Ofili's *Seven Deadly Sins* brought me to this quotation from an unpublished note from Walter Benjamin:

> Ornament is a model of the mimetic faculty. This abstraction is the perfected art of empathy. Do connections exist between the experiences of aura and those of astrology[?] Are there earthly creatures as well as things that gaze back from the stars? That actually only open up their gaze in the heavens? Are the stars with their glimpse from out of the distance the original phenomenon (*Urphänomen*) of aura?
>
> May one assume that the glimpse was the first mentor of the mimetic faculty? That the first coming into resemblance was completed by the glimpse? May one finally close the circle with the assumption that constellations of stars participated in the emergence of the ornament? That the ornament retains glimpses from the stars?

Walter Benjamin, Walter Benjamin Archive, MS 931, Berlin, Germany, trans. Esther Leslie, quoted in Frédéric Neyrat, "Walter Benjamin's Cosmos: Correspondence, Aura, and the Cosmo-geological Subject," *Mosaic: An Interdisciplinary Critical Journal* 54, no. 3 (2021): 76.

41. Benjamin, *On Hashish*, 35.

42. Wadada Leo Smith, "Notes on My Music (Part 1)," in *Notes (8 Pieces) Source a New World Music: Creative Music* (n.p.: Wadada Leo Smith, 1973).

43. See, e.g., Ekkehard Jost, *Free Jazz* (Boston, MA: Da Capo, 1974); George E. Lewis, "Improvised Music after 1950: Afrological and Eurological Perspectives," *Black Music Research Journal* 6, no. 1 (1996): 91–122; Jeff Pressing, "Free Jazz and the Avant-Garde," in *The Cambridge Companion to Jazz*, ed. Mervyn Cooke and David Horn (Cambridge: Cambridge University Press, 2002), 202–16; Scott De Veaux, "Constructing the Jazz Tradition: Jazz Historiography," *Black American Literature Forum* 25, no. 3 (1991): 525–60; Charles Hersch, "'Let Freedom Ring!' Free Jazz and African-American Politics," *Cultural Critique* 32 (1995): 97–123; Kwami Coleman, "Free Jazz and the 'New Thing' Aesthetics, Identity, and Texture, 1960–1966," *Journal of Musicology* 38, no. 3 (2021): 261–95.

44. Gerald L. Bruns, "On the Conundrum of Form and Material in Adorno's *Aesthetic Theory*," *Journal of Aesthetics and Art Criticism* 66, no. 3 (2008): 225. Emphasis original.

45. Walter Benjamin writes, "The collective is a body, too. And the physis that is being organized for it in technology can, through all its political and factual reality, only be produced in that image sphere to which profane illumination initiates us. Only when in technology body and image so interpenetrate that all revolutionary tension becomes bodily collective innervation, and all the bodily innervations of the

collective become revolutionary discharge, has reality transcended itself to the extent demanded by the *Communist Manifesto*." Benjamin, "Surrealism," 56. It is important to understand that Benjamin's collective is a nonrepresentational formation whose action is exclusively concerned with bringing itself about. See "Introduction: Constant Departure" herein.

    46. Urban Lasson, dir., *It Is Not My Music*, in BibiAudiofil2, "Don Cherry Swedish TV Documentary 1978," October 19, 2019, video, 57:51, https://www.youtube.com/watch?v=GZHgZ1K7V7s. Emphasis added.

    47. Laura Harris, *Experiments in Exile: C. L. R. James, Hélio Oiticica, and the Aesthetic Sociality of Blackness* (New York: Fordham University Press, 2018), 2; da Silva, "On Difference without Separability," 64–65. Folding this formulation but another way, we find ourselves in the proximity of J. Kameron Carter's writing of "a distinct cosmology of entangled aliveness, of entangled togetherness, that alternative we-ness that we might call *sociality in the flesh, sociality in black*. In this alternate we-ness, existence (or be-*ing*) generatively begins and ends with the generosity of entanglement, not with the presumptive logics and violent practices of individualized separability—the logics and practices that power the cosmology of (racial) capitalism." Carter, *Anarchy of Black Religion*, 18–19. Emphasis original. See also Ashon T. Crawley, *Blackpentecostal Breath: The Aesthetics of Possibility* (New York: Fordham University Press, 2016).

    48. Nathaniel Mackey, *School of Udhra* (San Francisco: City Lights Books, 1993), 43–44.

    49. Peter Szendy, *Listen: A History of Our Ears* (New York: Fordham University Press, 2009), 35, 36. To appreciate the ubiquity of Szendy's arrangers' listening practice, see also Martin Daughtry, "Listening beyond Sound and Life," in *The Oxford Handbook of the Phenomenology of Music Cultures*, ed. Harris M. Berger, Riedel Friedlind, and David VanderHamm (Oxford: Oxford University Press, 2023), 137–72.

    50. Cherry, quoted in Lasson, *It Is Not My Music*.

    51. This play with birdcall is not uncommon in the black experimental tradition. Eric Dolphy, in a beautiful conversation with John Coltrane for *DownBeat* on April 12, 1962, says, "At home [in California], I used to play, and the birds always used to whistle with me. I would stop what I was working on and play with the birds." Don DeMichael, "John Coltrane and Eric Dolphy Answer the Jazz Critics," *DownBeat*, April 12, 1962, 21. See also the footage of Roland Kirk in a zoo, with a child on his shoulders. LongTallYamlaJay, "Rahsaan Roland Kirk at the Zoo," September 23, 2010, video, 1:54, https://www.youtube.com/watch?v=VF5yN4_mkNs.

    52. Don Cherry, *Complete Communion*, Blue Note Records 22573, 1965, compact disc.

53. John Coltrane to Don DeMichael, June 2, 1962, quoted in Leonard L. Brown, "In His Own Words: Coltrane's Responses to Critics," in *John Coltrane and Black America's Quest for Freedom: Spirituality and the Music*, ed. Leonard L. Brown (Oxford: Oxford University Press, 2010), 17.

54. Cherry, quoted in Lasson, *It Is Not My Music*; Moten, "Subprime and the Beautiful," 238.

55. The Yorùbá "critic" is *gbẹ́nugbẹ́nu*—literally, "one who carves with one's mouth"—and so is "by necessity," according to Ọlábíyìí Yáì, an artist (*gbẹ́nàgbẹ́nà*). Yai, "Tradition," 32. See also "Introduction: Constant Departure" herein.

56. This formulation comes from Khatib, "To Win the Energies," 1.

57. To borrow from Adorno, our brilliance "constantly suspends itself as such. . . . [T]he essence of its coherence is that it does not cohere." Adorno, *Aesthetic Theory*, 143. Emphasis added.

58. Fred Moten, *All That Beauty* (Seattle: Letter Machine Editions, 2019), 76.

59. Cherry, quoted from Lasson, *It Is Not My Music*.

60. Adorno was critical of both the "irrational fetishization of rationali*st* construction" of integral serialism and the aleatory ego avoidance of Cagean experientialism. Of the former, Adorno complains, "Alienated and preestablished rules are blindly followed—as a good schoolboy might follow them—excluding any tension with subjectivity, without which there is as little art as truth." Theodor W. Adorno, *Essays on Music*, ed. Richard Leppert (Berkeley: University of California Press, 2002), 194. Emphasis added. Furthermore, in a formulation shared with Gyorgy Ligeti, he is struck by "the essential arbitrariness of the 'rationalistic' forms in which the originally pitch-based twelve-tone row was extended to the other parameters of music, and by virtue of which 'total determinacy comes to be identical with total indeterminacy,' at least experientially." Gyorgy Ligeti, "Metamorphoses of Musical Form," in *Source Readings in Musical History: The Twentieth Century*, ed. Robert P. Morgan (New York: W.W. Norton, 1998), 113, quoted in David Cunningham, "Notes on Nuance: Rethinking the Philosophy of New Music," *Radical Philosophy* 125 (May–June 2004): 19.

61. Theodor W. Adorno, *Quasi una Fantasia: Essays on Modern Music* (London: Verso, 1998), 272, 307. Marcus Zagorski writes,

> Schoenberg is praised by Adorno because, unlike the postwar serialists, he combines the 12-tone technique with traditional elements of musical language; the objective and subjective dimensions of material are mediated. Adorno cites the "expressive character" of Schoenberg's music and the use of techniques such as "thematic construction, exposition, transitions, continuation, fields of tension and release," and he claims, "it is only by means of these and related traditional categories that the coherence of the music, its sense, the authentic composition

[*das eigentliche Komponieren*], in so far as it is more than mere arrangement [*bloße Anordnung*], has been preserved in the midst of 12-tone technique." Marcus Zagorski, "'Nach dem Weltuntergang': Adorno's Engagement with Postwar Music," *Journal of Musicology* 22, no. 4 (2005): 693. Interestingly, it has been noted that free jazz bears greater resemblance to earlier twentieth-century permutations (expressionist-era Arnold Schoenberg, Igor Stravinsky, Béla Bartók) than it does the total organization of integral serialism and, although this might be more contentious, the aleatory composition of John Cage. See Gunther Schuller, *Musings: The Musical Worlds of Gunther Schuller* (Oxford: Oxford University Press, 1989); Steven Block, "Pitch-Class Transformation in Free Jazz," *Music Theory Spectrum* 12, no. 2 (1990): 181–202; Alfred Bennett Spellman, *Four Lives in the Bebop Business* (Milwaukee: Hal Leonard, 1985).

62. Max Paddison writes that Adorno's informal music "is not a prescription for composers to try to put into practice . . . but is really what I would call a 'prismatic concept'—that is to say, a multi-faceted concept that enables us to see things from different and unusual angles and in a new and unfamiliar light." Max Paddison, "Contemporary Music: Theory, Aesthetic, Critical Theory," in *Contemporary Music, Theoretical and Philosophical Perspectives*, ed. Max Paddison and Irène Deliège (Farnham: Ashgate, 2010), 8.

63. Adorno, *Quasi una Fantasia*, 272.

64. Paddison, "Contemporary Music," 5–7; Joris de Henau, "Towards an Aesthetics of the '(In)formel': Time, Space and the Dialectical Image in the Music of Varèse, Feldman and Xenakis" (PhD diss., Durham University, 2015), 65, 76–81, 234.

65. De Henau, "Towards an Aesthetics," 80.

66. Text provided by Städel Museum, accompanying the digital archive of *Injured Head*. Wols, *Injured Head*, ca. 1944, pen and black ink, watercolor and white glaze on mottled pink laid paper, 170 x 123 mm, Städel Museum, https://sammlung.staedelmuseum.de/en/work/injured-head.

67. De Henau, "Towards an Aesthetics," 80.

68. The spontaneous interplay of idiomaticity and autopoiesis, an enduring faculty of jazz practice, is deepened and extended with the new thing. Familiar phrasing, cadence, articulation, instrumentation, and, in some cases, even the head-solo-head convention remain and are further investigated as the scope of improvisational technique is extended. This practice that draws from existing language, convention, and material while allowing musicians to go where the music leads facilitates great expressivity. For more on idiomaticity and autopoiesis in the new thing, see Fumi Okiji, "Aesthetic Form in the New Thing / Aesthetic Sociality of *Musique Informelle*," in *Black Art and Aesthetics: Relationalities, Interiorities, Reckonings*, ed. Michael Kelly and Monique Roelofs (London: Bloomsbury, 2023),

137. See also Keren Omry, "Literary Free Jazz? *Mumbo Jumbo* and *Paradise*: Language and Meaning," *African American Review* 41, no. 1 (2007): 131; Sara Ramshaw, "Deconstructin(g) Jazz Improvisation: Derrida and the Law of the Singular Event," *Critical Studies in Improvisation / Études Critiques en Improvisation* 2, no. 1 (2006): 3, https://ssrn.com/abstract=2041321. Finally, the unfolding thoughts of these past few sections, and most particularly the "kinship" of experimental jazz and *musique informelle* proposed, are very much enabled by the musicological context provided by two texts—the indispensable Lewis, "Improvised Music after 1950," and what I consider to be its companion text, Benjamin Piekut, "Indeterminacy, Free Improvisation, and the Mixed Avant-Garde: Experimental Music in London, 1965–1975," *Journal of the American Musicological Society* 67, no. 3 (2014): 769–824.

69. The reference is to Paul Klee's monoprint *Angelus Novus* (1920).

70. Delphine Bière, Annie Claustres, and Pierre Dhainaut, *Wols, Dessins: Catalogue de l'exposition au LAAC de Dunkerque* (Malacoff: Arichibooks, 2021), 14, quoted in de Henau, "Towards an Aesthetics," 79.

71. William Parker, liner notes on William Parker Quartet, *Sound Unity*, AUM Fidelity AUM034, 2004, compact disc. Bassist William Parker has published several books, including collections of interviews with musicians and other artists and a number of meditations on musical practice. See, e.g., William Parker, *Conversations II: Dialogues and Monologues* (Paris: Rogue Art, 2015); William Parker, *Who Owns Music?* (Cologne: Buddy's Knife Jazzedition, 2007). See also Cisco Bradley, *Universal Tonality: The Life and Music of William Parker* (Durham: Duke University Press, 2021).

72. Might we not put Wols's "noodles" in constellation with Benjamin's image concept of the mosaic as another instance of what the latter terms "presentation" (*Darstellung*)? Hans-Jost Frey, in discussion of the peculiar rendering of "truth" we find in Benjamin, writes that "presentation must take place in such a way that an opening ensues onto what lies outside the cognitively accessible. The method demands the inclusion within the thought process of what cannot be mastered. This occurs through the 'renunciation of the uninterrupted course of intention.'" Hans-Jost Frey, "On Presentation," in *Walter Benjamin: Theoretical Questions*, ed. David S. Ferris (Stanford: Stanford University Press, 1996), 141.

73. Theodor W. Adorno, "Form in the New Music," *Music Analysis* 27, no. 2–3 (2008): 201. He continues, "Form has to be distinguished from whatever is formed; it is the epitome of what makes art art, of all the elements which organise a work of art as a meaningful thing in itself." Ibid.

74. "Adorno's idea of musical material appears in various forms throughout his output, and crystallizes aspects found in his thought more generally: the dialectics of history and nature, and the antagonistic relations of constraint and freedom

under modernity. Musical material, for Adorno, is all that faces the composer in the present as inherited from the past: formal schemes, instrumental forces, harmonic and melodic formulae and expectations, and so on." Samuel Wilson, "Notes on Adorno's 'Musical Material' During the New Materialisms," *Music and Letters* 99, no. 2 (2018): 262.

75. Adorno, *Quasi una Fantasia*, 307.

76. Adorno, *Quasi una Fantasia*, 322, 320. The very fact that Adorno is contravening his usual prohibition on positive utopic imaginings—that he is, in a sense, jumping the dialectic—is surprising, and while we welcome a lighter, possibly more optimistic tone, Adorno never sounds completely convinced of the legitimacy of his proposal. The movement of Western music at its journey's end did not lead to an informal music, and so his speculative (one might say artificial) offering must have been written in some ambivalence. As Raymond Geuss notes, "There is something *inherently* odd about Adorno's project in *'Vers une musique informelle'* of using this dialectical method to tell us where music must, could, might, or ought to go. Strictly speaking, a Hegelian dialectician should claim that the 'outcome' of a conflict, tension, contradiction, etc. can be seen to be 'rational' or 'logical' *only retrospectively*." Raymond Geuss, *Morality, Culture, and History: Essays on German Philosophy* (Cambridge: Cambridge University Press, 1999), 146. Emphasis original.

77. Adorno, *Quasi una Fantasia*, 307.

78. Eva Geulen, "'The Primacy of the Object': Adorno's *Aesthetic Theory* and the Return of Form," *New German Critique* 48, no. 2 (2021): 7.

79. Horkheimer and Adorno, *Dialectic of Enlightenment*, xii.

80. Rei Terada's discussion of Derrida's notion of the nonway has been important to my thinking here. Terada writes, "First, there is 'what clears the way' when the path is being cleared; second, 'what clears the way there where the way is not opened'; third (the counterpart, maybe, to the first), there is the possibility that the way is 'still blocked'; and fourth, as an alternative to blockage or clearance, a 'nonway,' in which a way does not emerge, but not because it is blocked." Terada, "Impasse as a Figure," 146.

81. Simone, Nobs, and Juassi, *Nina Simone*.

82. Adorno, *Critical Models*, 201, 202.

83. Benjamin, "Surrealism," 56.

84. Benjamin, "Surrealism," 56.

85. Benjamin, *On Hashish*, 24. In the closing stages of this project, I was really pleased to read Marcus Boon's excellent new book *The Politics of Vibration*. Although not directly concerned with intoxication, this work is engaging with comparable phenomena. In fact, Boon wrote the introduction to *On Hashish*, and at that time, he was likely working on a book about drug-fueled artistic practice. Marcus

Boon, *The Politics of Vibration: Music as a Cosmopolitical Practice* (Durham: Duke University Press, 2022). See also Marcus Boon, *The Road of Excess: A History of Writers on Drugs* (Cambridge, MA: Harvard University Press, 2005).

86. Benjamin, "Surrealism," 48.

87. Cannonball Adderley, "Love for Sale," on *Somethin Else*, Blue Note Records 49460, 1958, compact disc.

88. Ornette Coleman, *Something Else!!!!* Contemporary Records 25218616324, 1958, compact disc; Ornette Coleman, *The Shape of Jazz to Come*, Atlantic Records 8122731332, 1959, compact disc.

Bibliography

Abiodun, Rowland. "Verbal and Visual Metaphors: Mythical Allusions in Yorùbá Ritualistic Art of *Orí*." *Word and Image* 3, no. 3 (1987): 252–70.
Adeduntan, Ayo. *What the Forest Told Me: Yoruba Hunter, Culture and Narrative Performance*. Makhanda: National Inquiry Service Center, 2019.
Adéẹ̀kọ́, Adélékè. *Arts of Being Yorùbá: Divination, Allegory, Tragedy, Proverb, Panegyric*. Bloomington: Indiana University Press, 2017.
Adéẹ̀kọ́, Adélékè. "Decolonization without a Linguistic Turn Is like Drinking Sugar without Tea: Ọlábíyìí Babalọlá Joseph Yáì." *Journal of the African Literature Association* 15, no. 2 (2021): 308–20.
Adéẹ̀kọ́, Adélékè. "Oral Poetry and Hegemony: Yorùbá Oríkì." *Dialectical Anthropology* 26 (2001): 181–92.
Adeleke, Durotoye A. "The Yorùbá Fool Insignia: Beyond the Shakespearean Tradition." *Journal of Social Sciences* 21, no. 2 (2009): 105–15.
Adorno, Theodor W. *Aesthetic Theory*. Translated by Robert Hullot-Kentor. London: Continuum, 1997.
Adorno, Theodor W. *Critical Models: Interventions and Catchwords*. Translated by Henry W. Pickford. New York: Columbia University Press, 2005.
Adorno, Theodor W. *Essays on Music*. Edited by Richard Leppert. Berkeley: University of California Press, 2002.
Adorno, Theodor W. "Form in the New Music." *Music Analysis* 27, no. 2–3 (2008): 201–16.

Adorno, Theodor W. *Hegel: Three Studies*. Translated by Shierry Weber Nicholsen. Cambridge, MA: MIT Press, 1994.

Adorno, Theodor W. *An Introduction to Dialectics*. Translated by Nicholas Walker. Cambridge, MA: Polity, 2017.

Adorno, Theodor W. *Minima Moralia: Reflections from Damaged Life*. Translated by E. F. N. Jephcott. London: Verso, 2005.

Adorno, Theodor W. *Negative Dialectics*. Translated by E. B. Ashton. London: Routledge, 1973.

Adorno, Theodor W. *Notes to Literature*. Translated by Shierry Weber Nicholsen. 2 vols. New York: Columbia University Press, 1991–92.

Adorno, Theodor W. *Quasi una Fantasia: Essays on Modern Music*. London: Verso, 1998.

Agada, Ada. "Bewaji and Fayemi on God, Omnipotence and Evil." *Filosofia Theoretica: Journal of African Philosophy, Culture and Religions* 11, no. 1 (2022): 41–46.

Agada, Ada. "Complementarism and Consolationism: Mapping Out a 21st-Century African Philosophical Trajectory." *Synthesis Philosophica* 35, no. 1 (2020): 135–53.

Ajayi, Abiodun, and Olusegun Rotimi Faturoti. "Èjìgbòmẹkùn Market in Ilé-Ifẹ̀: Investigating the Nexus between the Mythical and Modern Era of the Yorùbá History." *Yoruba Studies Review* 5, no. 1–2 (2020): 1–18.

Apter, Andrew. *Black Critics and Kings: The Hermeneutics of Power in Yoruba Society*. Chicago: University of Chicago, 1992.

Balibar, Etienne. "Ideas of Europe: Civilization and Constitution." *Iris: European Journal of Philosophy and Public Debate* 1, no. 1 (2009): 3–17.

Balliett, Whitney. *American Musicians II: Seventy-One Portraits in Jazz*. Jackson: University Press of Mississippi, 2006.

Barber, Karin. *I Could Speak until Tomorrow: Oriki, Women and the Past in a Yoruba Town*. Edinburgh: Edinburgh University Press, 2020.

Bartlett, Andrew W. "Cecil Taylor, Identity Energy, and the Avant-Garde African American Body." *Perspectives of New Music* 33, no. 1–2 (1995): 274–93.

Beier, H. Ulli. "The Historical and Psychological Significance of Yoruba Myths." *Yoruba Studies Review* 1, no. 2 (2017): 204–10.

Benjamin, Walter. *Illuminations*. Translated by Harry Zohn. New York: Schocken Books, 2007.

Benjamin, Walter. *On Hashish*. Cambridge, MA: Harvard University Press, 2006.

Benjamin, Walter. *Origin of the German Trauerspiel*. Cambridge, MA: Harvard University Press, 2019.

Benjamin, Walter. *Selected Writings*. Edited by Marcus Bullock and Michael W. Jennings. 4 vols. Cambridge, MA: Belknap, 2004–6.

Benjamin, Walter. "Surrealism: The Last Snapshot of the European Intelligentsia." *New Left Review* 108 (1978): 47–56.

Bernasconi, Robert. "Hegel at the Court of the Ashanti." In *Hegel after Derrida*, edited by Stuart Barnett, 41–63. Milton Park: Routledge, 1998.

Bernasconi, Robert. "With What Must the Philosophy of World History Begin? On the Racial Basis of Hegel's Eurocentrism." *Nineteenth Century Contexts* 22, no. 2 (2000): 171–201.

Bernstein, Jay M. *Adorno: Disenchantment and Ethics*. Cambridge: Cambridge University Press, 2001.

Bernstein, Jay M. "Why Rescue Semblance? Metaphysical Experience and the Possibility of Ethics." In *The Semblance of Subjectivity: Essays in Adorno's Aesthetic Theory*, edited by Tom Huhn and Lambert Zuidervaart, 177–212. Cambridge, MA: MIT Press, 1997.

Best, Stephen. *None like Us: Blackness, Belonging, Aesthetic Life*. Durham: Duke University Press, 2019.

Block, Steven. "Pitch-Class Transformation in Free Jazz." *Music Theory Spectrum* 12, no. 2 (1990): 181–202.

Bobak, Mark J. "The Music of Cecil Taylor: An Analysis of Selected Piano Solos, 1973–1989." PhD diss., University of Illinois Urbana–Champaign, 1994.

Bonetto, Sandra. "Race and Racism in Hegel—an Analysis." *Minerva: An Internet Journal of Philosophy* 10 (2006): 5–64.

Boon, Marcus. *The Politics of Vibration: Music as a Cosmopolitical Practice*. Durham: Duke University Press, 2022.

Boon, Marcus. *The Road of Excess: A History of Writers on Drugs*. Cambridge, MA: Harvard University Press, 2005.

Borishade, Adetokunbo F. "The Study of African American Sermonics and Protest Rhetoric in Relation to the Yoruba Concepts of Oro (Hoo-ro) and Iwa." PhD diss., Temple University, 1993.

Bradley, Cisco. *Universal Tonality: The Life and Music of William Parker*. Durham: Duke University Press, 2021.

Brathwaite, Edward Kamau. "Dialect and Dialectic." *Bulletin of the African Studies Association of the West Indies*, no. 6 (December 1973): 89–99.

Brathwaite, Edward Kamau. "Kumina: The Spirit of African Survival in Jamaica." *Jamaica Journal* 42 (September 1, 1978): 44–63.

Brown, Leonard L. "In His Own Words: Coltrane's Responses to Critics." In *John Coltrane and Black America's Quest for Freedom: Spirituality and the Music*, edited by Leonard L. Brown, 11–32. Oxford: Oxford University Press, 2010.

Brown, Nahum. *Hegel on Possibility: Dialectics, Contradiction, and Modality*. London: Bloomsbury, 2020.

Brown, Nahum. "Transcendent and Immanent Conceptions of Perfection in Leibniz and Hegel." In *Transcendence, Immanence, and Intercultural Philosophy*, edited by Nahum Brown and William Franke, 183–205. Cham: Springer, 2016.

Bruns, Gerald L. "On the Conundrum of Form and Material in Adorno's Aesthetic Theory." *Journal of Aesthetics and Art Criticism* 66, no. 3 (2008): 225–35.

Buck-Morss, Susan. *Hegel, Haiti, and Universal History*. Pittsburgh: University of Pittsburgh, 2009.

Cahn, Michael. "Subversive Mimesis: T. W. Adorno and the Modern Impasse of Critique." In *Mimesis in Contemporary Theory: An Interdisciplinary Approach*, edited by Mihai Spariosu, 27–64. Philadelphia: John Benjamins, 1984.

Caillois, Roger. "Mimicry and Legendary Psychasthenia." In *The Edge of Surrealism: A Roger Caillois Reader*, edited by Claudine Frank, 91–103. Durham: Duke University Press, 2003.

Carter, J. Kameron. *The Anarchy of Black Religion: A Mystic Song*. Durham: Duke University Press, 2023.

Carter, J. Kameron. *Race: A Theological Account*. New York: Oxford University Press, 2008.

Casimir, Jean. *The Haitians: A Decolonial History*. Translated by Laurent Dubois. Chapel Hill: University of North Carolina Press, 2020.

Cervenak, Sarah J. *Black Gathering: Art, Ecology, Ungiven Life*. Durham: Duke University Press, 2021.

Chandler, Nahum Dimitri. "Of Exorbitance: The Problem of the Negro as a Problem for Thought." *Criticism* 50, no. 3 (2008): 345–410.

Chandler, Nahum Dimitri. *X—the Problem of the Negro as a Problem for Thought*. New York: Fordham University Press, 2013.

Chernoff, John M. "The Rhythmic Medium in African Music." *New Literary History* 22, no. 4 (1991): 1093–1102.

Ciccariello-Maher, George. "'So Much the Worse for the Whites': Dialectics of the Haitian Revolution." *Journal of French and Francophone Philosophy* 22, no. 1 (2014): 19–39.

Coleman, Kwami. "Free Jazz and the 'New Thing' Aesthetics, Identity, and Texture, 1960–1966." *Journal of Musicology* 38, no. 3 (2021): 261–95.

Comay, Rebecca, and Frank Ruda. *The Dash—the Other Side of Absolute Knowing*. Cambridge, MA: MIT Press, 2018.

Connell, Matt F. "Body, Mimesis and Childhood in Adorno, Kafka and Freud." *Body and Society* 4, no. 4 (1998): 69–81.

Crawley, Ashon T. *Blackpentecostal Breath: The Aesthetics of Possibility*. New York: Fordham University Press, 2016.

Crawley, Ashon T. "Stayed | Freedom | Hallelujah." In *Otherwise Worlds: Against Settler Colonialism and Anti-blackness*, edited by Tiffany Lethabo King, Jenell Navarro, and Andrea Smith, 27–37. Durham: Duke University Press, 2020.

Cuénot, Lucien. *La Genèse des espèces animales*. Paris: Félix Alcan, 1911.

Cunningham, David. "Notes on Nuance: Rethinking the Philosophy of New Music." *Radical Philosophy* 125 (May–June 2004): 17–28.

da Silva, Denise Ferreira. Foreword to *All Incomplete*, by Stefano Harney and Fred Moten, 5–11. London: Minor Compositions, 2021.

da Silva, Denise Ferreira. "On Difference without Separability." In *Incerteza viva*, edited by Jochen Volz, Júlia Rebouças, and Isabella Rjeille, n.p. São Paulo: Bienal Internacional de São Paulo, 2016. Exhibition catalog.

da Silva, Denise Ferreira. "1 (Life) ÷ 0 (Blackness) = ∞-∞ or ∞/∞: On Matter beyond the Equation of Value." *E-flux*, no. 79 (2017). https://www.e-flux.com/journal/79/94686/1-life-0-blackness-or-on-matter-beyond-the-equation-of-value/.

da Silva, Denise Ferreira. *Toward a Global Idea of Race*. Minneapolis: University of Minnesota, 2007.

da Silva, Denise Ferreira. *Unpayable Debt*. London: Sternberg, 2022.

Daughtry, Martin. "Listening beyond Sound and Life." In *The Oxford Handbook of the Phenomenology of Music Cultures*, edited by Harris M. Berger, Riedel Friedlind, and David VanderHamm, 137–72. Oxford: Oxford University Press, 2023.

DeMichael, Don. "John Coltrane and Eric Dolphy Answer the Jazz Critics." *Down-Beat*, April 12, 1962, 20–23.

de Henau, Joris. "Towards an Aesthetics of the *'(In)formel'*: Time, Space and the Dialectical Image in the Music of Varèse, Feldman and Xenakis." PhD diss., Durham University, 2015.

De Veaux, Scott. "Constructing the Jazz Tradition: Jazz Historiography." *Black American Literature Forum* 25, no. 3 (1991): 525–60.

Dewar, Andrew R. "Searching for the Center of a Sound: Bill Dixon's Webern, the Unaccompanied Solo, and Compositional Ontology in Post-songform Jazz." *Jazz Perspectives* 4, no. 1 (2010): 59–87.

Diop, Mati. "Atlantics Director Q&A." TIFF Originals. September 11, 2019. Video, 22:30. https://www.youtube.com/watch?v=Azsq_Ghojis&t=1143s.

Edwards, Brent Hayes. *Epistrophies: Jazz and the Literary Imagination*. Cambridge, MA: Harvard University Press, 2017.

Ellison, Ralph. *Shadow and Act*. New York: Vintage, 2011.

Fanon, Frantz. *Black Skin, White Masks*. New York: Grove, 2008.

Fanon, Frantz. *The Wretched of the Earth*. Translated by Richard Philcox. New York: Grove, 2004.

Felver, Christopher, dir. *Cecil Taylor: All the Notes*. Sausalito: Emotion Studios, 2004.

Fenves, Peter. *Points of Departure: Samuel Weber between Spectrality and Reading*. Evanston, IL: Northwestern University Press, 2016.

Finlayson, James Gordon. "Hegel, Adorno and the Origins of Immanent Criticism." *British Journal for the History of Philosophy* 22, no. 6 (2014): 1142–66.

Fong, Benjamin Y. *Death and Mastery: Psychoanalytic Drive Theory and the Subject of Late Capitalism*. New York: Columbia University Press, 2016.

Fong, Benjamin Y. "Hans Loewald and the Death Drive." *Psychoanalytic Psychology* 31, no. 4 (2014): 525–26.

Freud, Sigmund. *Beyond the Pleasure Principle*. London: Penguin, 2003.

Freud, Sigmund. *Beyond the Pleasure Principle*. In *The Standard Edition of the Complete Psychological Works of Sigmund Freud*, translated by James Strachey, 18:7–64. 24 vols. London: Hogarth Press, 1953–74.

Frey, Hans-Jost. "On Presentation." In *Walter Benjamin: Theoretical Questions*, edited by David S. Ferris, 139–64. Stanford: Stanford University Press, 1996.

Friedlander, Eli. "On the Musical Gathering of Echoes of the Voice: Walter Benjamin on Opera and the *Trauerspiel*." *Opera Quarterly* 21, no. 4 (2005): 631–46.

Friedlander, Eli. *Walter Benjamin: A Philosophical Portrait*. Cambridge, MA: Harvard University Press, 2012.

Geggus, David. "Slave Society in the Sugar Plantation Zones of Saint Domingue and the Revolution of 1791–93." *Slavery and Abolition* 20, no. 2 (1999): 31–46.

Geulen, Eva. "'The Primacy of the Object': Adorno's Aesthetic Theory and the Return of Form." *New German Critique* 48, no. 2 (2021): 5–21.

Geuss, Raymond. *Morality, Culture, and History: Essays on German Philosophy*. Cambridge: Cambridge University Press, 1999.

Giladi, Paul. "Hegel's Philosophy and Common Sense." *European Legacy* 23, no. 3 (2018): 269–85.

Givan, Benjamin. "Apart Playing: McCoy Tyner and 'Bessie's Blues.'" *Journal of the Society for American Music* 1, no. 2 (2007): 257–80.

Givan, Benjamin. "'The Fools Don't Think I Play Jazz': Cecil Taylor Meets Mary Lou Williams." *Journal of Musicology* 35, no. 3 (2018): 397–430.

Hahn, Susan Songsuk. *Contradiction in Motion: Hegel's Organic Concept of Life and Value*. Ithaca, NY: Cornell University Press, 2007.

Halbig, Christoph. "The Philosopher as Polyphemus? Philosophy and Common Sense in Hegel and Jacobi." *Internationales Jahrbuch des Deutschen Idealismus* 3 (2005): 261–82.

Harney, Stefano, and Fred Moten. *All Incomplete*. London: Minor Compositions, 2021.

Harney, Stefano, and Fred Moten. *The Undercommons: Fugitive Planning and Black Study*. London: Minor Compositions, 2013.

Harrington, Tony. "Three Seconds in the World of Cecil Taylor." *The Wire*, April 2018. https://www.thewire.co.uk/in-writing/essays/three-seconds-in-the-world-of-cecil-taylor-by-tony-herrington.

Harris, Laura. *Experiments in Exile: C. L. R. James, Hélio Oiticica, and the Aesthetic Sociality of Blackness*. New York: Fordham University Press, 2018.

Harris, Laura. "The Subjunctive Poetics of the Undocument: C. L. R. James's American Civilization." *Criticism* 58, no. 2 (2016): 205–30.

Harris, Laura. "What Happened to the Motley Crew? C. L. R. James, Hélio Oiticica, and the Aesthetic Sociality of Blackness." *Social Text* 30, no. 3 (2012): 49–75.

Hartman, Saidiya V. *Scenes of Subjection: Terror, Slavery, and Self-Making in Nineteenth-Century America*. Oxford: Oxford University Press, 1997.

Hartman, Saidiya V. "Venus in Two Acts." *Small Axe* 12, no. 2 (2008): 1–14.

Heard, Danielle C. "'Don't Let Me Be Misunderstood': Nina Simone's Theater of Invisibility." *Callaloo* 35, no. 4 (2012): 1056–84.

Hegel, Georg W. F. *Hegel's "Phenomenology of Spirit."* Translated by A. V. Miller. Oxford: Oxford University Press, 2004.

Hegel, Georg W. F. *Hegel's "Philosophy of Mind."* Translated by William Wallace. Oxford: Clarendon Press, 1894.

Hegel, Georg W. F. *Hegel's "Science of Logic."* Translated by A. V. Miller. New York: Humanities Press, 1976.

Hegel, Georg W. F. *Lectures on the Philosophy of History*. Translated by J. Sibree. London: G. Bell and Sons, 1914.

Hegel, Georg W. F. *Lectures on the Philosophy of World History*. Translated. H. B. Nisbet. Cambridge: Cambridge University Press, 1975.

Hegel, Georg W. F. *The Science of Logic*. Translated by George Di Giovanni. Cambridge: Cambridge University Press, 2010.

Henderson, Stephen. *Understanding the New Black Poetry: Black Speech and Black Music as Poetic References*. New York: William Morrow, 1973.

Hersch, Charles. "'Let Freedom Ring!' Free Jazz and African-American Politics." *Cultural Critique* 32 (1995): 97–123.

Horkheimer, Max, and Theodor W. Adorno. *Dialectic of Enlightenment*. Translated by Edmund Jephcott. Stanford, CA: Stanford University Press, 2002.

Hughes, Langston. *The Panther and the Lash*. Visalia: Vintage, 1992.

Hulatt, Owen. *Adorno's Theory of Philosophical and Aesthetic Truth*. New York: Columbia University Press, 2016.

Hulatt, Owen. "Reason, Mimesis, and Self-Preservation in Adorno." *Journal of the History of Philosophy* 54, no. 1 (2016): 135–52.

Huyssen, Andreas. "Of Mice and Mimesis: Reading Spiegelman with Adorno." *New German Critique* 81 (2000): 65–82.

Ijiomah, Chris O. *Harmonious Monism: A Philosophical Logic of Explanation for Ontological Issues in Supernaturalism in African Thought*. Bloomington, IN: Xlibris, 2016.

Ijiomah, Chris O. "Harmonious Monism: A System of a Logic in African Thought."

In *Logic and African Philosophy: Seminal Essays on African Systems of Thought*, edited by Jonathan O. Chimakonam, 269–94. Wilmington: Vernon, 2020.

Ikäheimo, Heikki. "Hegel's Concept of Recognition—What Is It?" In *Recognition—German Idealism as an Ongoing Challenge*, edited by Christian Krijnen, 11–38. Leiden: Brill, 2014.

Infante, Chad, Sandra Harvey, Kelly Limes Taylor, and Tiffany King. "Other Intimacies: Black Studies Notes on Native/Indigenous Studies." *Postmodern Culture* 31, no. 1 (2020). https://doi.org/10.1353/pmc.2020.0022.

Iton, Richard. *In Search of the Black Fantastic: Politics and Popular Culture in the Post-Civil Rights Era*. Oxford: Oxford University Press, 2008.

Iverson, Ethan. "All-Star Television: Charles Mingus, Cecil Taylor, Ralph Ellison, Martin Williams." *Journal of Jazz Studies* 13, no. 1 (2022): 47–63.

Iyer, Vijay. "Exploding the Narrative in Jazz Improvisation." In *Uptown Conversation: The New Jazz Studies*, edited by Robert O'Meally, Brent Hayes Edwards, and Farah Jasmine Griffin, 393–403. New York: Columbia University Press, 2004.

Jackson, Zakiyyah I. *Becoming Human: Matter and Meaning in an Antiblack World*. New York: New York University Press, 2020.

Jackson, Zakiyyah I. "Losing Manhood: Animality and Plasticity in the (Neo)slave Narrative." *Qui Parle: Critical Humanities and Social Sciences* 25, no. 1–2 (2016): 95–136.

James, C. L. R. *The Black Jacobins: Toussaint L'Ouverture and the San Domingo Revolution*. New York: Vintage, 1989.

James, C. L. R. *Nkrumah and the Ghana Revolution*. Edited by Leslie James. Durham: Duke University Press, 2022.

James, C. L. R. *Notes on Dialectics: Hegel, Marx, Lenin*. London: Alison and Busby, 1980.

Jay, Martin. "Mimesis and Mimetology: Adorno and Lacoue-Labarthe." In *The Semblance of Subjectivity: Essays in Adorno's Aesthetic Theory*, edited by Tom Huhn and Lambert Zuidervaart, 29–53. Cambridge, MA: MIT Press, 1997.

Jones, Jennie C., and Fred Moten. *Constant Structure*. Chicago: Arts Club of Chicago, 2020.

Jones, LeRoi (Amiri Baraka). *Black Music*. Brooklyn: Akashic Books, 2010.

Jost, Ekkehard. *Free Jazz*. Boston, MA: Da Capo, 1974.

Judy, R. A. *(Dis)forming the American Canon: African-Arabic Slave Narratives and the Vernacular*. Minneapolis: University of Minnesota Press, 1993.

Judy, R. A. "Introduction: On W. E. B. Du Bois and Hyperbolic Thinking." *Boundary 2* 27, no. 3 (Fall 2000): 1–35.

Judy, R. A. "Kant and the Negro." *Surfaces* 1, no. 8 (1991): 7–81.

Judy, R. A. "On the Question of Nigga Authenticity." *Boundary 2* 21, no. 3 (1994): 211–30.

Judy, R. A. *Sentient Flesh: Thinking in Disorder, Poiésis in Black*. Durham: Duke University Press, 2020.

Judy, R. A. "The Unfungible Flow of Liquid Blackness." *Liquid Blackness* 5, no. 1 (2021): 27–36.

Kania, Andrew. "All Play and No Work: An Ontology of Jazz." *Journal of Aesthetics and Art Criticism* 69, no. 4 (2011): 391–403.

Karera, Axelle. "Paraontology: Interruption, Inheritance, or a Debt One Often Regrets." *Critical Philosophy of Race* 10, no. 2 (2022): 158–97.

Kelley, Robin D. "Beyond the 'Real' World, or Why Black Radicals Need to Wake Up and Start Dreaming." *Souls* 4, no. 2 (2002): 51–64.

Kelley, Robin D. *Freedom Dreams: The Black Radical Imagination*. Boston, MA: Beacon, 2022.

Kelly, Michael. *Iconoclasm in Aesthetics*. Cambridge: Cambridge University Press, 2003.

Kernodle, Tammy L. *Soul on Soul: The Life and Music of Mary Lou Williams*. Champaign: University of Illinois Press, 2020.

Khatib, Sami. "Fantasy, Phantasmagoria, and Image-Space: Walter Benjamin's Politics of Pure Means." Paper presented at Phantasma und Politik, Hebbel am Ufer Theatre, Berlin, Germany, November 23, 2013. https://www.academia.edu/5257726/Fantasy_Phantasmagoria_and_Image_Space_Walter_Benjamins_Politics_of_Pure_Means.

Khatib, Sami. "'To Win the Energies of Intoxication for the Revolution': Body Politics, Community, and Profane Illumination." *Anthropology and Materialism: A Journal of Social Research* 2 (2014): 2–11.

King, Tiffany Lethabo, Jenell Navarro, and Andrea Smith, eds. *Otherwise Worlds: Against Settler Colonialism and Anti-blackness*. Durham: Duke University Press, 2020.

Kisukidi, Nadia Yala. "Décoloniser la philosophie: Ou de la philosophie comme objet anthropologique." *Présence Africaine* 2 (2015): 83–98.

Kotsko, Adam. "How to Read Žižek." *Los Angeles Review of Books*, September 2, 2012. https://lareviewofbooks.org/article/how-to-read-zizek/.

Kuykendall, Ronald. "Hegel and Africa: An Evaluation of the Treatment of Africa in the Philosophy of History." *Journal of Black Studies* 23, no. 4 (1993): 571–81.

Lasson, Urban, dir. *It Is Not My Music*. In BibiAudiofil2, "Don Cherry Swedish TV Documentary 1978," October 19, 2019. Video, 57:51. https://www.youtube.com/watch?v=GZHgZ1K7V7s.

Lawal, Babatunde. "Àwòrán: Representing the Self and Its Metaphysical Other in Yoruba Art." *Art Bulletin* 83, no. 3 (2001): 498–526.

Lawal, Babatunde. "Èjìwàpò: The Dialectics of Twoness in Yoruba Art and Culture." *African Arts* 41, no. 1 (2008): 24–39.

Le Glaunec, Jean-Pierre. *The Cry of Vertières: Liberation Memory and the Beginning of Haiti*. Translated by Jonathan Kaplansky. Kingston: McGill-Queen's University Press, 2020.

Lewis, George E. "Improvised Music after 1950: Afrological and Eurological Perspectives." *Black Music Research Journal* 6, no. 1 (1996): 91–122.

Loewald, Hans W. *Papers on Psychoanalysis*. New Haven: Yale University Press, 1989.

LongTallYamlaJay. "Rahsaan Roland Kirk at the Zoo." September 23, 2010. Video, 1:54. https://www.youtube.com/watch?v=VF5yN4_mkNs.

Macdonald, Iain. "Adorno's Modal Utopianism: Possibility and Actuality in Adorno and Hegel." *Adorno Studies* 1, no. 1 (2017): 1–12.

Macdonald, Iain. *What Would Be Different: Figures of Possibility in Adorno*. Stanford, CA: Stanford University Press, 2019.

Mackey, Nathaniel. *From a Broken Bottle Traces of Perfume Still Emanate*. New York: New Directions, 2010.

Mackey, Nathaniel. *School of Udhra*. San Francisco: City Lights Books, 1993.

Mackey, Nathaniel. *Splay Anthem*. New York: New Directions, 2006.

Marasco, Robyn. *The Highway of Despair: Critical Theory after Hegel*. New York: Columbia University Press, 2015.

Marcuse, Herbert. *One-Dimensional Man: Studies in the Ideology of Advanced Industrial Society*. Milton Park: Routledge, 2013.

Marriott, David. "No Lords A-leaping: Fanon, C. L. R. James, and the Politics of Invention." *Humanities* 3, no. 4 (2014): 517–45.

Marriott, David. "On Decadence: Bling Bling." *E-flux*, no. 79 (2017). https://www.e-flux.com/journal/79/94430/on-decadence-bling-bling/.

Marx, Karl. *The Economic and Philosophic Manuscripts of 1844*. Translated by M. Milligan. New York: International Publishers, 1964.

Mbembe, Achille. "Nicolas Sarkozy's Africa." Translated by Melissa Thackway. Africultures, August 7, 2007. https://africultures.com/nicolas-sarkozys-africa-6816/.

McCaskie, Tom. "Exiled from History: Africa in Hegel's Academic Practice." *History in Africa* 46 (2019): 165–94.

McGowan, Todd. *Emancipation after Hegel: Achieving a Contradictory Revolution*. New York: Columbia University Press, 2019.

McKittrick, Katherine. "Dear April: The Aesthetics of Black Miscellanea." *Antipode* 54, no. 1 (2022): 3–18.

McNeill, John Robert. *Mosquito Empires: Ecology and War in the Greater Caribbean, 1620–1914*. Cambridge: Cambridge University Press, 2010.

Mignolo, Walter. "Sylvia Wynter: What Does It Mean to Be Human?" In *Sylvia*

Wynter: On Being Human as Praxis, edited by Katherine McKittrick, 106–23. Durham: Duke University, 2015.

Mills, Jon. "Psyche as Inner Contradiction." *Continental Thought and Theory* 2, no. 4 (2019): 71–82.

Moten, Fred. *All That Beauty*. Seattle: Letter Machine Editions, 2019.

Moten, Fred. *Black and Blur*. Durham: Duke University Press, 2017.

Moten, Fred. "Blackness and Poetry." *Evening Will Come* 55 (July 2015). https://arcade.stanford.edu/content/blackness-and-poetry-0.

Moten, Fred. *In the Break: The Aesthetics of the Black Radical Tradition*. Minneapolis: University of Minnesota Press, 2003.

Moten, Fred. "is alone together how it feels to be free? ummm." *Interim* 37, no. 3–4 (Winter 2021). https://www.interimpoetics.org/373374/fred-moten.

Moten, Fred. "Notes on Passage (the New International of Sovereign Feelings)." *Palimpsest: A Journal on Women, Gender, and the Black International* 3, no. 1 (2014): 51–74.

Moten, Fred. "the red sheaves." In *Perennial Fashion, Presence Falling*, 2–20. Seattle: Wave Books, 2023.

Moten, Fred. *Stolen Life*. Durham: Duke University, 2018.

Moten, Fred. "The Subprime and the Beautiful." *African Identities* 11, no. 2 (2013): 237–45.

Moten, Fred. *The Universal Machine*. Durham: Duke University Press, 2018.

Muñoz, José E. "Toward a Methexic Queer Media." *GLQ: A Journal of Lesbian and Gay Studies* 19, no. 4 (2013): 564.

Neyrat, Frédéric. "Walter Benjamin's Cosmos: Correspondence, Aura, and the Cosmo-geological Subject." *Mosaic: An Interdisciplinary Critical Journal* 54, no. 3 (2021): 59–84.

Ogundipe, Ayodele. "Esu Elegbara, the Yoruba God of Chance and Uncertainty: A Study in Yoruba Mythology." PhD diss., Indiana University, 1978.

Ogunnaike, Oludamini. *Deep Knowledge: Ways of Knowing in Sufism and Ifa, Two West African Intellectual Traditions*. University Park: Pennsylvania State Press, 2020.

Oguntola-Laguda, Danoye. "Esu, the Individual, and the Society." Inaugural lecture at Lagos State University, Lagos, Nigeria, January 31, 2017. https://www.lasu.edu.ng/publications/inaugural_lectures/inaugural_57th_lecture_of_professor_danoye_oguntola_laguda.pdf.

Okediji, Moyo. *The Shattered Gourd: Yoruba Forms in Twentieth-Century American Art*. Seattle: University of Washington Press, 2003.

Okiji, Fumi. "Aesthetic Form in the New Thing / Aesthetic Sociality of *Musique Informelle*." In *Black Art and Aesthetics: Relationalities, Interiorities, Reckonings*, edited Michael Kelly and Monique Roelofs, 135–50. London: Bloomsbury, 2023.

Okiji, Fumi. "All Is Written." *Black One Shot* 15, no. 1 (2020). https://asapjournal.com/node/15-1-all-is-written-fumi-okiji/.

Okiji, Fumi. *Jazz as Critique: Adorno and Black Expression Revisited*. Stanford, CA: Stanford University Press, 2018.

Okoth, Kevin. "Resistance from Elsewhere." *London Review of Books* 44, no. 7 (April 2022). https://www.lrb.co.uk/the-paper/v44/n07/kevin-okoth/resistance-from-elsewhere.

Omry, Keren. "Literary Free Jazz? *Mumbo Jumbo* and *Paradise*: Language and Meaning." *African American Review* 41, no. 1 (2007): 127–41.

Osborne, Catherine. "The Repudiation of Representation in Plato's *Republic* and Its Repercussions." *Cambridge Classical Journal* 33 (1987): 53–73.

Oyewumi, Oyeronke. "The Translation of Cultures: Engendering Yoruba Language, Orature and World-Sense." In *Women, Gender, Religion: A Reader*, edited by Elizabeth A. Castelli and Rosamond C. Rodman, 76–97. London: Palgrave Macmillan, 2001.

Paddison, Max. "Contemporary Music: Theory, Aesthetic, Critical Theory." In *Contemporary Music, Theoretical and Philosophical Perspectives*, edited by Max Paddison and Irène Deliège, 1–16. Farnham: Ashgate, 2010.

Palm, Ralph. "Hegel's Contradictions." *Hegel Bulletin* 32, no. 1–2 (2011): 134–58.

Palmer, Tyrone S. "'What Feels More Than Feeling?' Theorizing the Unthinkability of Black Affect." *Critical Ethnic Studies* 3, no. 2 (2017): 31–56.

Parker, William. *Conversations II: Dialogues and Monologues*. Paris: Rogue Art, 2015.

Parker, William. Liner notes on William Parker Quartet, *Sound Unity*. AUM Fidelity AUM034, 2004, compact disc.

Parker, William. *Who Owns Music?* Cologne: Buddy's Knife Jazzedition, 2007.

Parker, William. "William Parker: Everything Is Valid." Interview by Eyal Hareuveni. All about Jazz, March 7, 2005. https://www.allaboutjazz.com/William-parker-everything-is-valid-william-parker-by-eyal-hareuveni.

Piekut, Benjamin. "Indeterminacy, Free Improvisation, and the Mixed Avant-Garde: Experimental Music in London, 1965–1975." *Journal of the American Musicological Society* 67, no. 3 (2014): 769–824.

Pressing, Jeff. "Free Jazz and the Avant-Garde." In *The Cambridge Companion to Jazz*, edited by Mervyn Cooke and David Horn, 202–16. Cambridge: Cambridge University Press, 2002.

Purtschert, Patricia. "On the Limit of Spirit: Hegel's Racism Revisited." *Philosophy and Social Criticism* 36, no. 9 (2010): 1039–51.

Quashie, Kevin. *Black Aliveness, or a Poetics of Being*. Durham: Duke University Press, 2021.

Ramshaw, Sara. "Deconstructin(g) Jazz Improvisation: Derrida and the Law of the Singular Event." *Critical Studies in Improvisation / Études Critiques en Improvisation* 2, no. 1 (2006): 1–19. https://ssrn.com/abstract=2041321.
Rankine, Claudia. *Citizen: An American Lyric*. Minneapolis, MN: Graywolf, 2014.
Richter, Gerhard. *Thinking with Adorno: The Uncoercive Gaze*. New York: Fordham University Press, 2019.
Robinson, Cedric J. *Black Marxism: The Making of the Black Radical Tradition*. Chapel Hill: University of North Carolina, 2020.
Robinson, Cedric J. *The Terms of Order: Political Science and the Myth of Leadership*. New York: State University of New York, 2016.
Rosemont, Franklin, and Robin D. Kelley. *Black, Brown, and Beige: Surrealist Writings from Africa and the Diaspora*. Austin: University of Texas Press, 2009.
Sacks, Jeffrey. "Introduction: Nonsense—Critique for the Times." *Critical Times* 6, no. 1 (2023): 1–14.
Schuller, Gunther. *Musings: The Musical Worlds of Gunther Schuller*. Oxford: Oxford University Press, 1989.
Scott, David. "On the Very Idea of a Black Radical Tradition." *Small Axe: A Caribbean Journal of Criticism* 17, no. 1 (2013): 1–6.
Sexton, Jared. "Affirmation in the Dark." *The Comparatist* 43 (2019): 90–111.
Shipp, Matthew. "Black Mystery School Pianists." New Music USA, December 18, 2020. https://nmbx.newmusicusa.org/black-mystery-school-pianists/.
Simone, Nina, Claude Nobs, and Raymond Juassi. *Nina Simone: Live at Montreux 1976*. Performed July 3, 1976. DVD. Directed by Claude Nobs and Raymond Juassi. London: Eagle Rock Entertainment, 2006.
Sinnerbrink, Robert. *Understanding Hegelianism*. Milton Park: Routledge, 2014.
Sithole, Tendayi. *Refiguring in Black*. Cambridge, MA: Polity, 2023.
Smith, Wadada Leo. "Notes on My Music (Part 1)." In *Notes (8 Pieces) Source a New World Music: Creative Music*, n.p. N.p.: Wadada Leo Smith, 1973.
Snead, James A. "Repetition as a Figure of Black Culture." In *Black Literature and Literary Theory*, edited by Henry Louis Gates Jr., 59–80. Milton Park: Routledge, 2016.
Soyinka, Wole. "Exile: Thresholds of Loss and Identity." *Caliban* 7, no. 1 (2000): 61–70.
Soyinka, Wole. *Of Africa*. New Haven: Yale University, 2012.
Spellman, Alfred Bennett. *Four Lives in the Bebop Business*. Milwaukee: Hal Leonard, 1985.
Stone, Alison. "Adorno, Hegel, and Dialectic." *British Journal for the History of Philosophy* 22, no. 6 (2014): 1118–41.
Stone Alison. "Hegel and Colonialism." *Hegel Bulletin* 41, no. 2 (2020): 247–70.

Szendy, Peter. *Listen: A History of Our Ears*. New York: Fordham University Press, 2009.
Taylor, Cecil. "Being Matter Ignited: An Interview with Cecil Taylor." Interview by Chris Funkhouser. Hambone 12 (1995). https://writing.upenn.edu/epc/authors/funkhouser/ceciltaylor.html.
Taylor, Cecil. "Cecil Taylor: African Code, Black Methodology." Interview by J. B. Figi. *DownBeat*, April 10, 1975, 12–14, 31.
Taylor, Cecil. "Cecil Taylor: This Music Is the Face of a Drum." Interview by Robert Levin. Robert Levin (website), April 9, 2009. https://robert-levin.com/2009/04/09/cecil-taylor-this-music-is-the-face-of-a-drum/.
Taylor, Cecil. "Sound Structure of Subculture Becoming Major Breath / Naked Fire Gesture." Liner notes on Cecil Taylor, *Unit Structures*. Blue Note Records BST 84237, 1966, LP.
Terada, Rei. "Hegel's Racism for Radicals." *Radical Philosophy* 2, no. 5 (2019): 11–22.
Terada, Rei. "Impasse as a Figure of Political Space." *Comparative Literature* 72, no. 2 (2020): 144–58.
Terada, Rei. *Metaracial: Hegel, Antiblackness, and Political Identity*. Chicago: University of Chicago Press, 2023.
Thompson, Robert Farris. "An Aesthetic of the Cool: West African Dance." *African Forum* 2, no. 2 (1966): 85–122.
"US Embassy Cables: Nicolas Sarkozy's Personal Diplomacy in Africa Is Hamfisted." *The Guardian*, August 13, 2008. https://www.theguardian.com/world/us-embassy-cables-documents/165955.
Vizcaíno, Rafael. "Sylvia Wynter's New Science of the Word and the Autopoetics of the Flesh." *Comparative and Continental Philosophy* 14, no. 1 (2022): 72–88.
Wagner, Bryan. *Disturbing the Peace: Black Culture and the Police Power after Slavery*. Cambridge, MA: Harvard University Press, 2009.
Weheliye, Alexander G. "The Grooves of Temporality." *Public Culture* 17, no. 2 (2005): 319–38.
Weheliye, Alexander G. *Habeas Viscus: Racializing Assemblages, Biopolitics, and Black Feminist Theories of the Human*. Durham: Duke University Press, 2014.
Wilderson, Frank B., III. *Afropessimism*. New York: Liveright, 2020.
Wilderson, Frank B., III. "Frank Wilderson, Wallowing in the Contradictions, Part 2." Interview by Percy Howard. Necessary Angel, July 14, 2010. https://percy3.wordpress.com/2010/07/14/frank-wilderson-wallowing-in-the-contradictions-part-2/.
Wilderson, Frank B., III. "Gramsci's Black Marx: Whither the Slave in Civil Society?" *Social Identities* 9, no. 2 (2003): 225–40.
Wilderson, Frank B., III. "'The Inside-Outside of Civil Society': An Interview with

Frank B. Wilderson, III." Interview by Samira Spatzek and Paula von Gleich. *Black Studies Papers* 2, no. 1 (2016): 4–22.

Wilderson, Frank B., III. *Red, White and Black: Cinema and the Structure of U.S. Antagonisms*. Durham: Duke University Press, 2008.

Wilderson, Frank B., III. "We're Trying to Destroy the World." Interview by Jared Ball, Todd Steven Burroughs, and Hate. Black Ink, February 10, 2018. https://black-ink.info/2018/02/10/were-trying-to-destroy-the-world/.

Wilderson, Frank B., III, Selamawit Terrefe, and Joy James. "An Ontology of Betrayal." Williams College. November 16, 2022. Video, 2:03:04. https://www.youtube.com/watch?v=8p3At6glozQ&t=5095s.

Wilson, Samuel. "Notes on Adorno's 'Musical Material' During the New Materialisms." *Music and Letters* 99, no. 2 (2018): 260–75.

Wols. *Injured Head*. Ca. 1944. Pen and black ink, watercolor and white glaze on mottled pink laid paper, 170 x 123 mm. Städel Museum. https://sammlung.staedelmuseum.de/en/work/injured-head.

Wynter, Sylvia. "Africa, the West and the Analogy of Culture: The Cinematic Text after Man." In *Symbolic Narratives / African Cinema: Audiences, Theory and the Moving Image*, edited by June Givanni, 25–78. London: British Film Institute, 2001.

Wynter, Sylvia. "The Ceremony Found: Towards the Autopoetic Turn/Overturn, Its Autonomy of Human Agency and Extraterritoriality of (Self-)Cognition." In *Black Knowledges / Black Struggles: Essays in Critical Epistemology*, edited by Jason R. Ambroise and Sabine Broeck, 184–252. Liverpool: Liverpool University Press, 2015.

Wynter, Sylvia. "The Ceremony Must Be Found: After Humanism." *Boundary 2* 12–13, no. 3–1 (1984): 19–70.

Wynter, Sylvia. "The Re-enchantment of Humanism: An Interview with Sylvia Wynter." Interview by David Scott. *Small Axe* 8, no. 120 (2000): 173–211.

Wynter, Sylvia. "Towards the Sociogenic Principle: Fanon, the Puzzle of Conscious Experience, of 'Identity' and What It's Like to Be 'Black.'" In *National Identity and Socio-political Change: Latin America between Marginalisation and Integration*, edited by Mercedes Duran-Cogan and Antonio Gomez-Moriana, 30–66. New York: Garland, 2000.

Wynter, Sylvia. "Unsettling the Coloniality of Being/Power/Truth/Freedom: Towards the Human, after Man, Its Overrepresentation—an Argument." *CR: The New Centennial Review* 3, no. 3 (2003): 265–69.

Wynter, Sylvia, and Katherine McKittrick. "Unparalleled Catastrophe for Our Species? Or, to Give Humanness a Different Future: Conversations." In *Sylvia Wynter: On Being Human as Praxis*, edited by Katherine McKittrick, 9–89.

Durham: Duke University Press, 2015.
Yai, Olabiyi. "African Ethnonymy and Toponymy: Reflections on Decolonization African Ethnonyms and Toponyms." *General History of Africa: Studies and Documents* 6 (1984): 39–50.
Yai, Ọlabiyi Babalọla. "In Praise of Metonymy: The Concepts of 'Tradition' and 'Creativity' in the Transmission of Yoruba Artistry over Time and Space." *Research in African Literatures* 24, no. 4 (1993): 29–37.
Yai, Olabiyi Babalola. "The Path Is Open: The Legacy of Melville and Frances Herskovits in African Oral Narrative Analysis." *Research in African Literatures* 30, no. 2 (1999): 1–16.
Yai, Olabiyi Babalola. "Tradition and the Yorùbá Artist." *African Arts* 32, no. 1 (1999): 32–93.
Zagorski, Marcus. "'Nach dem Weltuntergang': Adorno's Engagement with Postwar Music." *Journal of Musicology* 22, no. 4 (2005): 680–701.
Zalloua, Zahi. *Žižek on Race: Toward an Anti-racist Future*. London: Bloomsbury, 2020.
Zambrana, Rocío. "Actuality in Hegel and Marx." *Hegel Bulletin* 40, no. 1 (2019): 74–91.
Zambrana, Rocío. "Hegelian History Interrupted." *Crisis and Critique* 8, no. 2 (2021): 410–31.
Žižek, Slavoj. "Against the Populist Temptation." *Critical Inquiry* 32, no. 3 (2006): 551–74.
Žižek, Slavoj. *The Courage of Hopelessness: Chronicles of a Year of Acting Dangerously*. London: Penguin, 2017.
Žižek, Slavoj. *Disparities*. London: Bloomsbury, 2016.
Žižek, Slavoj. *First as Tragedy, Then as Farce*. London: Verso, 2009.
Žižek, Slavoj. "A Leftist Plea for 'Eurocentrism.'" *Critical Inquiry* 24, no. 4 (1998): 988–1009.
Žižek, Slavoj. "Sublimation and Dislocation: A False Choice." *International Journal of Žižek Studies* 16, no. 1 (2022): 1–5.

Discography

Adderley, Cannonball. *Somethin Else*. Blue Note Records 49460, 1958, compact disc.
Cherry, Don. *Complete Communion*. Blue Note Records 22573, 1965, compact disc.
Coleman, Ornette. *The Shape of Jazz to Come*. Atlantic Records 8122731332, 1959, compact disc.
Coleman, Ornette. *Something Else!!!!* Contemporary Records 25218616324, 1958, compact disc.
Holiday, Billie. *The Complete Original American Decca Recordings*. MCA Records 80100379, 2005, compact disc.
Malone, Slauson. *A Quiet Farwell, 2016-2018 (Crater Speak) / Vergangenheitsbewältigung (Crater Speak)*. Grand Closing GC001, 2022, Bandcamp.
Mingus, Charles. *The Clown*. Rhino Records 8122796415, 1957, compact disc.
Roberts, Matana. *River Run Thee*. Coin Coin 3. Constellation Records CST1101, 2015, compact disc.
Taylor, Cecil. *Always a Pleasure*. FMP CD69, 1996, compact disc.
Taylor, Cecil. *Unit Structures*. Blue Note Records BST 84237, 1966, LP.
Taylor, Cecil. *The World of Cecil Taylor*. Candid CJS 9006, 1961, LP.
Thomas, Pat, and XT. *"Akisakila" / Attitudes of Preparation (Mountains, Oceans, Trees)*. Edition Gamut EG01, 2021, 2 LPs.
William Parker Quartet. *Sound Unity*. AUM Fidelity AUM034, 2004, compact disc.
Williams, Mary Lou, and Cecil Taylor. *Embraced*. Pablo Live 2620 108, 1977, LP.

Index

Abiodun, Rowland, 82–83, 149n34
accents, 12, 20, 25–31
actuality, 2, 6, 12–13, 39, 42–44, 53, 62, 89–90, 102n1, 103n2, 123nn45–46, 138n81. *See also* actualization; deactualization
actualization: African, 35; black, 6, 21, 33–35, 42–44, 112n16; and the artwork, 71–72; of the fantastic, 93; and Hegelian dialectics, 21, 42–43, 55, 121n32, 123n46. *See also* actual; deactualization
aesthetic form. *See* form
aesthetics, 15, 37, 65–66, 71–73, 84–97; Yorùbá, 68. *See also* aesthetic form; aesthetic sociality
aesthetic sociality, 2, 86–94, 138n79. *See also* aesthetic form; aesthetics; blackess, aesthetic sociality of
Adderley, Cannonball, 95, 97
Adéẹ̀kọ́, Adélékè, 11–13, 102n79, 104n14, 105n25, 105n29, 106n30, 106nn32–34, 137n76, 138n83, 149n36, 149n38

Adeleke, Durotoye A., 41
Adorno, Theodor: 5–6, 34; and laws of historical movement, 8–10, 29; and possibilities, 42–44; on the artwork, 44–45, 69, 71–72; on Hegel's dialectic, 50, 54, 60 (*see also* Adorno on laws of historical movement; Adorno on possibilities); on mimesis, 64–71, 80; on aesthetic form, 71, 73, 84, 93–94; on *musique informelle*, 89–93
African thought, 8–14, 36–42, 82–83, 117n11, 118–119n20, 119n27, 120n30, 121nn35–38, 122n39–43, 128n14, 138n81, 147n28, 149nn34–38. *See also* Yorùbá
Agada, Ada, 41, 120n30, 121n36
aleatory composition, 89, 153n61
alogical logic, 1, 7–9, 33, 44. *See also* logical frugality
analogy, 80–81
anamnesis, 11, 47, 85–87, 95, 114n6
Angelus Novus, 91, 154n69

175

anschmiegen. See snuggle
anthem. See "Marseillaise, la"
anticolonial, 112n15, 127n11. *See also*
    Haitian Revolution
anxiety, 33, 40, 50–52, 57, 15n68. *See also*
    despair
apart playing, 48–49, 127n9
appositional complementarity, 41
Apter, Andrew, 38
arrangers, 86, 139n42, 151n49
art, 2, 6, 11–13, 15, 65, 69, 71–72, 83,
    90–93, 104n12, 105n29, 106n32,
    107n40. *See also* artwork
artwork, 6, 69, 71–73, 93–94, 105n29,
    125n61; "modal anomaly" of 44–45
àṣà (tradition), 13
Atlantics (2019), 39–40, 121n34. *See also*
    Diop, Mati; fantasy
autonomy, 48, 93
autopoiesis, 91, 153n68

babaláwo, 38–39, 125
bad faith, 32
Barber, Karin, 13, 138n81, 138n83
bebop, 96–97, 153n61
becoming human, 35–36, 103n9
Beethoven, Ludwig van, 24, 112n18. *See
    also* Ninth Symphony
Benjamin, Walter, 1, 3, 5, 11, 15–16, 91; on
    the organization of pessimism,
    14–15, 94; on image space and body
    space, 15, 107n40–41, 144n5, 146n13,
    150–151n45, 154n7; and mimesis, 65,
    107n36, 116n2, 127n10, 150n40; and
    musicality, 77, 79, 146n19; on
    Trauerspiel, 77–78, 145n7; on
    relationship, 80–81, 127m10, 147n25;
    and intoxication, 95, 149–150n40,
    155n85; and opportunity, 108n45;

and the nonsensuous standard,
    143n1; on *Darstellung*, 154n72;
    "Bequest," 10, 101n1
Bernstein, Jay, 44–45, 125n61
Best, Stephen, 68, 140n37
Billie's bent elbow, 9, 16, 73, 75, 101n1,
    108n45, 138n79, 14n1
black actualization. *See* actualization
blackened world, 6, 36, 41, 94
black methodology, 16, 72, 74, 108n44,
    127n49
blackness, 1–2, 9–10, 79, 103n9, 112n20,
    136n71; and Africa, 63–64, 81–82,
    115n44, 148n29; aesthetic sociality
    of, 86; and im/possibility 5, 16,
    31–32, 124–125n57; and the
    university, 23. *See also* blackened
    world
black noncitizenry, 5, 16, 63
black ontology, 6, 81–82, 103n9, 133n44.
    See also ontological totality
black radical tradition, 1, 27–28,
    108n49, 114n28, 124n55
black scholar, 23–24, 44–45, 125n57,
    132n34
black life, 6–11, 16, 34–36, 42–45, 81–82,
    124n55 148n31. *See also* aesthetic
    sociality; blackness, aesthetic
    sociality of; ontological totality
black mass, 16, 78. *See also* black life
black studies, 53, 94, 118n17, 137n78,
    147n27. *See also* black scholar; black
    study; university
black study, 6, 27, 31–32, 44–45, 101n1.
    See also black studies; black thought
black thought, 11, 32, 37, 44, 101n1; *See
    also* black scholar; black study
body space, 15–16, 77, 85–88, 95, 107n40,
    156n13. *See also* image space

Index

Bonaparte, Napoleon, 19–20, 109–110n1, 113n21
bondsman. *See* dialectic of lord and bondsman
Boudet, Jean, 22
Brathwaite, Edward K., 27, 31, 114n28, 118n16
brilliance, 1, 78, 83–85, 89, 92, 143n1, 145n10, 152n57. *See also* center of the sound
Buck-Morss, Susan, 24, 37, 113n20

Cahn, Michael, 66, 107n36, 107n90
Caillois, Roger, 65, 67–68, 140nn98–100, 141n103
Carter, J. Kameron, 103n11, 47n151. *See also* statelessness
Casimir, Jean, 29–30, 113n23, 115n38, 120n31, 127n11
Cecil Taylor Unit, 17; *See also* Taylor, Cecil
center of the sound, 78, 143n1, 145n10. *See also* brilliance
Chandler, Nahum D., 7–8, 22–23, 43–44, 102n1, 103nn6–9, 112n16, 124n53, 124n55, 134n58, 138n79
chants, 25, 29. *See also* howling
Cherry, Don, 78, 85–89, 96–97, 145n10
Christianity, 38–42, 114n29, 117n12, 119n27, 120n30–31. *See also* colonialism
Code Noir, 24–25
coldness, 94
Coleman, Ornette, 96–97, 156n88
collective being, 3, 15–16, 27, 89. *See also* body space; black mass; entanglement; flesh; ontological totality
colonialism 1, 8, 10, 36–43, 56–62, 81–82, 111n10, 112n15, 114n29, 118n17, 137n73; in Haiti, 19–31, 109n1, 110n4, 113n23. *See also* Christianity; Haitian Revolution
common sense, 37; African, 8–9, 121n36, 128n14; European, 36, 39, 49–50 (*see* Western); and Hegel's dialectic, 50–51, 128n12, 130n23, 130n25, 130–131n28; Western, 17, 32 (*see also* European); Yorùbá, 128n14. *See also* Yorùbá sense of being
complementarity of the contrary (incomplete), 28, 40–41, 121n36. *See also* contradiction
communion, 84, 88, 93, 143n1; complete, 61, 66, 71, 87–89, 93 151n52; paratactical, 47, 126n3
congregation, 11, 78, 87–88
constant departure, 12, 64, 101n1, 106nn31–32. *See also* dwelling
constellation, 12, 73, 83, 87, 143n1, 144n1, 150n40
contradiction, in the artwork, 71–73; and common sense, 32, 36, 50–52; and doubleness, 7, 33, 44, 124n55; and European thought, 39–41, 49; failure to be disturbed by, 2, 9, 37–41, 65, 121n36; and Hegel's dialectics, 10, 33, 49–64, 120–121n32, 123n48, 128n12, 131n31, 134n54, 134n62, 138n81, 155n76; and polytheism, 37–41; in Yorùbá sense of being, 8–9, 38, 40–41, 128n14. *See also* alogical logic; exorbitance; laws of noncontradiction; nonidentity; willful thing
correspondence(s), 13–16, 31, 37, 61, 64–65, 107n36, 140n37, 142n119; 144n5; nonsensuous, 16, 48–49, 73, 77–78, 85, 87, 92, 146n13; magical, 80, 83, 127n10

cosmogonies, 34–35
counterhumanism, 1, 35, 118n17
craters, 9, 16, 64. *See also* ditches
Crawley, Ashon T., 114n29, 151n47
Creole, 25, 29, 110n6, 113n21. *See also* dialect
Crête-à-Pierrot, battle for, 26–27
critical theory, 21, 52, 69, 101n1, 130n28, 139n87. *See also* Adorno, Theodor W.; Benjamin, Walter; Frankfurt School; Hegel, Georg W. F.; Horkheimer, Max
critical thought, modern German, 5–6, 10, 30, 62; Žižek's universalist genre of, 21; in the Western humanities, 31–32, Hegelian (*see* Hegel, Georg W. F.); European, 64. *See also* critical theory; Frankfurt School; black radical tradition; black study; black thought
Cuénot, Lucien, 68
cunning of reason, 21–24

damned of the earth, 35
da Silva, Denise Ferreira., 2, 8–10, 24, 63
deactualization, 1, 42–43. *See also* actuality; possibility
death instinct (drive), 68–70, 141nn108–109. *See also* mimesis
Declaration of the Rights of Man, 21–22. *See also* human rights
despair, 33, 54, 130nn24–28; want of, 10, 39 49–61
Dessalines, Jean-Jacques, 25–27, 112–113n20, 114n26
determination, 9, 15, 23, 32–33, 40, 49–50 59, 128n14, 144n5; *See also* exorbitance
dialect, dose of, 25–32; *See also* dialectic; accent

dialectic, 1–3, 9–11, 15, 33, 42–43, 65, 101n1, 118n12; and Africa, 54–55, 62, 111n12, 114n28 (*see also* Hegel on Africa); and black radicalism, 111n12; and common sense, 50–52, 130n23; and despair (*see* despair); and dialect, 31–32; and the Haitian Revolution, 22–31, 113n23, 114n26; of lord and bondsman, 59–61, 135nn68–69, 139n86; and mimesis, 66–67 and refusal (da Silva), 9–10; *See also* contradiction in Hegel's dialectics; dialectical openness; dialectical passion
dialectical openness, 42–43
dialectical passion, 50–51
Dialectic of Enlightenment, 68–69, 123n49, 135n71, 140n94, 141n105
Diop, Mati, 39–40. *See also* fantasy
ditches, 9, 16, 26, 29, 64. *See also* craters
double consciousness, 7, 43. *See also* doubleness
doubleness, 6–11, 16, 22–23, 43–44, 64, 124n55
doubling. *See* doubleness
Du Bois, W. E. B., 6–8

ecumenically human, 34–38; *See also* counterhumanism; Wynter, Sylvia
Èlà, 82. See also *òrìshà*
Ellison, Ralph, 48, 105n22, 126–127n8
engulfment, 24, 28, 31, 34–36, 38
ensemble, 47, 68, 86–87, 105n25, 117n12, 144n5, 145n10. *See also* congregation; communion
enslavement, 8, 10, 24–25, 30, 36, 56, 62, 81, 109n1, 110n4, 133n53, 147–148n29
entanglement, 11–12, 27, 83, 151n47
equivocation, 9. *See also* contradiction

Èṣù, 9, 40–41, 78, 104n12, 121n38, 122n39. *See also* Yorùbá pantheon

Eurocentrism. *See* common sense, European; common sense, Western; dialectic and the Haitian Revolution; European universal; European world; Hegel on Africa

European universal, 25–29

European world, 5–6, 23–24, 27, 33, 36, 41–42. *See also* blackened world

exorbitance 1, 6–10, 16, 42, 44, 48, 64, 78

extraterritoriality, 1, 27, 32, 94, 106n32; *See also* statelessness

ẹ̀ya (fragments), 13. *See also* àṣà; fragments; ìtàn; oríkì; ọ̀rọ̀

Fanon, Frantz, 1, 10, 14, 44

fantasy, 39–40, 66, 70, 103n1, 142n13; in the hold, 44. *See also* actuality, possibility

fascination, 8, 12, 16–17, 47–48, 53, 75–76, 80, 82, 89–91, 93–95, 140n94, 142n119

feeling, 35, 58, 75–82, 85, 93, 107n36, 127n25, 143n1, 145n10, 149n19, 148n33. *See also* kinship; musicality; relationship

Felver, Christopher, 73–74

flesh, 2, 27, 35–36, 61, 81, 114n29, 133n53, 151n47. *See also* entanglement

folkic, 77, 80, 89. *See also* ọ̀rọ̀

Fong, Benjamin Y., 69–70, 141n108, 141n111, 142n113

form, 6–7, 10–13, 21, 26, 28, 58, 66, 74, 91, 103n9; aesthetic, 71–73, 84–85, 90–93, 96, 143n1, 153n68; commodity, 65; dialectical, 1, 9–10; musical, 84, 89–92, 126n2;

paratactic, 63; particular, 26, 71–72; universal, 21, 23–24. *See also* musique informelle

fragments, 13–16, 65, 73, 76, 80, 88

freedom, 14, 21, 25–31, 44, 51, 53; of Hegelian Spirit, 55, 62, 133n53; of subjective composition, 92; universal, 112n20, 113n23, 114n26. *See also* French Revolution; Haitian Revolution

freedom song. *See* "Marseillaise, la"

French Revolution, 21, 24. *See* "Marseillaise, la"

Freud, Sigmund, 15, 65–66, 68–70, 141n108, 141n111

Friedlander, Eli, 78–79

gathering, 17, 27, 75, 83, 138n79, 148n31

gbẹ́nugbẹ́nu (critic), 2, 11–12, 88–89, 105n25, 105n29, 107n36, 152n55

gbẹ́nàgbẹ́nà (artist), 11–12, 105n25, 106n32, 107n36, 147n28, 152n55

Geulen, Eva, 93

Giladi, Paul, 50

Givan, Benjamin, 48

Hahn, Susan S., 50

Haiti, 19–32, 36, 110n4, 112n16, 112–113n20, 113n21, 113n23, 115n38, 120n31, 127n11 *See also* Haitian Revolution

Haitian Revolution, 19–32, 37. *See also*, Dessalines, Jean-Jacques; L'Ouverture, Toussaint

happenings, 17, 76, 84, 105n29. *See also* gatherings

Harney, Stefano, 10, 105n29, 137n75

Harris, Laura, 11, 104n14

Hartman, Saidiya, 2, 8, 21, 63

Heard, Danielle C., 78
Hegel, Georg W. H., 10, 41, 49–54, 64, 102–103n1, 104n18, 104n21, 107n36, 121n32, 128n14, 129n18, 134n62, 137n75; on Africans 10, 24, 36, 54–64, 72, 133n43, 135n71; cunning of reason, 21; philosophy of history, 24, 36, 54–56, 135n71, 138n80; theory of actuality, 42–43, 123n46. *See also* dialectic
Hegelian, left, 52–53, 128n12
Henderson, Stephen, 83
history, 1, 10–11, 28, 62, 64, 119n21; Chandler's philosophy of, 8; erasure from 105n22; and l'Histoire, 10, 104n18; universal (world), 7–8, 21, 39, 54–55, 59, 62 75, 113n20, 136n73, 139n86; of the vanquished, 1, 10, 29;. See also *Angelus Novus*; Hegel's philosophy of history; *ìtàn*; laws of historical movement
History of Dahomy (1793), 64
Holder, Will, 17, 105n25
Holiday, Billie, 9, 75, 120n31. *See also* Billie's bent elbow
Horkheimer, Max, 68–69, 80, 123n49, 135n71
Hughes, Langston, 78
Huyssen, Andreas, 65
Hulatt, Owen, 65–69
human, genres of the, 1. *See also* counterhumanism; Man; Wynter, Sylvia
humanism. *See* counterhumanism; human rights
human rights, 21–22, 24–26, 29–30, 112–113n20 *See also* Declaration of the Rights of Man; "Marseillaise, La"

Huyssen, Andreas, 65

identification. *See* identity
identity, 7, 15, 38, 43–44, 49, 53–55, 65, 80–81, 89 121n32, 124n57, 131n31, 143n1; European, 131n34. *See also* double consciousness; nonidentity
idiomaticity, 64–65, 91, 143n1, 153n68
Ifá, 38–39, 41, 83
Ijiomah, Chris O., 40
image space, 15, 85, 144n5, 145n13. *See also* body space
imagination, 2, 33–34, 42, 88, 90, 123n49, 136n73; and black death, 33, 115–116n1. *See also* actuality, fantasy, possibility
immanent critique, 5, 11, 63
impossibility, 15, 38, 78, 88, 96, 118n14, 123n46; blackness as space of, 2, 5–6, 16, 32, 44, 124–125n57, 147n28; of African humanity, 62. *See also* actuality; fantasy; possibility; potentiality
improvisation, 12–15, 23, 61, 63–64, 71, 73, 76, 79, 87, 91, 137n75, 140n37, 143n128, 153n68
incomplete, 11, 28, 89, 105n29
informal music. *See musique informelle*
independence. *See* Haitian Revolution
indeterminacy, 6, 11–12, 16, 33, 40, 90, 105n29, 152n60. *See also* determination
individuation, 7, 43–44, 77–78
intimacy, 60, 65–66, 69–71, 79, 85, 88, 95, 105n29. *See also* snuggle
intoxication, 12, 75, 83–84, 89, 92, 95, 149n40, 155n85; revolutionary, 17. *See also* profane illumination, 15, 95, 150n45; brilliance; center of the sound

Index

invention, 14–15, 44, 64, 104n18. *See also* leap
Invisible Man, 105n22
Islam, 37–38, 119n27
ìtàn (history), 2, 10–11, 31–32, 81, 105n23, 106nn31–32, 147n28. See also *oríkì; òrò*

James, C. L. R., 22, 26–28, 108–109n46, 110n7, 119n21, 138n83
jazz, 16, 47–48, 72, 53n68, 154n137; free, 84, 91, 96, 126n8, 145n10, 153n61
Jazz as Critique, 16, 101n1, 140n92
Jones, Hank, 96
Judy, R. A., 6–7, 9, 11, 122n38, 136n71, 148n30

kinship, 62, 78–82, 127n10, 143n1, 154n137. *See also* relationship
Kania, Andrew, 72
Khatib, Sami, 16–17, 152n56
Kotsko, Adam, 52–53

lack of insistence, 10, 38, 72, 128n14
lament, 76–80, 146n17, 146n19
Lasson, Urban, 87–88
law of noncontradiction, 7, 40, 43–44, 49, 121n32. *See also* contradiction
lawlessness, 10, 56, 136n71
laws of historical movement, 2, 9, 11, 29–31, 65. *See also* dialectic; Hegel, philosophy of history; history
leap, 14–15, 17, 26–27, 44, 64, 104n18, 138n83. *See also* ditches; craters
Le Glaunec, Jean-Pierre, 109n1, 110n6, 113n21
liminality, 5, 9, 30, 35, 40–41, 56. *See also* contradiction; doubleness
locality, 27, 34, 37–38, 54, 86

Loewald, Hans, 69–70, 141n108, 141n111, 142n113
logical exorbitance. *See* exorbitance
logical frugality, 3, 31. *See also* exorbitance; logical gluttony; parsimony
logical gluttony, 32, 47, 121n36. *See also* contradiction; logical frugality,
lord. *See* dialectic of lord and bondsman
L'Ouverture, Toussaint, 25–29, 110n4. *See also* Dessalines, Jean-Jacques; Haitian Revolution
love, 39, 77, 88, 93–97, 99, 134n59, 146n12
"Love for Sale," 95–96
Lyons, Jimmy, 47

Macdonald, Iain, 6, 42, 123n46
Mackey, Nathaniel, 73
Man, 1, 21, 34–35, 37, 117n9, 118n17, *See also* counterhumanism; Wynter, Sylvia
Marasco, Robyn, 50–52, 130n28
Marcuse, Herbert, 115–116n1
Marriott, David, 14–15, 104n18, 109n46
"Marseillaise, La", 20–22, 24, 29, 110n7, 112n16, 112n18, 113n21
Marx, Karl, 23, 28, 42, 53, 128n12
Mbembe, Achille, 137n73
Mehretu, Julie, 79–80, 146n21
Mercier, Lucie, 55
metaracial, 63
methexis, 71–72, 142n115
metonym 12–14, 25, 83. *See also* èya; *oríkì; òrò*
McKittrick, Katherine, 123n46
mimesis, 65 -72, 91, 107n36, 126n3, 139n88, 140n37, 141n105
modal anomaly, 6, 44

modal utopianism, 42, 44. *See also* Adorno, Theodor; Macdonald, Iain
modernity, 5, 8, 22, 24, 31, 35, 115n1, 118n17, 148n30, 155n74
monotheism, 37–39. *See also* Christianity; Islam; polytheism
Montreux Jazz Festival, 77
Moten, Fred 2, 9–10, 26–32, 37, 40, 63, 82, 88, 105n25, 126n3, 136n71, 137n75, 137n78, 138n83, 139–140n92 147n29 148n29, 148n33
musicality, 48, 77, 79 , 82, 93, 143n1. *See also* feeling; relationship
musicology, 66, 73, 84–85, 154n137
musique informelle, 89–90, 92–93, 153n62, 154n137, 155n76
mythology, 123n49; Greek, 61–62; white, 62–64;
Munster, Sebastian, 61

nation of community, 29. *See also* Carter, J. Kameron; Haiti; nation-state; statelessness
nation-state, 22, 30. *See also* Haitian Revolution
natural consciousness, 51–52, 55–58, 130nn24–25, 130–131n28. *See also* ordinary consciousness
natural reason, 34. *See* cunning of reason
negativity, 2, 32, 36–37, 49, 52–54, 57, 63–64, 92, 103n1, 105n29, 111n12, 119n27, 121n36 128n14, 130n24, 131nn31–32, 134n54, 138n79. *See also* nonrelation; dialectic; contradiction
new thing (music), 84, 96, 142n119, 153n68
Ninth Symphony, 25, 112n18
nommo, 35, 118n16. *See also* Word, new science of the

noncitizenry. *See* black noncitizenry
noncontradiction. *See* law of noncontradiction
nonidentity, 47, 53, 55, 65
nonrelation, 48, 51, 53, 55, 59, 68
nonrepresentational politics. *See* image space
nonsensuous, 14; correspondence, 16–17, 49, 77–78, 85–86, 92, 95–96; similarity, 80–81, 127n10; standard, 16, 66, 74–75, 86, 143n1, 145n13

objective Spirit, 58–59. *See also* dialectic; Hegel, Georg W. H.
Ofili, Chris, 83, 149–150n40
Okoth, Kevin, 27–28
ontological totality, 27–28, 148n29. *See also* collective being; flesh
opportunity, 57, 108n45. *See also* standard
order of politicality, 17, 28, 42
ornament, 149–150n40. *See also* mimesis; presentation
oríkì, 2, 9, 11–14, 40, 63–64, 88–89 137n76, 138n81. See also *ìtàn*; *ọ̀rọ̀*
òrìshà, 9, 40–41, 82–83m 149n34. *See also* Èlà; Èṣù; Ifá; Ọ̀rọ̀ (*òrìshà*)
ọ̀rọ̀, 2, 82–84, 149n34. *See also* accent; dialect; *àṣà*; *ẹ̀ya*; *ìtàn*; *oríkì*
Ọ̀rọ̀ (*òrìshà*), 82–84, 149n34. See also *òrìshà*; *ọ̀rọ̀*
outer noise, 29. *See also* center of the sound

Palm, Ralph, 129n21, 131n32
paratactical communion. *See under* communion
parataxis, 17, 31, 41, 47, 63, 126n3
Parker, Charlie, 98

Index

Parker, William, 78, 91, 144n10, 154n71
parsimony, 10, 23, 62, 65, 104n21
pessimism, organization of. *See under* Benjamin, Walter
play, 5, 11–14, 31–32, 47, 72–74, 70, 87–91, 96–97, 115n1, 142n119, 149n40, 151n51
poetics, 10–11, 47, 72–73, 84–85, 108n45, 109n49
political art, 15. *See also* art; artwork; image space
politics, nonrepresentational. *See* image space
Polyphemus, 57, 61–62, 135–136n71
polytheism, 37–40, 119n27. *See also* monotheism
position of noncommunicability, 44, 124n57
possibility, 6, 13–14, 17, 28–29, 33–34, 39–45, 62, 70, 89, 93, 97, 123n46, 138n79; fantastic, 16, 40–43, 90, 115n1, 116n4, 123n46; formal, 42; otherwise, 114n29; real, 2, 6, 16, 42–43, 93–94, 112n16, 123n45; unreal, 2, 42. *See also* actuality; fantasy; impossibility; potentiality
potentiality, 2, 10, 12–14, 22–23, 42–43, 54–57, 67, 73, 118n17, 132n40. *See also* actuality; impossibility; opportunity; possibility
presentation (*Darstellung*), 154n72. *See also* mimesis; ornament
profane illumination, 15, 95, 150n45. *See also* intoxication
primordial density, 68–71
Purtschert, Patricia, 55–57

Quashie, Kevin, 33, 116n1

racial difference, 41, 62
racial thinking, 53. *See also* Hegel on Africans; common sense, European; common sense, Western
Rankine, Claudia, 33, 115–116n1
real possibilities. *See under* possibilities
realism, 39–40, 49. *See also* surrealism
recognition, 12–14, 35, 42, 48–49, 60–61, 122n44, 135n68. *See also* actualization, dialectic of lord and bondsman
reconcilement, 2, 14, 62, 65, 71, 73, 118n12, 120n30, 124n55, 126n4, 131n31. *See also* contradiction
refusal, radical praxis of, 1, 9–10
relational ontology, 48, 60. *See also* dialectic
representation, 35–37, 42, 65, 90–91, 107n36, 144n5; counterrepresentation, 14; nonrepresentation, 15, 90; of origin, 34–35; overrepresentation, 21; politics of, 35; postrepresentational art, 90–91
revolution, 14–15, 17, 25, 28–29, 52, 95, 112n18, 118n17, 132n40, 138n79, 150–151n45. *See also* French Revolution; Haitian Revolution; "Marseillaise, La"
revolutionary spontaneity, 15. *See also* leap
rhythm, 11, 20, 29, 85–85, 136n73
Roberts, Matana, 76–77, 144n5
Robinson, Cedric J., 1, 5–6, 27–28, 31, 37, 105n29, 111n12, 137n78, 148n29
Rochambeau, General de, 19–20

Saint-Domingue. *See* Haiti
Scott, David, 27

self-preservation, 60, 66–71, 88, 104n20, 124n49
semblance, 33, 45, 116n1
sense of being, 7–8, 22–23, 38, 43–44, 112n16. *See also* Chandler, Nahum; doubleness; Yorùbá sense of being
serialism, 89, 152n60, 154n61. *See also* determination; indeterminacy
Sexton, Jared, 17
Shipp, Matthew, 17
similarity, 80–81, 143n1; nonsensuous, 80, 127n10. *See also* relationship
Simone, Nina, 77–78, 94, 145–146n12
slavery. *See* enslavement
Smith, Bessie, 84
Smith, Wadada L., 84
snuggle, 2, 9, 11, 16, 31, 47, 74, 115n44, 117n11, 126n3, 138n81, 139n88; Adorno's, 64–67, 71–72, 140n94, 140n100, 142n119. *See also* intimacy; mimesis; relationship
social cauldron, 22, 37, 111n12, 137n78. *See also* modernity
soul, 82, 93, 112n15, 148n33. *See also* feeling; kinship; musicality; relationship
sound, 13, 20, 25–26, 28–29, 64, 74, 76–78, 82–87, 96–97, 105n22, 140n94, 142n119, 143n128, 144n5, 145n10, 146n19. *See also* center of the sound; "Marseillaise, La"; outer noise
Soyinka, Wole, 38, 40
Snead, James, 63
speculative thought, 32, 39, 49, 51–53, 128n14, 134n62. *See also* Hegel, Georg W. F.; laws of historical movement; possibility; potentiality
Spillers, Hortense, 2, 27, 114n29. *See also* flesh

Spirit (Hegel), 21, 36, 51–55, 58–59, 62, 71, 103n1. *See also* dialectic; Hegel, Georg W. F.
standard, 16–17, 20, 25, 29, 80, 95–96, 108n45; nonsensuous, 16, 66, 74–75, 86, 143n1. *see also* Tin Pan Alley composition; àṣà; aesthetic form; aesthetic sociality; Billie's bent elbow; black methodology; èya; ìtàn; oríkì; òrò; relationship; snuggle; soul; vexillum
statelessness, 1, 8–9, 30, 54, 103n11. *See also* black noncitizenry
subjunctive comportment, 44. *See also* subjunctive poetics
subjunctive poetics, 11, 125n59, 148n29
surrealism, 15, 94–95
Szendy, Peter, 86, 151n49

Taylor, Cecil 16–17, 47–49, 63, 65, 72–75, 87, 105n25, 126nn-3, 126–127n8, 127n11, 142n119, 143n128
Terada, Rei, 53–63, 72, 104n20, 118l4, 132n40, 138n79, 139n86, 155n80
Thomas, Pat, 17
Tin Pan Alley composition, 16. *See also* standard
tradition. *See* àṣà; black radical tradition
tragedy, 78–79, 99
Trauerspiel. *See* tragedy
twoness. *See* doubleness

überspülen, 93–94
undocumenting, 9, 16, 105n29
Universal history. *See under* history
universality, 21–30, 34–40, 42, 52, 54, 57–59, 62–63, 86, 111n10, 112n18, 112–113n20, 113n23, 120n30, 131n34. *See also* history, universal

university, the, 23–24. *See also* black scholar; black studies
unreality, 2, 6, 42–45, 84. *See also* actuality; fantasy; impossibility; possibility

Vertières, Battle of, 19–20
Verwandtschaft. *See* relationship
vexillum, 14, 75, 142n1. *See also* standard

Weheliye, Alexander G., 105n22
West, the, 1, 17, 21, 30–37, 39, 42, 62, 111n12, 116n1, 119n20, 148n29. *See also* Man, modernity
Western modernity. *See* modernity
Wilderson, Frank B., 44, 122n44, 124n57, 147n27
Williams, Mary Lou, 47–49, 66, 125n3, 127n11
Wols (Alfred Otto Wolfgang Schulze), 90–92, 154n72
Word, new science of the, 34–36; See also *nommo; ọ̀rọ̀*
world history. *See under* history

writing, 26, 28, 35, 86, 99, 122n39
Wynter, Sylvia, 33–38, 114n29, 117n9, 117n12, 118n17, 120n30, 123n46

XT, 17

Yáì, Ọlábíyìí 2, 10–14, 105n29, 106nn31–32, 107n36, 138n83, 147n28, 148n31, 152n55
Yorùbá, aesthetics, 11–13, 63, 68–69, 101n1, 106n32, 107n36, 147n28, 152n55; and blackness, 115n44; episteme, 81; pantheon (See *òrìshà*); sense of being, 8, 38–41, 81, 104n14, 120n30, 122n39, 128n14, 148n31. See also *àṣà;* common sense, Yorùbá; *ìtàn; oríkì; ọ̀rọ̀*

Zalloua, Zahi, 132n40
Zambrana, Rocío, 30, 111n10, 113n23, 132n34
Žižek, Slavoj, 21–29, 52–53, 112n18, 113nn20–21, 113n23, 114n26, 132n34, 132n40

The authorized representative in the EU for product safety and compliance is:
Mare Nostrum Group B.V.
Mauritskade 21D
1091 GC Amsterdam
The Netherlands
Email address: gpsr@mare-nostrum.co.uk

KVK chamber of commerce number: 96249943

The authorized representative in the EU for product safety and compliance is:
Mare Nostrum Group
B.V Doelen 72
4831 GR Breda
The Netherlands

www.ingramcontent.com/pod-product-compliance
Lightning Source LLC
Chambersburg PA
CBHW030110170426
43198CB00009B/567